The Way of Virtue

The Way of Virtue

Franco Anzures Martinez

2021

*"For all those who hunger
for the wisdom of God."*

Table of Contents

Introduction

We live in what seems to be a morally dark and confusing moment in history, as we are witnesses of exceptional times since ideologies are preferred to philosophy; political correctness seems more valuable than the truth; pleasure, popularity, and financial success are the basis of the self-esteem of our society. In short, we could say that our egoism is usurping the place of God.

All the spiritual chaos or all the sum of injustices that we observe in the world is strongly related to the lack of attention or consideration to one of the most interesting and wondrous branches of philosophy: Ethics.

Most of us start to get serious about ethics once we meet someone either extremely good or extremely evil. Admittedly, there are plenty "heavenly" or "hellish" experiences in this world; and certainly, going through some of those situations is what usually leads us to wake up and discover the great relevance of the ethical, moral, and spiritual realities; which is fascinating because we began to inquire about the true meaning of the words good and evil.

The incredible thing is that our interpretation or judgment of those words is what defines our philosophy and purpose of life. For In the end, we will try do what we consider to be good, and we will try not to do what we consider to be evil.

The main goal of philosophizing or reflecting on ethics (good and evil – right and wrong) is to gain a realistic and idealistic understanding of what is good in life.

First, realistic because an ethical theory must be seen, identified, and confirmed in an evident way throughout the history of humanity; it must be easily and strongly related to our personal and social lives. And secondly, idealistic because an ethical theory should also point to a universal better way of living, and consequently, it should lead to a more meaningful and satisfying human existence.

This book will try to explain objectively the reason why the Christian understanding of good and evil is so realistic and idealistic, and therefore reliable. I will do my best to explain why the spiritual teachings of Christ are so functional, worthy, and valuable; for they are very accessible and reasonable lessons that convey an exceptional and unparalleled moral meaning.

This book is mainly grounded on many philosophical and theological writings. In short, I can say that ethics is about virtues and vices; it is about our existence, our circumstances, our purpose, our conscience, our behavior, and ultimately, about love.

If you are a believer in Christ, I encourage you to immerse yourself in these writings and to discover or rediscover the great value of our spiritual heritage. I can truly tell you that our moral belief system is splendidly designed and arranged by God. I hope this book helps you clarify your ideas regarding holiness, and by doing so, you can come closer to live it fully.

If you are not a believer in Christ, I invite you to explore and reflect on some of the central ethical ideas of the most read and studied book of all time, the Bible. Also, it would be especially useful if you approached these writings with both critical thinking and an open heart, for I believe that you can find many valuable ideas thanks to the remarkable people quoted throughout this book. We Christians are sometimes far from exemplifying a truly Christian life, and therefore, it would be helpful for you to challenge us to live up to our own ethical or spiritual standards.

If you are young, I encourage you to read this book and then contrast it with any other ethical, philosophical, religious, or ideological system. I encourage you to become wise as soon as possible. I hope you surprise most of the adults through your excellent moral behavior. Because regardless of your background, or your future role in society, you will always be able to show your spiritual leadership, through your virtues, through your love.

This book is divided into 3 Parts:

The first part reflects on God and the human being's nature; for these are the starting points to understand human ethics origin and foundation. It is important to note that, without such knowledge, we could not affirm the identity of good and evil, and therefore, we would not be certain in our understanding of virtues and vices. In philosophy and theology, these topics are mainly associated with Metaphysics, Ontology, and Anthropology.

The second part deals in depth with the main virtues and the main vices; and how these qualities of our soul guide our lives and lead us on radically opposite paths. The ideas and thoughts about virtues have the potential to transform our lives, for, in them, we can find with great clarity the traits that constitute human excellence. In philosophy and theology, this is known primarily as Ethics.

The third part deals with introspection and the practical way to achieve spiritual development; it mainly considers what inner transformation means and how our spiritual maturity affects, benefits, enhances our communities, and contributes to the overall society.

I hope this book helps you become a better person and motivates you to develop a great friendship with God.

God bless you!

Part 1

"The soul needs to follow something in order to give birth to virtue: this something is God: if we follow Him we shall live aright."
Saint Augustine

Chapter 1: The Puzzle of Ethics

"Morality, like art, consists in drawing a line somewhere."
G. K. Chesterton

A book about ethics-spirituality might sound a bit boring. Yet, I hope to demonstrate that idea as false. Ethics is extremely exciting and intriguing; viewed with the right lenses, it will always cause our intellect to wonder. Ethics is about understanding how the most complex beings on this planet attain and discover the meaning and value of life.

If you think about it, the quality of our life is directly influenced and governed by the so-called ethical principles. For it is true that every human being, and every human organization, has some sort of ethical standards of what should be done and what shouldn't, of what is right, and what is wrong.

Admittedly, all spiritual or rational beings discover in themselves the capacity to distinguish what is good, positive, and constructive, and what is evil, negative, and destructive. It is simply fascinating understanding, comparing, and contrasting the different moral-ethical views people, organizations, philosophical theories, and religions have.

The exciting thing is that there must be at least some ethical ideals that are complementary and functional to each other. However, we can regularly notice many polemical disputes where people hold certain ethical ideals that are contradictory and dysfunctional with each other. But precisely because of that, the scope of ethics is to discover and clarify the strongest, most logical, and most reliable ethical principles, norms, or laws that human beings share. And for that, we will look at the basics of ethical analysis.

"If no set of moral ideas were truer or better than any other, there would be no sense in preferring civilized morality to savage morality." C.S. Lewis

Ethics *can be broadly divided in 3 areas.*

Figure 1 Elements of Human Ethics.

A.- Analyzing human **circumstances**.

Here we analyze the given natural realities, external influences, and/or any human conditions. We take to account mainly things like personal capabilities and possibilities and particular situations.

*Circumstances are either **favorable** or **unfavorable.***

B.- Analyzing human **spirituality**.

Here we analyze the conscience and the free will. It's mainly about what we think, what we feel, and what we want. It's either a good use of free will or an evil use of free will.

*Spirituality is either **good** or **evil**.*

C.- Analyzing human **actions**.

Here we analyze the specific actions and their consequences or impact on other beings and overall life.

*Actions are either **positive** or **negative**.*

Human ethics is about finding what perfects human life; it is mainly related to spirituality or morality, but it also considers circumstances and actions.

Ethics has **3** main ideals:

1.- Inspiring and teaching people how to use their free will or their spirit for the good.

2.- Promoting the actions that carry the greatest number of positive consequences or the ones that will most transform reality for the good.

3.- Making circumstances favorable so that people can have the opportunity to develop their potential for the good.

A simple example can be useful to make this analysis clearer.

Suppose that 3 people want to donate money.

Persons A, B, and C give $100 each to 3 different charities.

Now imagine A and C wanted to avoid tax as their primary purpose for the donation. It would only be B who was authentically generous, for only he was truly conscious of doing something good.

Principle #1 Spirituality or morality carries in itself the essence of ethical merit.

Now let us imagine the work of Charity A was to the maintenance of a local park. The work of charity B was taking care of orphan kids. And the work of Charity C was to save some animals from the ocean. All charities perform actions of positive value, yet B is making the most positive actions out of the 3.

Principle #2 The more positive the consequences of actions are, the more ethical merit they deserve.

And finally, imagine that they were all consciously wanting to help, yet A had $ 900 available, B had $ 600 available, and C had $ 300 available. By performing the same action under the same use of freedom, we can understand that C was more generous because he gave more given his circumstances.

Principle #3 Given circumstances can increase or decrease ethical merit.

That was a simple example, but it's sufficient for the purpose of explaining an overview of ethics. We all know that real human ethics are incredibly more complex, and yet, they are also commonsensical because they are embodied into our very nature. For to perceive ethics is, in the end, the most human thing to do.

Also, this analysis inevitably gives us a glimpse into why the ethical truths are so enigmatic. For to know someone's personal merit or demerit, first, we would need to understand his or her circumstances, conditions, and situation perfectly. After that, we would have to know their inner realities, what they knew, what they felt, and what they wanted. And finally, to have a clear view of their actions and their respective consequences or impact on overall life… Not easy, right.

This book won't try to do the humanly impossible task of solving the enigma of discovering someone's moral value. However, it will try to delve mainly into the second category of ethics, on what we humans consider to be the good and evil drama, which is related to spiritual virtues and vices.

For virtues and vices are the qualities of our beings that we can choose, accept, reject, develop, or change. They are intimately and mostly dependent on God and our free will.

At this point, you might consider yourself or not a be a believer in God, nonetheless, you have something you consider to be your moral authority, and therefore you have some sort of god and you have some sort of good and evil criteria. The exciting part is to know how real, precise, and clear those assumptions are.

We typically take our moral-ethical authority or our god as one of the 3 following options.

A) Yourself. A Relativist.

"If you do not worship God, you worship something, and nine times out of ten it will be yourself." Fulton Sheen

This ethical theory assumes that each is his own moral authority. It infers that everyone has some sort of self-ethical standards that apply only to themselves. People with this mindset hold that spirituality is relative and has no absolute or universal qualities. In a way, they defend a kind of anarchy applied to ethics. Here each person is considered as a god, and for the same reason, no one has authority to tell anyone what is good or what is evil.

The problem with this mentality is that if we genuinely live by it, life would become a battle of egos, the human experience would be turned into something chaotic and cruel. Imagine if, for some people, it was okay according to their own spiritual standards to be greedy, prideful, dishonest, or to steal, murder, or rape. We can quickly realize this philosophical view of life is insufficient and inefficient to produce order and human flourishing.

We can consistently notice that most the people who did atrocious things excuse themselves into some sort of self-righteousness. Most of the crimes and injustices can be traced to people who thought they were their own dictators of right and wrong.

People with this mentality are right to think that we all participate in the ethical sphere in a deeply personal and unique form and that we ought to be responsible for ourselves. For we can't control the free will of others. But that simply does not mean that we are our own gods or our own moral authorities.

B) Any human organization or accord.

"Right is right, even if everyone is against it, and wrong is wrong, even if everyone is for it." William Pen

This ethical theory assumes that what we socially construct and agree upon should be the moral-ethical authority. This means that ethics are laws purely invented by humans, and therefore, they can be designed or redesigned at our will through agreements and decrees.

This people think that legality and common agreement means morality. They assume that what is decided by democracy is right, or by a monarchy is right, or by a dictatorial state is right. They give each community the ability to determine their own ethical principles.

The problem that arises here is that human agreements are not sufficient to make the good things good and the evil things evil. Again, we could design a community or an organization where the ethical laws don't judge as wrong to be greedy, prideful, dishonest or to steal, murder, and rape. Yet, those realities would remain ethically evil or wrong.

People with this mentality are usually right in arguing that people should participate in discovering and applying ethical laws. They also are right in saying that human agreements, decrees, and laws have value, for they can help a society attain order and prosperity. But that doesn't mean that the legal entities are our ethical-moral authorities. Nor that the people that rule can absolutely determine what good or evil constitutes to the others.

C) God, the transcendental moral authority.

"The authority required by the moral order derives from God." CCC

This ethical theory assumes that there is a divine moral law that binds all humanity. It infers that we all have some sort of moral law within ourselves in which we participate personally and socially. Assuming this moral authority implies accepting that the laws of ethics are to be discovered and not invented.

This view assumes that good and evil are universal, and that it was God who drew those lines. Religions give this moral authority to their respective deities or gods, and that's why it is so interesting to analyze and compare the ethical theories and principles of the many religions and philosophies.

Regularly the people who have this view sustain that God established a Divine Moral Law which rules all humanity from within, yet it respects our free will. It is not easy to understand who or what God is, but we recognize it must be some greater, something beyond human beings, yet something that makes humanity live in complete bliss.

The problem with this theory is that people can exchange the transcendental identity of God for some insufficient and twisted human-made selfish ideas. Precisely, this is what is known as taking God's name in vain.

The previous problem can be complemented by the fact that people can take an unserious approach towards God. And by not taking sufficient inquiry into the real God, they will end up following void and superficial philosophies of life.

That's why the next chapter will be about that quest for the true identity of God. For only a transcendental God can sustain a logical, functional, and universal ethical system.

"If there's no God, all is permitted." Dostoyevsky

Chapter 2: The Quest for God

"The mystery of human existence lies not in just staying alive, but in finding something to live for." Dostoevsky

What we think about God is of utmost importance and relevance to understanding human morality. Only God is capable of establishing a perfect moral order; only in Him does ethics acquire an absolute and universal identity.

God is necessary to understand good and evil. Without Him, the good and the evil would end up being a matter of simple personal taste. Trying to define or justify human morality by discarding the idea of God makes no sense, for all moral systems need some kind of moral authority.

It is interesting that, in the history of humanity, the most remarkable tragedies have arisen due to the distortion or elimination of the genuine concept of God; because it is precisely in the lie or the negation of God where we could rationalize all kinds of injustices and evils.

It is fascinating how what we assume about God greatly influences who we are and what we do. If you think about it, most of our desires are oriented towards what we choose as our life priority or as our moral authority; that's why clarifying God's identity is essential when we speak of morality, precisely because that is the idea that sustains everything that we understand as good or evil; and therefore, that is the idea that guides our lives.

The Idea of God

We know that God is a mystery that surpasses everything we can imagine and comprehend, but that does not mean that we do not know anything about God. It means that it is always little what we can understand due to our limitations and his perfection. Yet still, God's concept is the most meaningful and beautiful idea that we aspire to know.

It is essential to clarify what we conceive about God's definition to understand and get the most out of this book. If we assume a similar meaning when we speak about God, most of the arguments will make sense. Otherwise, we could fall into an almost endless word-play due to the term's versatility and complexity.

God's truth is the main foundation of the book. Philosophy and the-ology have made the most significant advances in the knowledge of God; and for this reason, these are the sciences that we must con-sider to establish a description of the idea of God.

Figure 2 Sciences that Seek to Understand the Concept of God.

God in Philosophy

It is interesting to note that philosophy knows the questions that direct us to God but does not know the answers. Precisely looking for the answers to these questions is doing philosophy. This intellectual quest towards the knowledge of reality is a theodicy in which we are all inclined to participate, simply because we are human beings.

Philosophically, we are all looking for answers to the questions about God. We do it directly or indirectly; consciously, or unconsciously.

Philosophy defines that there are 4 crucial questions that direct us to the philosophical idea of God:

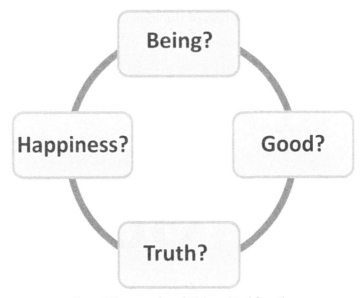

Figure 3 Transcendental Philosophical Questions.

"When we seek The Perfect Being, Truth, Good or Happiness, we seek God, whether we know it or not." Unknown

- <u>*What is the most perfect being among all those that exist?*</u>

The philosopher Leibniz represents the search for God as a perfect being. In the book: *Théodicée,* Leibniz argues and describes how only in God we find perfection, but that due to the smallness and limitations of our humanity, it is often difficult for us to understand God.

Leibniz and his philosophy could represent the relationship of God's concept to the perfection of a being.

"Love is this affection that makes us enjoy the perfections of what we love, and there is nothing more perfect than God, nor is there anything more charming. The perfections of God are those of our souls, only that he possesses them without limits; it is an ocean, from which only a few drops have reached us. There is in us some power, some knowledge, some goodness; but in God all these things are given in their integrity. We love order, proportion, harmony, and painting and music are samples of this: but God is the entire order, always keeps the exactness of proportions, constitutes universal harmony and all beauty is an expansion of his irradiations."[1]

God is the Perfect Being.

* *What good has the most value and is the most desirable?*

The philosopher Plato represents the search for the good in life. In the book The Republic, Plato argues that the idea of the good is the supreme concept that governs everything we can think or desire. Plato and his philosophy could represent the divine value of good in our lives.

"What is this knowledge superior to all others and what is its object? In no way and you can ask, I said; after all, you've heard me ad nauseam, and now you either have no memory or whatever seems more likely, you're just trying to hinder me with objections. I am inclined towards the latter, because you have heard me say many times that the idea of the good is the object of the most sublime knowledge and that justice and the other virtues owe their usefulness and all their advantages to this idea. You know very well that this, more or less, is what I have to tell you now, adding that we do not know this idea except imperfectly and that, if we did not get to know it, everything else would be of no use to us; just as the

---

[1]Leibniz, Gottfried Wilhelm. Teodicea (Illustrated) (Siltolá, Recovered Classics). Editions of La Isla de Siltolá. Kindle Edition.

possession of anything is useless to us without the possession of the good. Do you think, indeed, that it is advantageous to possess something, whatever it is, if it is not good, or to know all things except what is beautiful and good? "[2]

God is the greatest Good.

- *What is that truth that contains all the others and explains all the others?*

The philosopher Socrates represents this search and natural defense of truth. In the book, *The Apology of Socrates*, we encounter the story of an innocent person who, on a death trial, prefers to be faithful to the truth and assume death than to live as a liar. Socrates and his philosophy could represent the divine value that truth has in our lives.

"Because having not feared the shameful lie that I am going to give you at this moment, pretending that I am not eloquent, is the height of impudence, unless they do not call the one who tells the truth eloquent. If this is what they want, I confess that I am a great speaker; but I am not in his way; because, I repeat, they have not said a single true word, and you are going to know the pure truth from my mouth, no, by Zeus!, in a harangue dressed in brilliant sentences and chosen words, as are the speeches of my accusers, but in a simple and spontaneous language; because I rest in the confidence that I tell the truth and none of you should expect anything else from me."[3]

God is the absolute Truth.

---

[2]Plato. Plato's Complete Works - The Republic Complete (Spanish Edition). ATOZ Classics. Kindle Edition.

[3]Socrates. Plato's Complete Works - The Apology of Socrates (Spanish Edition). ATOZ Classics. Kindle Edition.

- *What is the reality that leads us to the greatest happiness?*

The philosopher Aristotle represents the search for happiness in life. In his book: *Nicomachean Ethics,* we find arguments about the importance and causes of joy. Aristotle and his philosophy could represent the value of happiness in life.

"Let us also say that happiness, to be the thing most worthy of our desire, does not need to be added to any other. If anything were added, it is clear that the smallest addition of goods would suffice to make it even more desirable, because in such a case what is added forms a superior and incomparable sum of goods, since a greater good is always more desirable than a lesser good. Therefore, happiness is certainly a definitive, perfect, and self-sufficient thing, since it is the end of all possible acts of man."[4]

God is the maximum Happiness.

Philosophy establishes that God must be the greatest and most worthy thing that human beings can aspire to know, feel, desire or experience: Perfect Being - Truth - Good - Happiness. Philosophically no one is an atheist because we all have life priorities, and in some way, we all want something associated with these philosophical ideals.

"I have examined most philosophical systems and have seen that none will work without God." James Clerk Maxwell

---

[4]Aristotle. Complete works of Aristotle. Nicomachean Ethics. (Spanish Edition). Kindle Edition.

God in Theology

On the other hand, theology is also interested in the same questions, only that the answers to those questions come from God's personal revelation to humanity. In Christianity, God reveals himself in 3 divine persons that make up the Holy Trinity.

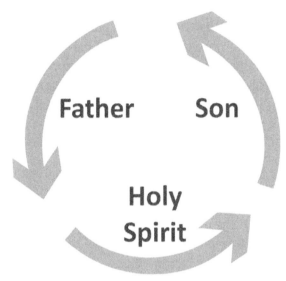

Figure 4 The Holy Trinity: 3 Persons 1 God.

God according to Theology is:

Holy: *Good, Benevolent, Loving, Just, Merciful and Faithful.*

Perfect: *It lacks nothing, it has all the excellence in itself.*

Creator: *The only one who creates everything that exists; the author of life; the author of visible and invisible realities (material and immaterial or physical and spiritual). Nobody created God because his existence is Absolute.*

Unlimited: *It has no limits of any kind.*

Immortal: *It cannot cease to exist.*

Infinite: *He has neither beginning nor end, but He himself is the beginning and the end.*

Necessary: *That all reality depends on its existence and its essence.*

Supreme Moral Authority: *Author of the Divine Moral Law and absolute judge of all actions done by beings endowed with free will.*

Omnipotent: *He can do everything.*

Omniscient: *He knows everything.*

Omnipresent: *Everything exists in Him. He is in everything.*

Mysterious: *The totality of God will always exceed our understanding.*

In Christianity, these beliefs are grounded in the Judeo-Christian revelation of God in the Bible and expressed on the Creed. Precisely these beliefs are known as the dogmas or the truths of faith. They are the essential and indispensable statements about God that constitute the richness and beauty of Christian theology.

Apostles' Creed

I believe in God, the Father almighty, creator of heaven and earth.

I believe in Jesus Christ, his only Son, our Lord. He was conceived by the power of the Holy Spirit and born of the Virgin Mary. He suffered under Pontius Pilate, was crucified, died, and was buried. He descended into hell. On the third day he rose again. He ascended into heaven and is seated at the right hand of the Father. He will come again to judge the living and the dead.

I believe in the Holy Spirit, the holy catholic Church, the communion of saints, the forgiveness of sins, the resurrection of the body, and the life everlasting.

The Identity of God

The identity of God is both his divine persons with their qualities revealed through theology (Father, Son, and the Holy Spirit) and his universal features intuited and reasoned through philosophy (Being, Good, Truth and Happiness). When speaking of God, these two great realities will always be implicit.

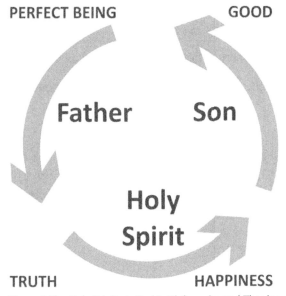

Figure 5 The Holy Trinity is God in Philosophy and Theology.

"The greatest romance one can find is to fall in love with God. The greatest journey one could embark on is to seek Him. The greatest achievement one can obtain is to find Him." Saint Augustine

1 Chronicles 29:11 Yours, LORD, is the greatness and the power and the glory and the majesty and the splendor, for everything in heaven and earth is yours. Yours, LORD, is the kingdom; you are exalted as head over all.

Chapter 3: The Human Being

"Nature is the art of God." Dante Alighieri

God is the author of our nature and our capabilities, and so, it is impossible to deeply understand human beings without God. Just as a work of art is fully explained by its author, so our humanity is fully explained by God.

Genesis 1:26 Then God said, 'Let us make mankind in our image, in our likeness, so that they may rule over the fish in the sea and the birds in the sky, over the livestock and all the wild animals, and over all the creatures that move along the ground.' 27 So God created mankind in his own image, in the image of God he created them; male and female he created them.

Wisdom 2:23 For God created man incorruptible, and to the image of his own likeness he made him.

The Unity of Soul and Body

The human being, formed by the unity of the soul and the body (spiritual and material substance), has different faculties. It is through these capacities that the human being fully experiences the divine mystery of life. These individual capacities conform to the uniqueness of human life; they enable and guide our unique participation in history and destiny.

1.- <u>Intelligence</u>: Ability to think, know, understand, imagine, judge, reason, and reflect.

2.- <u>Will</u>: Ability to desire, choose, decide, and want.

3.- <u>Affectivity</u>: Ability to feel, project, and transmit emotions, attitudes, and sentiments.

4.- <u>Sensitivity</u>: Ability to experience through the five senses of the body (Sight, Sound, Smell, Taste, and Touch).

"Everything that happens in the soul is manifested in the body."
Leibniz

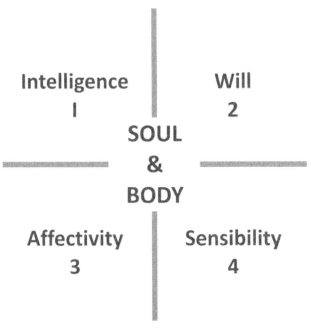

Figure 6 Human Faculties or Capacities.

Thanks to the four dimensions of the human nature, we humans participate in a passive and proactive manner in life. We are affected by reality, and at the same time, we affect reality.

All our potential as beings is grounded and related with the union of these faculties. Saint Thomas Aquinas thought that we can distinguish but not separate the human faculties because, ultimately, they are all united and form the uniqueness of a person.

These faculties act in unity in the conscience. Indeed, that is the "place" where our personality is formed; and our history unfolds.

The Conscience

Conscience is represented in the Bible by the human heart, and it is closely related to the parts or areas of conscience that we will be analyzing afterwards.

Conscience: Mental activity of the subject that allows him to feel present in the world; allows him to perceive and know reality personally; It fundamentally enables us to think, feel, and will.

In the following biblical phrases, we can understand why the heart represents the human conscience.

Proverbs 27:19 As water reflects the face, so one's life reflects the heart.

Proverbs 4:23 Above all else, guard your heart, for everything you do flows from it.

Deuteronomy 6:5 Love the LORD your God with all your heart and with all your soul and with all your strength. 6 These commandments that I give you today are to be on your hearts.

Proverbs 3:3 Let love and faithfulness never leave you; bind them round your neck, write them on the tablet of your heart. 4 Then you will win favor and a good name in the sight of God and man.

Sirach 30:16 There is no riches above the riches of the health of the body: and there is no pleasure above the joy of the heart.

Psalm 37:4 Take delight in the LORD, and he will give you the desires of your heart.

Sirach 26:4 Rich or poor, if his heart is good, his countenance shall be cheerful at all times.

Romans 5:5b because God's love has been poured out into our hearts through the Holy Spirit, who has been given to us.

Our **conscience** or our **heart** is the continual relationship between the **conscious** and the **subconscious**, which influence each other to reflect a unique personality.

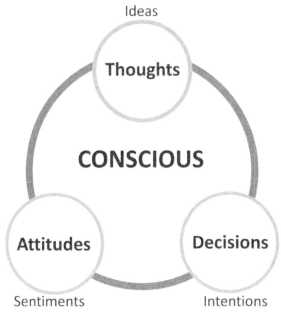

Figure 7 Conscience – Conscious.

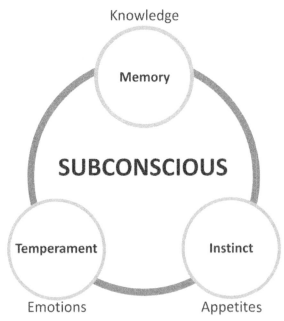

Figure 8 Conscience – Subconscious.

Conscious: The part of the conscience that allows us to be in control of our attention and our mental activity. It is also the reflective knowledge of things, and it is what allows us to apperceive or to voluntarily control our perceptions. It enables us to be aware or to feel awake towards some reality. (thoughts-attitudes-decisions).

Subconscious or unconscious: The part of our conscience that contains emotions, knowledge, and appetites that we do not fully perceive, yet they influence or affect the way we behave. (memory-temperament-instinct)

Our **memory** contains what we know but what we are not always aware of, which is knowledge. **Thoughts** are ideas, concepts, reasonings, and/or mental images about some reality. Ideas are the immaterial components of thought.

One might think that memory is more related to the subconscious while thoughts to the conscious.

Temperament is like our natural emotional structure; it is our dominant tendency among the four Choleric-Blood-Melancholic-Phlegmatic temperaments. **Attitudes** are the way we feel and dispose ourselves towards some reality.

It might be thought that the temperament is more related to the subconscious while attitudes to the conscious.

Instincts are appetites for something (pleasure, pain, corporal impulses); they do not necessarily originate in the person's will. **Decisions** are the most proper part of the person; they are intentions or inner choices that originate in the person and guide him to an end.

It might be thought that the instinct is more related to the subconscious while decisions to the conscious.

Some aphorisms related to intelligence.

"The world of ideas affects the physical world, think well, and you will act well." Plato

"Not participating in this search for ideas is living like ants instead of men." Mortimer Adler

"Our life always expresses the result of our dominant thoughts." Søren Kierkegaard

"Crooked thinking leads to crooked living." Bob Phillips

"Change your thoughts and change your world." Norman Vincent Pale

"If you don't act like you think, you will end up thinking like you act." Blaise pascal

"The world we have created is a process of our thought. It cannot be changed without changing the way we think." Albert Einstein

"The mind concerns itself with four things: these are good and evil, life and death. They all begin in the mind." Sirach 37:17

"Knowing their thoughts, Jesus said, 'Why do you entertain evil thoughts in your hearts?" Matthew 9:4

"Immediately Jesus knew in his spirit that this was what they were thinking in their hearts, and he said to them, 'Why are you thinking these things?" Mark 2:8

Some aphorisms related to affectivity.

"The heart has its reasons which reason knows not." Blaise Pascal

"Emotions or passions are forces that motivate us to pursue good or avoid evil." CCC 1763

"Passions are morally good when they contribute to a good action, evil in the opposite case." CCC 1768

"Every sentiment is the perception of a truth." Leibniz

"It is simply a mistake to dismiss all emotions as defending their unbridled activity." Joseph Massman

"May the God who gives endurance and encouragement give you the same attitude of mind toward each other that Christ Jesus had." Romans 15:5

"Our greatest freedom is the freedom to choose our attitude." Viktor Frankl

Some aphorisms related to our will.

"Some desire is necessary to keep life in motion." Samuel Johnson

"The self-indulgent man craves for all pleasant things... and is led by his appetite to choose these at the cost of everything else." Aristotle

"It is our choice of good or evil that determines our character, not our opinion of good or evil." Aristotle

"The content of your character is your choice. Day by day, what you choose, what you think and what you do is who you become."
Heraclitus

"Excellence is never an accident. It is always the result of high intention, sincere effort, and intelligent execution; it represents the wise choice of many alternatives – choice, not chance, determines your destiny." Aristotle

"Decisions, not conditions, determine what a man is."
Viktor Frankl

"With every choice we move either closer to God or farther away from him." Peter Kreeft

"God writes the story of our lives with the pen strokes of our own free choices." Peter Kreeft

"For it is God who is at work in you, enabling you both to will and to work for his good pleasure." Philippians 2:13

After knowing and reflecting on certain fundamental realities about the human conscience, we find that everything we do consciously is considered moral or spiritual because it is directed towards good or evil. That is why ethics, or the realization of moral duty through our free will is the main plot of every human life.

The Free Will

Free will is the human's ability to determine himself as a being; it is a freedom that is limited by our own being. It is the quality that constitutes us as moral or spiritual beings. Free to think, feel, decide, or do; for better or for worse. Free will is the most powerful and mysterious reality in our human nature; it is formed mainly by the union of the four faculties of human nature:

1.- Freedom in thoughts. (intelligence)

2.- Freedom in decisions. (will)

3.- Freedom in attitudes. (affectivity)

4.- Freedom in our actions. (sensibility)

Figure 9 Human Responsibility.

Free will allows us to participate in life in a personal and transcendental way. Basically, what we do or stop doing will have definitive consequences in life. No human can know or predict with absolute certainty what people will do with their free will, but only the Creator. The truth is that God, by giving us free will, made our existence a great little mystery.

"*External circumstances can strip us of everything but one thing: the freedom to choose how to respond to those circumstances.*"
Viktor Frankl

"*Between stimuli and response there is a space. In that space is our power to choose our response. In our response lies our growth and our freedom.*" *Viktor Frankl*

"*Most people love freedom when it means being able to do whatever they feel like doing. But they don't love freedom when it means the responsibility of making moral choices and living with the results.*" *Peter Kreeft*

Free will is an incredibly special gift, it was given by God when he created us in his image and likeness. God created us for the purpose of loving. God gave us the ability to understand and choose what we want in life. God makes a proposal to man, which is the fundamental proposal of human freedom.

Sirach 15:17 Before each person are life and death, and whichever one chooses will be given.

Proverbs 11:19 Truly the righteous attain life, but whoever pursues evil finds death.

Ezekiel 18:20 The righteousness of the righteous will be credited to them, and the wickedness of the wicked will be charged against them.

God offers us to participate in his will, which is a free and perfect love. He gave us these freedoms, not for us to minimize or nullify them, but to make the most of them and use them for good, that is, for us to be responsible for solving and facing the problems and challenges of life.

Free will changes all the cause-effect dynamics; it frees us from the absolute conditioning that would arise from the circumstances. This reality is the simple explanation of why people with almost identical stimuli or circumstances respond in such different and contrasting ways.

If there would be no free will, then we would simply be a consequence of the things that happen to us. We could not really change anything; neither in us nor outside of us. Without free will, responsibility would only be an illusion. There would be neither merit nor guilt, neither justice nor injustice, neither good nor evil, neither truth nor lies; we would be simple victims of destiny.

"Philosophers and sociologists and psychologists who teach that we are not really free to make choices but are rather "determined" (caused, pushed around passively and unfreely) by our environment and our heredity, are causing more damage to the human moral conscience than a war would." Peter Kreeft

Human beings universally live and experience moral dilemmas; because they are part of the everyday life and are related to an infinity of situations. From the smallest moments that seem insignificant to the most crucial moments that are, in fact, clearly significant. Living implies a continual ethical dilemma, where we are indeed free to choose between good or evil.

Sirach 13:25 A man's heart changes his countenance, either for good or for evil. 26 The mark of a happy heart is a cheerful face.

Indeed, the proof what we do with our free will is materialized through our behavior. For we are known by our actions, and our actions have a source in our conscience. As the classical Latin phrase portrays it: "Agere sequitur esse." Doing follows being.

The Human Behavior

In one of the simplest and most important teachings to understand the human being, Jesus tells us that the fruits (our behavior) have their cause or origin in the tree (our conscience), and therefore, it is clarified and affirmed the intimate unity between who we are and what we do. Our moral/spiritual identity is based on that personal unity.

Luke 6:43 'No good tree bears bad fruit, nor does a bad tree bear good fruit. 44 Each tree is recognized by its own fruit. People do not pick figs from thornbushes, or grapes from briers. 45 A good man brings good things out of the good stored up in his heart, and an evil man brings evil things out of the evil stored up in his heart.

Matthew 12:33 'Make a tree good and its fruit will be good, or make a tree bad and its fruit will be bad, for a tree is recognized by its fruit. 34 You brood of vipers, how can you who are evil say anything good? For the mouth speaks what the heart is full of. 35 A good man brings good things out of the good stored up in him, and an evil man brings evil things out of the evil stored up in him.

If we reflect on these words, we can understand that who we are on the inside, we manifest it on the outside and that our life is a consequence and a projection of what happens in our conscience.

It is interesting to note the relationship between conscience and human actions. Saint Thomas Aquinas thought that proper human deeds are those that we carry out according to free will, that is, in freedom.

"The highest manifestation of life consists in this: that a being governs its own actions." Saint Thomas Aquinas

"Let's not forget that the causes of human actions are often immeasurably more complex and varied than our later explanations of them." Dostoyevsky

Figure 2 Behavior - Projection of Conscience.

In the scheme, when we refer to **words**, we refer to what we say or express. To speak is precisely to externalize what happens in conscience. Words are linguistic units endowed with meaning.

When we talk about **actions**, we are referring to the things we do. It is in our deeds where we concretize the realities of our conscience and manifest our morality or spirituality. **Habits** are actions that we repeatedly do. The continuous union of our conscience and our actions is what we understand by **conduct** or **behavior**.

Some aphorisms about words.

"Its fruit discloses the cultivation of a tree; so a person's speech discloses the cultivation of his mind. Never praise anyone before you hear him talk; that is the real test." Sirach 27:6-7

"The tongue has the power of life and death, and those who love it will eat its fruit." Proverbs 18:21

"Have you seen a man hasty to speak? More can be expected of a fool than of him." Proverbs 29:20

"The wise speak because they have something to say; fools because they have to say something." Plato

"When you have something to say, silence is a lie."
Jordan Peterson

"Better one word in time than a hundred out of time."
Miguel de Cervantes

"Kind words may be short and easy to say, but their echoes are truly endless." Saint Teresa of Calcutta

"All truth, whoever says it, comes from the Holy Spirit."
Saint Thomas Aquinas

"The heart of the righteous weighs its answers, but the mouth of the wicked gushes evil." Proverbs 15:28

"Do not let any unwholesome talk come out of your mouths, but only what is helpful for building others up according to their needs, that it may benefit those who listen." Ephesians 4:29

"Anyone who is never at fault in what they say is perfect, able to keep their whole body in check." James 3:2b

"But I tell you that everyone will have to give account on the day of judgment for every empty word they have spoken."
Matthew 12:36

Some aphorisms about actions.

"Good actions give strength to ourselves and inspire good actions in others." Plato

"The greatness of a life can only be estimated by the multitude of its actions. We should not count the years; it is our actions which constitute our life." Leibniz

"Don't explain your philosophy. Embody it." Epictetus

"Dear children, let us not love with words or speech but with actions and in truth." James 3:18

"And God is able to bless you abundantly, so that in all things at all times, having all that you need, you will abound in every good work." 2 Corinthians 9:8

"Everyone who does evil hates the light, and will not come into the light for fear that their deeds will be exposed. But whoever lives by the truth comes into the light, so that it may be seen plainly that what they have done has been done in the sight of God." John 3:20

"Anyone who does what is good is from God. Anyone who does what is evil has not seen God." 3 John 1:11b

Some aphorisms about habits and conduct or behavior.

"Happiness does not consist in pastimes and amusements but in virtuous activities." Aristotle

"We are what we repeatedly do. Excellence, then, is not an act, but a habit." Aristotle

"Moral excellence is the result of habit. We become righteous by performing acts of justice; temperate, performing acts of temperance; brave, performing acts of bravery." Aristotle

"Resist temptations in the beginning, and unlearn the evil habit lest perhaps, little by little, it lead to a more evil one."
Thomas A Kempis

"Habit is a second nature that destroys the first." Blaise pascal

"Habits are formed by the repetition of particular acts. They are strengthened by an increase in the number of repeated acts. Habits are also weakened or broken, and contrary habits are formed by the repetition of contrary acts." Mortimer Adler

"Behavior is a mirror in which everyone shows his image."
Johann Wolfgang Goethe

"We needed to stop asking about the meaning of life and instead think of ourselves as those who were being questioned by life – daily and hourly. Our answer must consist, not in talk and meditation, but in right action and right conduct." Viktor Frankl

"I the LORD search the heart and examine the mind, to reward each person according to their conduct, according to what their deeds deserve." Jeremiah 17:10

After taking some time to meditate and understand the basics of human behavior, it will be time to delve into the unparalleled teachings of Christianity on the study of what is morally right and wrong, good or evil.

Chapter 4: Christian Ethics

"Good must be done and sought, evil must be avoided. On this precept all the other precepts of moral law are founded."
Saint Thomas Aquinas

There are 3 levels of the knowledge about good and evil:

1.- The Natural Moral Law: Knowledge of good and evil through the presence of God in our conscience, especially through right use of reason.

> Romans 2:12a All who sin apart from the Law will also perish apart from the Law.

2.- The Jewish Moral Law: Knowledge of good and evil through divine revelation to the Jewish people, especially through the 10 Commandments.

> Romans 3:20 the knowledge of sin exists through the Law.

3.- The Christian Moral Law or the Law of Love: Knowledge of good and evil through the eternal words of Jesus.

> John 15:22 If I had not come and spoken to them, they would not be guilty of sin; but now they have no excuse for their sin.

The unity of these 3 Laws is what we consider to be:
Divine Moral Law.

God is the author of this Law, and its purpose is to make people good. It is interesting to note that the Divine Moral Law is universal, and that we all have a certain degree of knowledge about it, which is why it demands or commands us to do the right thing proportionally to our understanding of it.

"Freedom consists not in doing what we like, but in having the right to do what we ought." Pope John Paul II

The fulfillment of Divine Moral Law is what we call:

virtue.

The transgression of the Divine Moral Law is what we call:

sin or **vice.**

The word virtue originates from the Greek word "areté," which means excellence. In Christianity, excellence or perfection is holiness. Virtues are the essence of holiness; they are the excellencies or perfections of human beings. Virtues are the mystical union of our will with the will of God and of our soul with the Spirit of God.

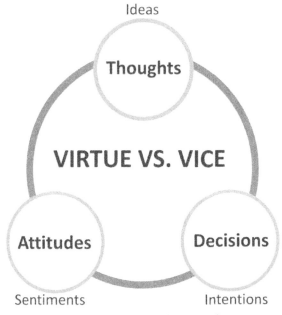

Figure 11 Virtuous or Vicious Conscience.

Good (virtues) and evil (vices) are qualities of the conscience and of the free will (Thoughts-Attitudes-Decisions) which are manifested through behaviors (Words-Actions-Habits).

Figure 12 Virtuous or Vicious Behavior.

Virtues are always qualities of the soul of positive value; they always contribute for the good somehow, while vices have a negative value; they always drive us away and deprive us of the authentic good. The words sin and vice are synonyms. In theology, the word sin is used more, while in philosophy, the word vice is used more, but in the end, both words seek to represent and express the reality of a moral or ethical evil.

Virtues and vices are also understood as qualities of our souls. They are like spiritual principles that are manifested in our conscience and our behavior. A clear and concise example is that a humble person (good-positive characteristic) lives manifesting humble thoughts, attitudes, decisions, words, actions, and habits. The same towards vices, a prideful person (evil-negative characteristic) lives manifesting prideful thoughts, attitudes, decisions, words, actions, and habits.

Virtues are always based on and agree with the voice of God in the conscience (The Natural Moral Law), the Ten commandments (The Jewish Moral Law), and the teachings of Jesus (The Christian Moral Law or the Law of Love).

Natural Moral Law

God, being an infinite Spirit, manifests Himself universally in the human being's conscience and appears as a "voice" that leads us to discern between good and evil. The simple fact of intuiting that we should do something good, or that we should reject something evil (moral duty) shows the presence of that divine voice.

Wisdom 12:1 For your immortal spirit is in all things.

It is like an inner inclination or motion, which guides the conscience to the purpose of life, which is love. God is the one who speaks to us in those moments. He alerts us about evil things and prompts us to do good things. God's Spirit always guides us to seek the good and reject the evil.

Sirach 37:13 Listen carefully to what your own heart tells you, since nothing is more faithful to you than it. - But above everything else, pray to the Most High, so that he may make your path straight in truth.

The Spirit of God probes all hearts, knows everything that happens to us at all times. He knows our conscience to perfection. God universally communicates to the human souls about what is right and what is wrong.

1 Chronicles 28:9b For the LORD searches every heart and understands every desire and every thought.

Psalm 33:13 From heaven the LORD looks down and sees all mankind; 14 from his dwelling-place he watches all who live on earth 15 he who forms the hearts of all, who considers everything they do.

"Two things fill the mind with ever-increasing wonder and awe, the more often and the more intensely the mind of thought is drawn to them: the starry heavens above me and the moral law within me."
Immanuel Kant

"Everything that helps to preserve human life and prevents its destruction belongs to natural moral law." Saint Thomas Aquinas

Moses and the 10 Commandments

God gave an ethical Law in physical form to the Jewish people: The Ten Commandments. God communicates to us through these divine precepts the standard of life that he wants for us. Being faithful to his commandments will be to be faithful to God himself.

Exodus 34:28 Moses was there with the LORD forty days and forty nights without eating bread or drinking water. And he wrote on the tablets the words of the covenant – the Ten Commandments.

Deuteronomy 6:1 These are the commands, decrees and laws the LORD your God directed me to teach you to observe in the land that you are crossing the Jordan to possess, 2 so that you, your children and their children after them may fear the LORD your God as long as you live by keeping all his decrees and commands that I give you, and so that you may enjoy long life. 3 Hear, Israel, and be careful to obey so that it may go well with you and that you may increase greatly in a land flowing with milk and honey, just as the LORD, the God of your ancestors, promised you. 4 Hear, O Israel: the LORD our God, the LORD is one. 5 Love the LORD your God with all your heart and with all your soul and with all your strength. 6 These commandments that I give you today are to be on your hearts. 7 Impress them on your children. Talk about them when you sit at home and when you walk along the road, when you lie down and when you get up. 8 Tie them as symbols on your hands and bind them on your foreheads. 9 Write them on the door-frames of your houses and on your gates.

Deuteronomy 5:29 Oh, that their hearts would be inclined to fear me and keep all my commands always, so that it might go well with them and their children for ever!

Deuteronomy 12:28 Be careful to obey all these regulations I am giving you, so that it may always go well with you and your children after you, because you will be doing what is good and right in the eyes of the LORD your God.

Deuteronomy 30:11 Now what I am commanding you today is not too difficult for you or beyond your reach.

THE TEN COMMANDMENTS

1. I AM THE LORD YOUR GOD: YOU SHALL HAVE NO OTHER GODS BEFORE ME YOU SHALL WORSHIP THE LORD YOUR GOD AND HIM ONLY SHALL YOU SERVE.

2. YOU SHALL NOT TAKE THE NAME OF THE LORD YOUR GOD IN VAIN.

3. REMEMBER THE SABBATH DAY, TO KEEP IT HOLY. SIX DAYS YOU SHALL LABOR, AND DO ALL YOUR WORK; BUT THE SEVENTH DAY IS A SABBATH TO THE LORD YOUR GOD.

4. HONOR YOUR FATHER AND YOUR MOTHER.

5. YOU SHALL NOT KILL.

6. YOU SHALL NOT COMMIT ADULTERY.

7. YOU SHALL NOT STEAL.

8. YOU SHALL NOT BEAR FALSE WITNESS AGAINST YOUR NEIGHBOR.

9. YOU SHALL NOT COVET YOUR NEIGHBOR'S WIFE.

10. YOU SHALL NOT COVET YOUR ANYTHING THAT IS YOUR NEIGHBOR'S.

Figure 13 Jewish Moral Law.

"God wrote on the tables of the Law what men did not read in their hearts." Saint Augustine

Romans 7:12 So then, the law is holy, and the commandment is holy, righteous and good.

Romans 13:8 "Love fulfils the law" Let no debt remain outstanding, except the continuing debt to love one another, for whoever loves others has fulfilled the law. 9 The commandments, 'You shall not commit adultery,' 'You shall not murder,' 'You shall not steal,' 'You shall not covet,' and whatever other command there may be, are summed up in this one command: 'Love your neighbor as yourself.' 10 Love does no harm to a neighbor. Therefore love is the fulfilment of the law.

Deuteronomy 8:1 Be careful to follow every command I am giving you today, so that you may live and increase and may enter and possess the land that the LORD promised on oath to your ancestors. 2 Remember how the LORD your God led you all the way in the wilderness these forty years, to humble and test you in order to know what was in your heart, whether or not you would keep his commands.

James 2:10 For whoever keeps the whole law and yet stumbles at just one point is guilty of breaking all of it. 11 For he who said, 'You shall not commit adultery,' also said, 'You shall not murder.' If you do not commit adultery but do commit murder, you have become a law-breaker.

The 10 commandments are the standard and ideal of justice in the Jewish religion; they are meant to be a concrete guide that encourages good works and prohibits bad ones. Interestingly, good-hearted people will find no problem in the logic, value, and obedience to this Law; any human being can realize that everything would be much better if we all acted without transgressing it. Anyone who does not have a good heart can read them and find resistance to recognize their value. Consequently, he will refuse to obey them and think that following them is a burden that causes him unhappiness and damages his freedom.

Ezequiel 33:17 'Yet your people say, "The way of the LORD is not just." But it is their way that is not just.

In most of the Old Testament stories, we see an inner struggle in the different biblical characters to lead a life according to the ten commandments, which are God's will. In Jewish tradition, the word righteous was used to indicate a person who lived according to the Law, someone who loved and honored its precepts.

Deuteronomy 6:25 And if we are careful to obey all this law before the LORD our God, as he has commanded us, that will be our righteousness.'

The commandments are the most practical and concrete guide to the will of God; they convey a mystery of blessing. Living in accordance with them is essential to maintaining a good relationship with God. We will always have the opportunity to discover and confirm their unique and divine value through experience.

Proverbs 3:1 My son, do not forget my teaching, but keep my commands in your heart, 2 for they will prolong your life many years and bring you peace and prosperity.

Psalm 119:10 I seek you with all my heart; do not let me stray from your commands.

1 Corinthians 7:19b Keeping God's commands is what counts.

Psalm 119:1 Blessed are those whose ways are blameless, who walk according to the law of the LORD. 2 Blessed are those who keep his statutes and seek him with all their heart – 3 they do no wrong but follow his ways.

Ecclesiastes 12:13 Now all has been heard; here is the conclusion of the matter: fear God and keep his commandments, for this is the duty of all mankind. 14 For God will bring every deed into judgment, including every hidden thing, whether it is good or evil.

Jesus and the Law of Love

Much of what Jesus came to teach at a moral-spiritual-ethical level is condensed in what we call the Law of love. This means that everything is based and summarized on the love of God and the love of neighbor.

Matthew 22:34 Hearing that Jesus had silenced the Sadducees, the Pharisees got together. 35 One of them, an expert in the law, tested him with this question: 36 'Teacher, which is the greatest commandment in the Law?' 37 Jesus replied: '"Love the Lord your God with all your heart and with all your soul and with all your mind." 38 This is the first and greatest commandment. 39 And the second is like it: "Love your neighbor as yourself." 40 All the Law and the Prophets hang on these two commandments.'

It is easy to recognize that love is something spiritually necessary. Universally we could affirm it, but the difficult thing is to love with the depth that Jesus taught us. This shows that the problem is not so much in believing that love is the solution to the most transcendent issues in life, but in understanding love as God understands it and loving as God loves us. In the following passage, we find Christianity's fundamental invitation with great clarity and simplicity.

John 15:9 'As the Father has loved me, so have I loved you. Now remain in my love. 10 If you keep my commands, you will remain in my love, just as I have kept my Father's commands and remain in his love. 11 I have told you this so that my joy may be in you and that your joy may be complete. 12 My command is this: love each other as I have loved you. 13 Greater love has no one than this: to lay down one's life for one's friends. 14 You are my friends if you do what I command. 15 I no longer call you servants, because a servant does not know his master's business. Instead, I have called you friends, for everything that I learned from my Father I have made known to you. 16 You did not choose me, but I chose you and appointed you so that you might go and bear fruit – fruit that will last – and so that whatever you ask in my name the Father will give you. 17 This is my command: love each other.

Jesus, in the Sermon on the Mount, preaches that he did not come to abolish the Law, but to bring it to its fullness, that is, to raise Jewish ethics to even higher levels, both on justice and mercy. It is important to note that the teachings of Jesus have perfect continuity with the 10 Commandments and that there is a divine union between the Law and the virtues that Jesus teaches us.

Matthew 5:17 'Do not think that I have come to abolish the Law or the Prophets; I have not come to abolish them but to fulfil them. 18 For truly I tell you, until heaven and earth disappear, not the smallest letter, not the least stroke of a pen, will by any means disappear from the Law until everything is accomplished. 19 Therefore anyone who sets aside one of the least of these commands and teaches others accordingly will be called least in the kingdom of heaven, but whoever practices and teaches these commands will be called great in the kingdom of heaven.

Jesus, in the Gospels, teaches us that not only external acts must be considered ethical, but also the internal consent of good or evil. In this way, he delves into the Law's teachings to affirm its unity with human conscience.

Matthew 5:21 'You have heard that it was said to the people long ago, "You shall not murder, and anyone who murders will be subject to judgment." 22 But I tell you that anyone who is angry with a brother or sister, will be subject to judgment. Again, anyone who says to a brother or sister, "Raca," is answerable to the court. And anyone who says, "You fool!" will be in danger of the fire of hell.

Matthew 5:27 'You have heard that it was said, "You shall not commit adultery." 28 But I tell you that anyone who looks at a woman lustfully has already committed adultery with her in his heart.

The great message of the Bible is the invitation is to become perfect or holy (saints).

Leviticus 19:1 The LORD said to Moses, 2 'Speak to the entire assembly of Israel and say to them: "Be holy because I, the LORD your God, am holy.

Leviticus 11:44 I am the LORD your God; consecrate your-selves and be holy.

1 Thessalonians 4:3a It is God's will that you should be   sanctified.

1 Peter 1:15 but as he who called you is holy, be holy your-selves in all your conduct; 16 since it is written, "You shall be holy, for I am holy."

Matthew 5:48 Be perfect, therefore, as your heavenly Father is perfect.

Matthew 19:21 Jesus answered, 'If you want to be perfect, go, sell your possessions and give to the poor, and you will have treasure in heaven. Then come, follow me.'

Human perfection begins by following God and culminates in the likeness of our love with the love of Christ. To love either God or our neighbor is to participate in the divine life. The ideal of Christian love is to live and experience Christlike holiness. To love like Christ means to be Alter Christus - Ipse Christus.

John 13:34 'A new command I give you: love one another. As I have loved you, so you must love one another.

John 14:23 Jesus replied, 'Anyone who loves me will obey my teaching. My Father will love them, and we will come to them and make our home with them. 24 Anyone who does not love me will not obey my teaching. These words you hear are not my own; they belong to the Father who sent me.

John 14:15 'If you love me, keep my commands. 16 And I will ask the Father, and he will give you another advocate to help you and be with you for ever – 17 the Spirit of truth. The world cannot accept him, because it neither sees him nor knows him. But you know him, for he lives with you and will be in you.

1 John 4:7 Dear friends, let us love one another, for love comes from God. Everyone who loves has been born of God and knows God. 8 Whoever does not love does not know God, because God is love.

The Grace of the Holy Spirit

You could say that the teachings of Jesus are even more demanding than the 10 Commandments. But they are also, in a way, easier to fulfill due to the divine grace that He gives us.

We find a text by Saint Paul that speaks to us about the grace of God that was granted through Jesus Christ. For it is the Holy Spirit who allows us to love and to live in holiness or in the commonly known state of grace.

Romans 8:1 Therefore, there is now no condemnation for those who are in Christ Jesus, 2 because through Christ Jesus the law of the Spirit who gives life has set you free from the law of sin and death. 3 For what the law was powerless to do because it was weakened by the flesh, God did by sending his own Son in the likeness of sinful flesh to be a sin offering. And so he condemned sin in the flesh, 4 in order that the righteous requirement of the law might be fully met in us, who do not live according to the flesh but according to the Spirit. 5 Those who live according to the flesh have their minds set on what the flesh desires; but those who live in accordance with the Spirit have their minds set on what the Spirit desires. 6 The mind governed by the flesh is death, but the mind governed by the Spirit is life and peace. 7 The mind governed by the flesh is hostile to God; it does not submit to God's law, nor can it do so. 8 Those who are in the realm of the flesh cannot please God. 9 You, however, are not in the realm of the flesh but are in the realm of the Spirit, if indeed the Spirit of God lives in you. And if anyone does not have the Spirit of Christ, they do not belong to Christ. 10 But if Christ is in you, then even though your body is subject to death because of sin, the Spirit gives life because of righteousness.

All virtues always presuppose and are based on the existence of divine grace, which, as its name implies, is a kind of free gift from God. Without the grace of God, we cannot exist or be virtuous. Virtues always require our participation, that is, the use of our free will. God is seeking to be in communion with us, He wants to do all kinds of good in/with us.

Through virtues, God perfects our being with his love. Humans do not create virtues; they are given, infused, and taught by God. Virtues are the overwhelming proof of the full presence of the Holy Spirit in our souls. It could even be said that the greater the virtue, the greater the communion with God. Virtues are the essence and the beauty of an authentical Christian life.

In Christianity, good and evil are understood as mutually exclusive ends of life. The Bible proposes that there are only two ways to live life. Spiritual warfare is real, and it results from these two ways of living that go in opposite directions.

"There are only two kinds of people in the end: those who say to God, 'Thy will be done', and those to whom God says, in the end, 'Thy will be done'." C.S. Lewis

Choice 1 is to live according to the Spirit of God. which entails being virtuous by living according to the demands of love and working all kinds of good deeds.

Choice 2 is to live according to the flesh, which implies being vicious and pursuing all type of egoistical goals, which, as a matter of fact, are contrary to love.

Galatians 6:7 Do not be deceived: God cannot be mocked. A man reaps what he sows. 8 Whoever sows to please their flesh, from the flesh will reap destruction; whoever sows to please the Spirit, from the Spirit will reap eternal life.

In the next part, we will delve into the general or systematic contradiction between living according to the Spirit of God and living according to the flesh. We will understand why God's will is good, and the opposite is evil; we will comprehend why evil, philosophically, is the privation of a good.

Life According to the Spirit of God - Good

The human being has as his life purpose the encounter with God (Summun Bonum). From that union, love is born in our hearts; consequently, goodness appears, and it directs us on the path of truth, from where friendships are born, which leads us to happiness and to reciprocity in love. The immense value of spiritual life is contained in this union of goods lived according to the Will of God.

Figure 3 Good - Living According to the Spirit of God (Inner Heaven).

Virtues will be our means to choose the good of life according to the Spirit of God. Only through virtue can we enjoy the beauty of life. In the Bible, we find some passages that indicate the characteristics of a virtuous and blessed life.

James 1:17 Every good and perfect gift is from above, coming down from the Father of the heavenly lights, who does not change like shifting shadows.

Proverbs 11:23 The desire of the righteous ends only in good.

Proverbs 21:21 Whoever pursues righteousness and love finds life, prosperity and honor.

Galatians 5:22 But the fruit of the Spirit is love, joy, peace, forbearance, kindness, goodness, faithfulness, 23a gentleness and self-control.

1 Timothy 6:11 But you, man of God, flee from all this, and pursue righteousness, godliness, faith, love, endurance and gentleness.

Ephesians 5:9 for the fruit of the light consists in all goodness, righteousness and truth.

Micah 6:8 He has shown you, O mortal, what is good. And what does the LORD require of you? To act justly and to love mercy and to walk humbly with your God.

Colossians 3:12 Therefore, as God's chosen people, holy and dearly loved, clothe yourselves with compassion, kindness, humility, gentleness and patience.

Matthew 5:3 'Blessed are the poor in spirit, for theirs is the kingdom of heaven. 4 Blessed are those who mourn, for they will be comforted. 5 Blessed are the meek, for they will inherit the earth. 6 Blessed are those who hunger and thirst for righteousness, for they will be filled. 7 Blessed are the merciful, for they will be shown mercy. 8 Blessed are the pure in heart, for they will see God. 9 Blessed are the peacemakers, for they will be called children of God. 10 Blessed are those who are persecuted because of righteousness, for theirs is the kingdom of heaven. 11 'Blessed are you when people insult you, persecute you and falsely say all kinds of evil against you because of me.

Life According to the Flesh - Evil

By rejecting good (living according to the Spirit), human beings cause disunity with God, resulting in an egoism; consequently, malice arises and leads us on the path of lies where enmities and unhappiness are born. The value of spiritual life is ruined due to the privation of goods according to Will of God.

Figure 4 Evil - Living According to the Flesh (Inner Hell).

Vices or sins will be the means to evil or to the rejection of God; their consequences will always be series of misfortunes and tragedies. In the Bible, we find other passages that indicate the characteristics of a vicious or wicked life.

Galatians 5:19 The acts of the flesh are obvious: sexual immorality, impurity and debauchery; 20 idolatry and witchcraft; hatred, discord, jealousy, fits of rage, selfish ambition, dissensions, factions 21 and envy; drunkenness, orgies, and the like. I warn you, as I did before, that those who live like this will not inherit the kingdom of God.

2 Timothy 3:3 But mark this: there will be terrible times in the last days. 2 People will be lovers of themselves, lovers of money, boastful, proud, abusive, disobedient to their parents, ungrateful, unholy, 3 without love, unforgiving, slanderous, without self-control, brutal, not lovers of the good, 4 treacherous, rash, conceited, lovers of pleasure rather than lovers of God.

Matthew 23:13 'Woe to you, teachers of the law and Pharisees, you hypocrites! You shut the door of the kingdom of heaven in people's faces. You yourselves do not enter, nor will you let those enter who are trying to. 15 'Woe to you, teachers of the law and Pharisees, you hypocrites! You travel over land and sea to win a single convert, and when you have succeeded, you make them twice as much a child of hell as you are. 16 'Woe to you, blind guides! You say, "If anyone swears by the temple, it means nothing; but anyone who swears by the gold of the temple is bound by that oath." 17 You blind fools! Which is greater: the gold, or the temple that makes the gold sacred? 18 You also say, "If anyone swears by the altar, it means nothing; but anyone who swears by the gift on the altar is bound by that oath." 19 You blind men! Which is greater: the gift, or the altar that makes the gift sacred? 20 Therefore, anyone who swears by the altar swears by it and by everything on it. 21 And anyone who swears by the temple swears by it and by the one who dwells in it. 22 And anyone who swears by heaven swears by God's throne and by the one who sits on it. 23 'Woe to you, teachers of the law and Pharisees, you hypocrites! You give a tenth of your spices – mint, dill and cumin. But you have neglected the more important matters of the law – justice, mercy and faithfulness. You should have practiced the latter, without neglecting the former. 24 You blind guides! You strain out a gnat but swallow a camel. 25 'Woe to you, teachers of the law and Pharisees, you hypocrites! You clean the outside of the cup and dish, but inside they are full of greed and self-indulgence. 26 Blind Pharisee! First clean the inside of the cup and dish, and then the outside also will be clean. 27 'Woe to you, teachers of the law and Pharisees, you hypocrites! You are like whitewashed tombs, which look beautiful on the outside but on the inside are full of the bones of the dead and everything unclean. 28 In the same way, on the outside you appear to people as righteous but on the inside you are full of hypocrisy and wickedness. 29 'Woe to you, teachers of the law and Pharisees, you hypocrites! You build tombs for the prophets and decorate the graves of the righteous. 30 And you say, "If we had lived in the days of our ancestors, we would not have taken part with them in shedding the blood of the prophets." 31 So you testify against yourselves that you are the descendants of those who murdered the prophets. 32 Go ahead, then, and complete what your ancestors started! 33 'You snakes! You brood of vipers! How will you escape being condemned to hell?

Sin or vice in general

"Whenever you try to break God's moral law, you end up breaking yourself and hurting others – all while proving His Law in the process." Ravi Zacharias

Sin will be the conscious action that goes against God's voice in conscience (Natural Law), and the Ten commandments (Jewish Law) and Love (Christian Law). Sin is the transgression of Divine Moral Law, and therefore an injustice. Sin is a conscious or voluntary act, contrary to love and to the will of God.

Romans 2:12 All who sin apart from the law will also perish apart from the law, and all who sin under the law will be judged by the law. 13 For it is not those who hear the law who are righteous in God's sight, but it is those who obey the law who will be declared righteous. 14 (Indeed, when Gentiles, who do not have the law, do by nature things required by the law, they are a law for themselves, even though they do not have the law. 15 They show that the requirements of the law are written on their hearts, their consciences also bearing witness, and their thoughts sometimes accusing them and at other times even defending them.) 16 This will take place on the day when God judges people's secrets through Jesus Christ, as my gospel declares.

1 John 5:17a All wrongdoing is sin.

1 John 3:4 Everyone who sins breaks the law; in fact, sin is lawlessness.

Tobias 12:10 But those who live a life of sin and wickedness are their own worst enemies.

Sirach 19:21 Better is a man that hath less intelligence, and wanted understanding, with the fear of God, than he that abounded in understanding, and transgressed the law of the most High.

The main problem is that as we fall into sin and grow in our moral vices, the conscience darkens and becomes wicked.

Wisdom 4:12 For the fascination of wickedness obscures what is good, and roving desire perverts the innocent mind.

The more we grow in sin, the less we can hear and perceive God. When we sin, we lose communion with God, which is what allows us to see the true good. If the sin is severe, we end up distorting our moral criteria. The Bible alerts us to this spiritual tragedy and warns us that this state of inner darkness is totally harmful to the person and to his neighbor.

Isaiah 5:20 Woe to those who call evil good and good evil, who put darkness for light and light for darkness, who put bitter for sweet and sweet for bitter.

Original sin

The idea of original sin comes from Jewish-Christian beliefs. It symbolizes or represents the reality of a kind of tendency or inclination towards evil, which arises in human nature as a consequence of the first human sin that is recorded in the book of Genesis. It is like a weakness around selfishness that affects us during our lives. It is a kind of nature that moves us towards sin or vice. That is why loving is so complicated and challenging for us.

"What Revelation makes known to us is confirmed by our own experience. For when man looks into his own heart he finds that he is drawn towards what is wrong and sunk in many evils which cannot come from his good creator. Often refusing to acknowledge God as his source, man has also upset the relationship which should link him to his last end, and at the same time he has broken the right order that should reign within himself as well as between himself and other men and all creatures." Gaudium et Spes - Paul VI

The provenance of sin

Vice or sin is the central ethical problem in philosophy and theology. Sin has three primary sources, for temptations can arise from ourselves, from a demon, or from another person.

The first source is the flesh; it means the inclination, weakness, or attraction towards evil (vices – sins), that we have within our being.

Mathew 26:41 'Watch and pray so that you will not fall into temptation. The spirit is willing, but the flesh is weak.'

Galatians 5:17 For the flesh desires what is contrary to the Spirit, and the Spirit what is contrary to the flesh. They are in conflict with each other, so that you are not to do whatever you want.

The second source of temptation is demons; Greek, Jewish and Christian, philosophical systems assume that demons exist. They are beings that belong to the spiritual realm but can also participate in the physical world; demons were angels, but they are wagging a lost war against God, so they tempt or seduce humans into sin or vice to lead them towards damnation.

Ephesians 6:12 For our struggle is not against flesh and blood, but against the rulers, against the authorities, against the powers of this dark world and against the spiritual forces of evil in the heavenly realms.

1 Peter 5:8 Be alert and of sober mind. Your enemy the devil prowls around like a roaring lion looking for someone to devour.

Luke 4:40 At sunset, the people brought to Jesus all who had various kinds of illness, and laying his hands on each one, he healed them. 41 Moreover, demons came out of many people, shouting, 'You are the Son of God!' But he rebuked them and would not allow them to speak, because they knew he was the Messiah.

The third source is known as the world; it represents the social pressure that originates in people engaged or committed to some sort of evil; with some kind of vice or sin.

1 John 2:15 Do not love the world or anything in the world. If anyone loves the world, love for the Father is not in them. 16 For everything in the world – the lust of the flesh, the lust of the eyes, and the pride of life – comes not from the Father but from the world. 17 The world and its desires pass away, but whoever does the will of God lives for ever.

James 4:4 Don't you know that friendship with the world means enmity against God? Therefore, anyone who chooses to be a friend of the world becomes an enemy of God.

John 15:18 'If the world hates you, keep in mind that it hated me first. 19 If you belonged to the world, it would love you as its own. As it is, you do not belong to the world, but I have chosen you out of the world. That is why the world hates you.

It is vital to understand why God allows evil in a finite way. For everything that God allows, even evil, is for a greater good. God has infinite power and can heal, repair, and restore for all evil. Nothing escapes his divine providence. While we are in this life, it will be difficult to imagine how God will solve everything and make all things new, but we know that only God has total control over destiny. The reign or dominion of evil is only temporary, while the Kingdom of God lasts forever. Saint Augustine, in a simple phrase, presents this Christian belief in a masterful way.

"God, being the highest good, would in no way allow some kind of evil in his works, unless, because he is omnipotent and good, he draws good out of evil. This belongs to the infinite goodness of God, who can allow evil to draw a good out of it." Saint Augustine

Part 2

*"The battleline between good and evil
runs through the heart of every man."*
Aleksander Solzhenitsyn

Chapter 5: The Contrast Between Virtues and Vices

"Ponder the fact that God has made you a gardener, to root out vice and plant virtue." Saint Catherine of Siena

The in-depth knowledge of the virtues and the vices will help us to understand the moral logic of God and to discover, as Saint Thomas Aquinas said, "all sin and vice are a form of stupidity." Indeed, by understanding the consequences of living by these spiritual qualities, we will realize that living in vices is absurd, silly, and meaningless. While living in virtue is logical, intelligent, and full of meaning.

The knowledge of virtues and vices is generally ignored and underestimated; we rarely achieve to identify them with precision and clarity in us or in the people around us.

The book: *The Road to Character* talks about how moral vocabulary has been lost. People think and use less the spiritual words, which reflects the moral decline of a part of our society.

The situation is that not merely the use has been lost, but also the essence and meaning of vices and virtues. Morality has fallen into a kind of relativism, where the moral-ethical criterion is not considered logical nor objective. Those who defend moral relativism usually end up arguing that being humble, generous, or prudent (virtuous) and being proud, greedy, or foolish (vicious) are equivalent, and that is an evidently false and unsustainable judgment.

You will realize the incredible contrast that exists between each virtue and its corresponding vice; they are means that lead us to totally different ends. The consequences of living one way or another are radically opposite.

Virtues and vices are clearly explained and understood in the New Testament, but they are manifested universally throughout human history. In all cultures, and at all times, there have been perseverant, patient, and wise persons, as well as lazy, impatient, and vain persons.

Humanity naturally tends to give merit to virtues and devalue vice. In some way, all justice systems manifest that duality between what deserves merit and what deserves punishment. There is a great diversity of virtues, and all exist for the Greater good and the Common good (The Glory of God).

"Happiness is obtained through virtue; it is a good achieved by man's own will." Saint Thomas Aquinas

"Remember our words, then, and whatever is your aim let virtue be the condition of the attainment of your aim; and know that without this all possessions and pursuits are dishonorable and evil." Plato

"The most virtuous are those who content themselves with being virtuous without seeking to appear so." Plato

"The superior man thinks always of virtue; the common man thinks of comfort." Confucius

"Honor is the reward of virtue." Cicero

"Dignity does not consist in possessing honors, but in the consciousness that we deserve them." Aristotle

"The proper good of man is the activity of the soul directed by virtue; and if there are many virtues, directed by the highest and most perfect of all." Aristotle

Love - Fundamental Virtue

Love makes all virtues good; it is the highest and most excellent virtue that man can achieve. Love is the only reality that fulfills the human heart; it is the only way to glimpse or envision an eternal joy, and it is the essence of the beauty of the Kingdom of Heaven. Thomas Aquinas said that to love is to will the good of the other.

"Life isn't about having, it's about being." Nick Vujicic

"Love is not just something that happens to you: it is a certain special way of being alive." Thomas Merton

Figure 5 The Way of Virtue – The Beauty of Life.

"And over all these virtues put on love (charity), which binds them all together in perfect unity." Colossians 3:14

The main thing would be to say that all the virtues are evident manifestations of love in our being. If our love is real, it will always be transformed into some virtue. Loving is not an easy thing, but it is something simple; it is something that from the most capable person to the most limited (intellectually and affectively speaking) can live. Loving is within reach of all humanity because God gave us that power and made us for that purpose.

The importance of this virtue is humanly indisputable and indispensable; therefore, it has been a topic always present. A series of renowned authors have expressed famous phrases that can help us to glimpse the immense value of the virtue of love:

"Love is to the soul what health is to the body."
Saint Thomas Aquinas

"Love is the only force capable of changing the heart of man and of all humanity." Benedict XVI

"Charity is the queen of virtues. As the thread intertwines pearls, so charity to the other virtues; when the thread breaks, the pearls fall. That is why when charity is lacking, virtues are lost."
Saint Pio of Pieltrecina

"Love embodies the life of all virtues and expresses the most intimate substance of all holiness." Dietrich Von Hildebrand

"We cannot do great things on this Earth, only small things with great love." Saint Teresa of Calcutta

"Love is the highest and most essential goal to which the human being can aspire... the fullness of human life is in love and is realized through it." Viktor Frankl

"Success, like happiness, is the unexpected side effect of personal dedication to a cause greater than oneself." Viktor Frankl

"If you want to know a person, do not ask him what he thinks but what he loves." Saint Augustine

"Love has to be put into action, and that action is service. Whatever form we are, able or disabled, rich or poor, it is not how much we do, but how much love we put in the doing."
Saint Teresa of Calcutta

"The soul that walks in love neither tires nor gets tired."
Saint John of the Cross

"What is done for love is never small." Chiara Lubich

"In the twilight of our life we will be judged in love."
Saint John of the Cross

"To love is to find your own happiness in the happiness of another."
Leibniz

"True love grows with difficulties, false love fades."
Saint Thomas Aquinas

"Love is a precious pearl that, if it is not possessed, the rest of things are of no use, and if it is possessed, everything else is left over."
Saint Augustine

"The spiritually evolved individual is an individual capable of extraordinary love and, with his extraordinary love, comes extraordinary joy." Scott Peck

"Charity is the center that unites the community with God and all its members with each other; contributes to the union of hearts and links them indissolubly to God." Saint Vincent of Paul.

"Merit consists only in the virtue of charity, flavored with the light of true discretion without which the soul is worth nothing."
Saint Catherine of Siena

"It is truly great who has great charity." Thomas of Kempis

"Charity revives those who are spiritually dead."
Saint Thomas Aquinas

"To love someone means to see them as God intended them."
Dostoyevsky

"Where charity reigns, there is happiness." Saint John Bosco

"Do not wait to be perfect to love, it will be love what perfects you."
Fr. Nelson Medina

"I really only love God as much as I love the person I love the least."
Dorothy Day

"Every work of authentic charity is then a concrete manifestation of God's love for men and thus becomes a proclamation of the Gospel." Benedict XVI

"External work without charity does not benefit, but what is done with charity, however little and despicable it may be, becomes all fruitful." Thomas a Kempis

"Love leads to happiness. Only those who have it are promised eternal bliss. And without it, everything else is insufficient." Saint Thomas Aquinas

Finally, Saint Thomas Aquinas said: "You cannot be good for a long time without being happy, nor can you be happy for a long time without being good." Indeed, we cannot imagine a good person who does not love; moreover, the word good is precisely designated to people who love. Being virtuous means living good by following God who is Good.

Virtue is when our conscience and our behavior are directed to the GOOD.

"The virtuous person tends toward the good with all his sensory and spiritual powers; he pursues the good and chooses it in concrete actions." CCC 1803

Love vs Egoism

Love is...	Egoism is...
The universal reason for being and for existing.	Self-deception about being and existing.
The purpose of free will and freedom.	The waste of free will and freedom.
The beginning and end of all virtue.	The beginning and end of all vice.
What deserves merit, honor, and reward.	What deserves demerit, dishonor, and correction or punishment.
Spiritual life and communion with God.	Spiritual death and disunity with God.

"Charity is the theological virtue by which we love God above all things for his own sake, and our neighbor as ourselves for the love of God." CCC 1822

The universal reason for being and for existing.

Love is why reality exists instead of absolute nothingness; it is why the Creator worked the creation. Human love is forever indebted to divine love. We, humans, have the opportunity and responsibility to respond to God's love, which has always existed. Biblical revelation affirms that the meaning of life for all creatures is to love and glorify the Holy Creator. We can fully trust that our mission in life is to love and that the most important and transcendent thing we can do is: to live with charity. We know that what makes life experiences valuable, beautiful, and perfect is only love. We know that God is really pleased and joyful when we love. Saint Paul affirms this by saying that we should not live for ourselves but for God, who, as we saw in the first part, is the source of all good. He is always holy and always perfect.

Romans 14:7 For none of us lives for ourselves alone, and none of us dies for ourselves alone. 8 If we live, we live for the Lord; and if we die, we die for the Lord. So, whether we live or die, we belong to the Lord. 9 For this very reason, Christ died and returned to life so that he might be the Lord of both the dead and the living.

Colossians 3:23 Whatever you do, work at it with all your heart, as working for the Lord, not for human masters, 24 since you know that you will receive an inheritance from the Lord as a reward. It is the Lord Christ you are serving.

Romans 12:9 Love must be sincere. Hate what is evil; cling to what is good. 10 Be devoted to one another in love. Honor one another above yourselves. 11 Never be lacking in zeal, but keep your spiritual fervor, serving the Lord.

Acts 17:28 For in him we live and move and have our being.

The purpose of free will and freedom.

Free will must exist for us to be able to love, that is why the denial of free will implies the denial of love. The divine goal of our liberty in thoughts, attitudes, decisions, expressions, and actions is charity.

Free will achieves freedom only through love. Only he who loves is truly free.

Romans 6:22 But now that you have been set free from sin and have become slaves of God, the benefit you reap leads to holiness, and the result is eternal life.

Galatians 5:13 You, my brothers and sisters, were called to be free. But do not use your freedom to indulge the flesh; rather, serve one another humbly in love.

1 Peter 2:15 For it is God's will that by doing good you should silence the ignorant talk of foolish people. 16 Live as free people, but do not use your freedom as a cover-up for evil; live as God's slaves. 17 Show proper respect to everyone, love the family of believers, fear God, honor the emperor.

2 Corinthians 3:17 Now the Lord is the Spirit, and where the Spirit of the Lord is, there is freedom.

The beginning and end of all virtue.

Love is also the essence of every virtue; it is like a force that leads our conscience and actions towards all kinds of good. Everything that we consider as virtue is an actual manifestation of love. For all virtues reflect the beauty and complementarity of the various forms of love. Truly in a transcendent way, we are called to experience complete joy by personifying all virtues.

1 Corinthians 13:4 Love is patient, love is kind. It does not envy, it does not boast, it is not proud. 5 It does not dishonor others, it is not self-seeking, it is not easily angered, it keeps no record of wrongs. 6 Love does not delight in evil but rejoices with the truth. 7 It always protects, always trusts, always hopes, always perseveres.

1 Peter 4:8 Above all, love each other deeply, because love covers over a multitude of sins.

In the Gospel, Jesus explains that the greatest love is to lay down one's life for one's friends, and his own story ends up being a literal demonstration of such love. The life of Christ is a unique and divine testimony of what fully loving really means, and that is why the gospels are the most incredible love story ever written.

John 15:13 Greater love has no one than this: to lay down one's life for one's friends.

We may not face the decision to lay down our lives in a life-or-death situation; however, through virtues, we still have the possibility to lay down our lives for others every day in imitation of Christ.

1 John 3:16 This is how we know what love is: Jesus Christ laid down his life for us. And we ought to lay down our lives for our brothers and sisters.

Ephesians 5:1 Follow God's example, therefore, as dearly loved children 2 and live a life of love, just as Christ loved us and gave himself up for us as a fragrant offering and sacrifice to God.

1 John 4:12b but if we love one another, God lives in us and his love is made complete in us.

What deserves merit, honor, and reward.

Love is what universally deserves merit; it is what we should always admire and recognize as heroic and venerable. Its effects are always fruitful and awe-inspiring. The highest human honor should always be given to the virtue of love.

Philippians 4:8 Finally, brothers and sisters, whatever is true, whatever is noble, whatever is right, whatever is pure, whatever is lovely, whatever is admirable – if anything is excellent or praiseworthy – think about such things.

Romans 13:7 Give to everyone what you owe them: if you owe taxes, pay taxes; if revenue, then revenue; if respect, then respect; if honor, then honor.

Romans 2:10a but glory, honor and peace for everyone who does good.

Sirach 10:28 My child, honor yourself with humility, and give yourself the esteem you deserve.

In one of the most demanding, paradoxical, and unique teachings of Christianity, Jesus teaches us that the merit of charity comes to excellence in the love for our human enemies.

We can do nothing more remarkable than that, since the more adverse the circumstances, the more heroic our love will be. That is why loving our enemies is so supernatural and exceptional.

We have all encountered people who are difficult to love, and clearly, the more vicious a person is, the more difficult it is to love them, but it is also when they need our love the most and it is what Christ is demanding for us.

By loving our enemies, Jesus is not only talking about our attitude, but of complete love, truly full in all types of virtues, which requires of all our faculties.

Luke 6:32 'If you love those who love you, what credit is that to you? Even sinners love those who love them. 33 And if you do good to those who are good to you, what credit is that to you? Even sinners do that. 34 And if you lend to those from whom you expect repayment, what credit is that to you? Even sinners lend to sinners, expecting to be repaid in full. 35 But love your enemies, do good to them, and lend to them without expecting to get anything back. Then your reward will be great, and you will be children of the Most High, because he is kind to the ungrateful and wicked. 36 Be merciful, just as your Father is merciful.

Interestingly, all that God offers us and asks of us is to love. Saint Augustine wisely prayed, "Lord, give me what you ask of me and ask me what you will." God will reward us at the end of our life based on love. The only way to happily face death is to know that we have lived loving; that we have renounced our egoism to seek the good of God and of our neighbor.

Ephesians 6:8 because you know that the Lord will reward each one for whatever good they do, whether they are slave or free.

Sirach 16:15a All mercy shall make a place for every man according to the merit of his works.

Sirach 11:26 It is easy for the Lord to pay back people according to their ways in the hour of death.

Revelation 22:11 Let the one who does wrong continue to do wrong; let the vile person continue to be vile; let the one who does right continue to do right; and let the holy person continue to be holy.' 12 'Look, I am coming soon! My reward is with me, and I will give to each person according to what they have done. 13 I am the Alpha and the Omega, the First and the Last, the Beginning and the End. 14 'Blessed are those who wash their robes, that they may have the right to the tree of life and may go through the gates into the city.

Spiritual life and communion with God.

We could define love as the spiritual life. To love is to live! This what Jesus is talking about when he declares that he has come so that we may have the fullness of life.

John 10:10b I have come that they may have life, and have it to the full.

Finally, communion with God means giving him his place as God in our lives, it means doing his will and living by and for God. There is a space in our hearts that only He can fill.

1 John 4:16 And so we know and rely on the love God has for us. God is love. Whoever lives in love lives in God, and God in them.

Egoism - Fundamental Vice

Selfishness is the idolatry of oneself, and idolatry is putting something at the center of our lives other than God, which goes against the first and most important commandment of the Divine Law. We are not our gods; both responsibility and moral duty come only from God. Selfishness or egoism is the belief that personal fulfillment can be achieved without love or virtue; and it is assuming that we can be good without God.

"Egoism is not self-love, but an inordinate passion for oneself."
Aristotle

Figure 6 The Way of Vice – The Tragedy of Life.

"Selfish people are incapable of loving others, but they are not capable of loving themselves either." Erich Fromm

"Unless you crucify your ego, you cannot be my follower, Jesus says. This move – This terrible move – has to be the foundation of the spiritual life." Robert Barron

Without a doubt, love cannot dwell nor develop in a heart that clings on its selfishness, which closes on itself and becomes the dictator of its own good. It is essential to understand that all vices derive from egoism and that our lack of love will always turn into a vice. Selfishness is precisely that absence of love, and when there is no love in our hearts, our experiences turn from negative to dramatic.

We find some phrases that help us understand that selfishness is the main enemy of love:

"Wars come from egoism and selfishness." Fulton J. Sheen

"One of the biggest diseases in the world is selfishness."
Saint Teresa of Calcutta

"The poison of selfishness is what destroys the world."
Saint Catherine of Siena

"Egoism is the source and summary of all faults and miseries."
Thomas Carlyle

"Every man must decide whether to walk in the light of creative altruism or in the darkness of destructive selfishness."
Martin Luther King

"Where selfishness reigns, love cannot dwell." Billy Graham

"Selfishness is blind." Mahatma Gandhi

"As selfishness and complaint pervert the mind, love with its joy clears and sharpens vision." Helen Keller

"As poor as the table is that lacks bread, so the most exemplary life is empty if it lacks love." Saint Anthony of Padua

"I understood that without love all works are nothing, even the most brilliant." Saint Teresa of Lisieux

"Selfishness is the death of society and families." Jeronimo Usera

"What is hell? I maintain that it is the suffering of being unable to love." Dostoevsky

"Great achievement is usually born of great sacrifice and is never the result of selfishness." Napoleon Hill

"He who is indifferent to life and death is that he does not love."
Saint Augustine

"He who does not love is already dead."
Saint John of the Cross

Selfishness or egoism is the primary spiritual evil; it is from where all kinds of vices develop. If we think about it, usually, the adjective evil is used to denote a person who lacks love. Selfishness, although it sometimes appears to be something functional-beneficial, in the end, is full of false promises and disastrous consequences. Because of egoism and its related vices, many people have destroyed and ruined the most valued realities of their lives.

Vice is when our conscience and our behavior
are directed towards evil.

"It is human to sin, but diabolic to persist in sin."
Saint Catherine of Siena

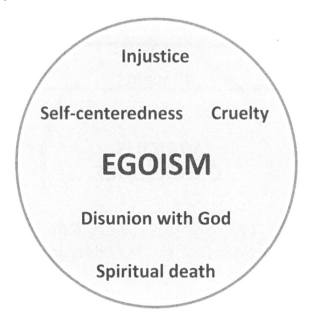

"This is what the LORD says: 'Cursed is the one who trusts in man, who draws strength from mere flesh and whose heart turns away from the LORD." Jeremiah 17:5

Self-deception about being and existing.

The Bible considers the sin or vice of selfishness as the primary manifestation of evil. Precisely, the first human sin mentioned in the Bible is the catastrophic lie of Satan to the woman.

This lie entails two fundamental fallacies: 1) it implies a distrust of God as God. 2) it suggests the belief that humans can become equal to God. Believing in these two ideas constitutes the self-deception of selfishness.

All evils could be reduced to these two perverse principles, a wrong understanding of God and a false understanding of the self. Love, Truth, Good are realities that transcend us in an absolute way; believing that we can be more relevant in our own life than God is absurd. What is the meaning of life if there is no Good, Love, and Truth?

Genesis 2:15 The LORD God took the man and put him in the Garden of Eden to work it and take care of it. 16 And the LORD God commanded the man, 'You are free to eat from any tree in the garden; 17 but you must not eat from the tree of the knowledge of good and evil, for when you eat from it you will certainly die.'

Genesis 3:3 Now the snake was more crafty than any of the wild animals the LORD God had made. He said to the woman, 'Did God really say, "You must not eat from any tree in the garden"?' 2 The woman said to the snake, 'We may eat fruit from the trees in the garden, 3 but God did say, "You must not eat fruit from the tree that is in the middle of the garden, and you must not touch it, or you will die." ' 4 'You will not certainly die,' the snake said to the woman. 5 'For God knows that when you eat from it your eyes will be opened, and you will be like God, knowing good and evil.'

"In that sin man preferred himself to God and by that very act scorned him. He chose himself over and against God, against the requirements of his creaturely status and therefore against his own good" CCC 398

In this life, we face the same temptation to rebel before God to allow ourselves to be carried away by our egoism. Believing that life is primarily about us is an empty belief that mimics the Genesis story. By denying God, we lose our true identity and the meaning of our existence. Jesus, in the Gospel, affirms one of the most challenging truths of Christianity, which also refers to the spiritual battle against our ego.

Mark 8:35 For whoever wants to save their life will lose it, but whoever loses their life for me and for the gospel will save it. 36 What good is it for someone to gain the whole world, yet forfeit their soul? 37 Or what can anyone give in exchange for their soul? 38 If anyone is ashamed of me and my words in this adulterous and sinful generation, the Son of Man will be ashamed of them when he comes in his Father's glory with the holy angels.'

Juan 12:25 Anyone who loves their life will lose it, while anyone who hates their life in this world will keep it for eternal life. 26 Whoever serves me must follow me; and where I am, my servant also will be. My Father will honor the one who serves me.

After these readings, it may be an excellent time to clarify a great contradiction between what is considered self-love according to God and self-love according to the world (Egoism). As Christians, we are morally obliged to seek our good, which can only be understood through the Spirit of God. Furthermore, self-love must be equivalent to the love of neighbor only behind the love of God. God's will is both; to care for our own good and to care for the good of others. This Christian belief is clearly expressed in both the Old Testament and the New Testament.

Leviticus 19:18 Do not seek revenge or bear a grudge against anyone among your people, but love your neighbor as yourself. I am the LORD.

Matthew 22:36 'Teacher, which is the greatest commandment in the Law?' 37 Jesus replied: "Love the Lord your God with all your heart and with all your soul and with all your mind." 38 This is the first and greatest commandment. 39 And the second is like it: "Love your neighbor as yourself."

The waste of free will and freedom.

If moral duty, responsibility, justice, and love are not the purpose of having free will, then we are doomed to live in absolute chaos, in which the law of the jungle rules. We all know what happens when we think that our free will is the maximum end on itself; it merely causes all types of sins in which we become slaves.

Saint Paul teaches this in one of his letters. It is typical for us to think that we have already freed ourselves from moral laws or that we are above universal good and evil. But we usually do that simply to end up justifying our immoral behavior, in which we are vile slaves of our selfishness.

If we reflect honestly, we may discover that we have never really felt free and whole when we have excused ourselves in our free will to end up doing something evil.

Romans 6:20 When you were slaves to sin, you were free from the control of righteousness. 21 What benefit did you reap at that time from the things you are now ashamed of? Those things result in death!

Using our free will to end up being selfish is the most crystal-clear sign of irresponsibility; it is the waste of our life because, really, the wages of sin is death.

Romans 6:23 For the wages of sin is death, but the gift of God is eternal life in Christ Jesus our Lord.

The beginning and end of all vice.

It is essential to learn to reject and expel all kinds of egoistic thoughts, attitudes, and decisions from within. Because if we do not, we will end up doing all sorts of injustices and cruelties. We find in the Bible a passage that categorically states that we should avoid doing anything out of selfishness and vanity. Christian philosophy is firm in its forceful rejection of all kinds of ego-based behaviors.

Philippians 2:3a Do nothing out of selfish ambition or vain conceit.

In a forceful rejection of modern utilitarianism, which drives us always to be looking for our benefit, our advantage, our pleasure, our comfort, our luxuries, Biblical wisdom invites us to think, serve and seek the good of others.

1 Corinthians 10:24 No one should seek their own good, but the good of others.

The benefit to which it refers is the good of the person, which does not necessarily imply fulfilling the whims of others or doing what others want. But to seek the greater good and the will of God for the other. If we think about it, loving and being virtuous is what can generate the greatest "utility" for human beings; it is what could give us the most progress in the shortest time, while the utility according to ego is insipid, monotonous, and superficial; growth, joy, and peace are always in shortage.

What deserves demerit, dishonor, and correction or punishment.

If there is something that denigrates the human person, it is sins or vices. If anything deserves demerit in human behavior or conduct, it is precisely living rejecting love and indulging in all kinds of selfishness. Saint Paul teaches us that if we do not act with love, even if we do very showy or portentous things, in reality, our actions are empty and do not deserve any merit.

1 Corinthians 13:1 If I speak in the tongues of men or of angels, but do not have love, I am only a resounding gong or a clanging cymbal. 2 If I have the gift of prophecy and can fathom all mysteries and all knowledge, and if I have a faith that can move mountains, but do not have love, I am nothing. 3 If I give all I possess to the poor and give over my body to hardship that I may boast, but do not have love, I gain nothing.

Complementarily, in the book of Sirach, we find an insightful passage that clarifies the injustice of flattering, honoring, or admiring those who are under immoral behaviors; and who do not seek the real good. Although it may seem obvious, there is often ideological warfare through the media that misconstrues reality; therefore, it is not easy to discern. But if we look closely at the fame and honor bestowed by the world, we can see that most of those honors are empty in the eyes of wisdom.

Sirach 10:23 It is not right to despise one who is intelligent but poor, and it is not proper to honor one who is sinful.

God, who is always perfect in justice and mercy, is willing to educate us so that we learn to love and turn away from sin and vices. As a parent, God is continually seeking to help us, and we must learn to accept his will, even when it comes as a correction in love. If we reject the discipline that comes from God, the only thing left for us is to expect dishonor and punishment.

Psalm 26:2 Test me, LORD, and try me, examine my heart and my mind.

Deuteronomy 8:5 Know then in your heart that as a man disciplines his son, so the LORD your God disciplines you.

Hebrews 12:4 In your struggle against sin, you have not yet resisted to the point of shedding your blood. 5 And have you completely forgotten this word of encouragement that addresses you as a father addresses his son? It says, 'My son, do not make light of the LORD's discipline, and do not lose heart when he rebukes you, 6 because the LORD disciplines the one he loves, and he chastens everyone he accepts as his son.' 7 Endure hardship as discipline; God is treating you as his children. For what children are not disciplined by their father? 8 If you are not disciplined – and everyone undergoes discipline – then you are not legitimate, not true sons and daughters at all. 9 Moreover, we have all had human fathers who disciplined us and we respected them for it. How much more should we submit to the Father of spirits and live! 10 They disciplined us for a little while as they thought best; but God disciplines us for our good, in order that we may share in his holiness. 11 No discipline seems pleasant at the time, but painful. Later on, however, it produces a harvest of righteousness and peace for those who have been trained by it.

Job 5:17 'Blessed is the one whom God corrects; so do not despise the discipline of the Almighty. 18 For he wounds, but he also binds up; he injures, but his hands also heal.

Wisdom 12:2 Therefore you correct little by little those who trespass, and you remind and warn them of the things through which they sin, so that they may be freed from wickedness and put their trust in you, O Lord.

Revelation 3:19 Those whom I love I rebuke and discipline. So be earnest and repent.

Proverbs 15:32 Those who disregard discipline despise themselves, but the one who heeds correction gains understanding.

Spiritual death and disunity with God.

We can be sure that God does not tempt us and that if he allows us to live and experience temptations; it is because he is going to give us the strength to resist them so that we have no excuse at any time to consent to evil and accept it as part of our lives.

James 1:13 When tempted, no one should say, 'God is tempting me.' For God cannot be tempted by evil, nor does he tempt anyone; 14 but each person is tempted when they are dragged away by their own evil desire and enticed. 15 Then, after desire has conceived, it gives birth to sin; and sin, when it is full-grown, gives birth to death.

1 Corinthians 10:13 No temptation has overtaken you except what is common to mankind. And God is faithful; he will not let you be tempted beyond what you can bear. But when you are tempted, he will also provide a way out so that you can endure it.

Finally, every vice or sin; is a sign of rupture in our unity with God. When we sin, we go against God's will, and it implies an inevitable loss of love in our hearts. Saint Paul clearly tells us that we cannot let sin reign in our lives. We must fight internally against the evils that drive us to commit all kinds of injustices.

Romans 6:12 Therefore do not let sin reign in your mortal body so that you obey its evil desires. 13a Do not offer any part of yourself to sin as an instrument of wickedness.

1 John 1:6 If we claim to have fellowship with him and yet walk in the darkness, we lie and do not live out the truth. 7 But if we walk in the light, as he is in the light, we have fellowship with one another, and the blood of Jesus, his Son, purifies us from all sin.

1 John 3:14b Anyone who does not love remains in death.

The Virtuous and Vicious Cycles

"If the glory of God is man fully alive, then virtues are the qualities of the fully living soul." Unknown

Interestingly with the virtues and vices that we will analyze in the following pages, it also happens as in the parable of the talents. We could think that virtue attracts virtue and vice attracts vice. The more we grow in one virtue, the more opportunities we have to develop other virtues; and the more we grow in one vice, the more likely it will be to develop other vices. We tend to polarize ourselves between good and evil through our actions, and for that reason, some people earn so much honor due to their virtues, while others accumulate so much infamy because of their vices.

Matthew 25:14 -The parable of the bags of gold- 'Again, it will be like a man going on a journey, who called his servants and entrusted his wealth to them. 15 To one he gave five bags of gold, to another two bags, and to another one bag, each according to his ability. Then he went on his journey. 16 The man who had received five bags of gold went at once and put his money to work and gained five bags more. 17 So also, the one with two bags of gold gained two more. 18 But the man who had received one bag went off, dug a hole in the ground and hid his master's money. 19 'After a long time the master of those servants returned and settled accounts with them. 20 The man who had received five bags of gold brought the other five. "Master," he said, "you entrusted me with five bags of gold. See, I have gained five more." 21 'His master replied, "Well done, good and faithful servant! You have been faithful with a few things; I will put you in charge of many things. Come and share your master's happiness!" 22 'The man with two bags of gold also came. "Master," he said, "you entrusted me with two bags of gold: see, I have gained two more." 23 'His master replied, "Well done, good and faithful servant! You have been faithful with a few things; I will put you in charge of many things. Come and share your master's happiness!" 24 'Then the man who had received one bag of gold came. "Master," he said, "I knew that you are a hard man, harvesting where you have not sown and gathering where you have not scattered seed. 25 So I was afraid and went out and hid your gold in the ground. See, here is what belongs to you." 26 'His master replied, "You wicked, lazy servant! So you knew that I harvest where I have not sown and gather where I have not scattered seed? 27 Well then, you should have put my money on deposit with the bankers, so that when I returned I would have received it back with interest. 28 ' "So take the bag of gold from him and give it to the one who has ten bags. 29 For whoever has will be given more, and they will have an abundance. Whoever does not have, even what they have will be taken from them. 30 And throw that worthless servant outside, into the darkness, where there will be weeping and gnashing of teeth."

This law that is fulfilled in the parable is also fulfilled in many areas of life. One of those realms is spirituality or morality. If we do not bear fruit through our virtues during our lifetime, we end up losing them.

The people on the right way (heaven) develop and accumulate virtues, while the people who are on the wrong track (hell) develop and accumulate vices.

Chapter 6: The Divine Lights

"If God can use a man without arms and legs to be His hands and feet, then He will certainly use any willing heart!" Nick Vujicic

Faith and hope are the highest and most mystical virtues after love; they uniquely reveal our faithfulness to God, and therefore the power of God. These virtues are known as theological because they have the Perfect Being as their object; and consequently, they are the most perfect in the hierarchy. These virtues are only known through the teachings of Judaism and Christianity. They do not remove nor cancel any of the other human virtues,' but rather, they elevate them to a supernatural meaning.

CCE: 1812 The human virtues are rooted in the theological virtues, which adapt man's faculties for participation in the divine nature: for the theological virtues relate directly to God. They dispose Christians to live in a relationship with the Holy Trinity. They have the One and Triune God for their origin, motive, and object.

This segment will analyze the contrast between theological virtues and their opposite vices. It will try to answer and demonstrate why they are so valuable and influential in our lives. The Bible is clearly inviting us to always be prepared to talk about our faith and our hope.

1 Peter 3:15b Always be prepared to make a defense to any one who calls you to account for the hope that is in you, yet do it with gentleness and reverence. 16 and keep your conscience clear, so that, when you are abused, those who revile your good behavior in Christ may be put to shame.

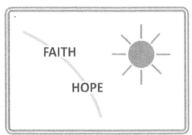

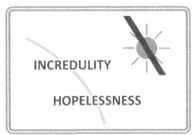

Faith vs. Incredulity

Faith is...	Incredulity is...
Wanting to know God.	Not wanting to know God.
To discern God.	Not to discern God.
To believe in God.	Not to believe in God.
To trust in God.	Not to trust in God.
To live for God.	Not to live for God.
To do good.	Not doing good.
To contemplate God.	Not to contemplate God.

"Faith is like a bright ray of sunshine. It allows us to see God in all things, as well as all things in God." Saint Francis of Sales

Wanting to know God.

*"God does not expect us to submit our faith to him without reason,
but the very limits of our reason make faith a necessity."*
Saint Augustine

Faith is reasonably the most mysterious virtue of all. It is a particular virtue of humans; it leads us directly to a mystical union with God. Faith begins with the knowledge of God and ends in the fullness of the encounter with God.

Sirach 25:12 The fear of the Lord is the beginning of his love: and faith is the beginning of cleaving unto him.

Faith is the existential and transcendental quest to find an answer to the 4 philosophical questions about God. It means searching for the Being, Truth, Good, and Happiness, and therefore searching for Love.

Matthew 7:7 'Ask and it will be given to you; seek and you will find; knock and the door will be opened to you. 8 For everyone who asks receives; the one who seeks finds; and to the one who knocks, the door will be opened.

The philosopher Pascal, in a brilliant thought, portrays the human quest for knowledge of God: "There are only three types of people; those who have found God and serve him; those who have not found God and seek him, and those who live not seeking or finding him. The first ones are rational and happy; the second ones are rational and unhappy, and the third ones irrational and unhappy."

Seeking and knowing God is something mysterious because we can find him in countless realities. Still, we can search for him in two primary sources:

1.- His Word.

Just as we know people through their words, we also know God through His. Faith is the answer to the Truth that is the Living Word of God. Our knowledge of God increases mainly through listening or reading the Holy Scriptures. The Word of God is full of life and meaning, and it is what ignites our faith in the quest for love.

Romans 1:16 For I am not ashamed of the gospel, because it is the power of God that brings salvation to everyone who believes: first to the Jew, then to the Gentile. 17 For in the gospel the righteousness of God is revealed – a righteousness that is by faith from first to last, just as it is written: 'The righteous will live by faith.'

Romans 10:17 Consequently, faith comes from hearing the message, and the message is heard through the word about Christ.

2 Timothy 3:15 and because since childhood you have known Sacred Scripture, which can give you the wisdom that leads to salvation through faith in Christ Jesus.

Faith is complemented and developed with the religious experience of knowing and feeling God's love for us, which is the Bible's central message. In Scripture, we find a passage that shows the immense love that God has for each one of us.

1 John 4:10 This is love: not that we loved God, but that he loved us and sent his Son as an atoning sacrifice for our sins.

2.- His people.

We can also know God through human experiences because He continually reveals himself to everyone through the people and circumstances of daily life. The opportunity is hidden in sincerely asking ourselves what messages from God are being revealed through the people around us. Faith increases especially in the encounter with someone close to God, with people who live and reflect an authentic faith through their virtues and testimony of life.

"The main way that God chooses to communicate us a message is our neighbor." Saint Thomas Aquinas

To discern God.

Discerning God is about placing our belief in Him and not in some reality smaller than Him, for we all are guided by beliefs, but we do not all believe the same things, and thus different beliefs lead to diverse destinations. That's why it is crucial to distinguish where we are setting our faith because this virtue only has order and only makes sense in Him. Indeed, only God is worthy of faith.

In the following text, we are encouraged to continually make spiritual discernments because this virtue is exclusively related to the true God and taught mainly by Jesus Christ, who is the authentic teacher of faith.

1 John 4:1 Dear friends, do not believe every spirit, but test the spirits to see whether they are from God, because many false prophets have gone out into the world. 2 This is how you can recognize the Spirit of God: every spirit that acknowledges that Jesus Christ has come in the flesh is from God, 3 but every spirit that does not acknowledge Jesus is not from God. This is the spirit of the antichrist, which you have heard is coming and even now is already in the world. 4 You, dear children, are from God and have overcome them, because the one who is in you is greater than the one who is in the world. 5 They are from the world and therefore speak from the viewpoint of the world, and the world listens to them. 6 We are from God, and whoever knows God listens to us; but whoever is not from God does not listen to us. This is how we recognize the Spirit of truth and the spirit of falsehood.

To believe in God.

Believing for humans comes naturally; it is an act that involves mainly our intelligence and our will, it is primarily related to a vision about the future; it works as a conviction in the face of an uncertain but possible reality.

Hebrews 11:1 Now faith is confidence in what we hope for and assurance about what we do not see. 2 This is what the ancients were commended for. 3 By faith we understand that the universe was formed at God's command, so that what is seen was not made out of what was visible.

1 Corinthians 5:7 For we live by faith, not by sight.

We have the unique opportunity to believe in God because of his wisdom-filled parables in the Bible, the historical miracles, and the prophecies fulfilled in Jesus Christ.

A parable serves as an example:

Matthew 13:24 Jesus told them another parable: 'The kingdom of heaven is like a man who sowed good seed in his field. 25 But while everyone was sleeping, his enemy came and sowed weeds among the wheat, and went away. 26 When the wheat sprouted and formed ears, then the weeds also appeared. 27 'The owner's servants came to him and said, "Sir, didn't you sow good seed in your field? Where then did the weeds come from?" 28 'An enemy did this, he replied. 'The servants asked him, "Do you want us to go and pull them up?" 29 "No," he answered, "because while you are pulling up the weeds, you may uproot the wheat with them. 30 Let both grow together until the harvest. At that time I will tell the harvesters: first collect the weeds and tie them in bundles to be burned; then gather the wheat and bring it into my barn."

Matthew 13:36 Then he left the crowd and went into the house. His disciples came to him and said, 'Explain to us the parable of the weeds in the field.' 37 He answered, 'The one who sowed the good seed is the Son of Man. 38 The field is the world, and the good seed stands for the people of the kingdom. The weeds are the people of the evil one, 39 and the enemy who sows them is the devil. The harvest is the end of the age, and the harvesters are angels. 40 'As the weeds are pulled up and burned in the fire, so it will be at the end of the age. 41 The Son of Man will send out his angels, and they will weed out of his kingdom everything that causes sin and all who do evil. 42 They will throw them into the blazing furnace, where there will be weeping and gnashing of teeth. 43 Then the righteous will shine like the sun in the kingdom of their Father. Whoever has ears, let them hear.

A miracle that serves as an example:

John 9:9 As he went along, he saw a man blind from birth. 2 His disciples asked him, 'Rabbi, who sinned, this man or his parents, that he was born blind?' 3 'Neither this man nor his parents sinned,' said Jesus, 'but this happened so that the works of God might be displayed in him. 4 As long as it is day, we must do the works of him who sent me. Night is coming, when no one can work. 5 While I am in the world, I am the light of the world.' 6 After saying this, he spat on the ground, made some mud with the saliva, and put it on the man's eyes. 7 'Go,' he told him, 'wash in the Pool of Siloam' (this word means 'Sent'). So the man went and washed, and came home seeing. 8 His neighbors and those who had formerly seen him begging asked, 'Isn't this the same man who used to sit and beg?' 9 Some claimed that he was. Others said, 'No, he only looks like him.' But he himself insisted, 'I am the man.' 10 'How then were your eyes opened?' they asked. 11 He replied, 'The man they call Jesus made some mud and put it on my eyes. He told me to go to Siloam and wash. So I went and washed, and then I could see.' 12 'Where is this man?' they asked him. 'I don't know,' he said. The Pharisees investigate the healing 13 They brought to the Pharisees the man who had been blind. 14 Now the day on which Jesus had made the mud and opened the man's eyes was a Sabbath. 15 Therefore the Pharisees also asked him how he had received his sight. 'He put mud on my eyes,' the man replied, 'and I washed, and now I see.' 16 Some of the Pharisees said, 'This man is not from God, for he does not keep the Sabbath.' But others asked, 'How can a sinner perform such signs?' So they were divided. 17 Then they turned again to the blind man, 'What have you to say about him? It was your eyes he opened.' The man replied, 'He is a prophet.' 18 They still did not believe that he had been blind and had received his sight until they sent for the man's parents. 19'Is this your son?' they asked. 'Is this the one you say was born blind? How is it that now he can see?' 20 'We know he is our son,' the parents answered, 'and we know he was born blind. 21 But how he can see now, or who opened his eyes, we don't know. Ask him. He is of age; he will speak for himself.' 22 His parents said this because they were afraid of the Jewish leaders, who already had decided that anyone who acknowledged that Jesus was the Messiah would be put out of the synagogue. 23 That was why his parents said, 'He is of age; ask him.' 24 A second time they summoned the man who had been blind. 'Give glory to God by telling the truth,' they said. 'We know this man is a sinner.' 25 He replied, 'Whether he is a sinner or not, I don't know. One thing I do know. I was blind but now I see!' 26 Then they asked him, 'What did he do to you? How did he open your eyes?' 27 He answered, 'I have told you already and you did not listen. Why do you want to hear it again? Do you want to become his disciples too?' 28 Then they hurled insults at him and said, 'You are this fellow's disciple! We are disciples of Moses! 29 We know that God spoke to Moses, but as for this fellow, we don't even know where he comes from.' 30 The man answered, 'Now that is remarkable! You don't know where he comes from, yet he opened my eyes. 31 We know that God does not listen to sinners. He listens to the godly person who does his will. 32 Nobody has ever heard of opening the eyes of a man born blind. 33 If this man were not from God, he could do nothing.' 34 To this they replied, 'You were steeped in sin at birth; how dare you lecture us!' And they threw him out. Spiritual blindness 35 Jesus heard that they had thrown him out, and when he found him, he said, 'Do you believe in the Son of Man?' 36 'Who is he, sir?' the man asked. 'Tell me so that I may believe in him.' 37 Jesus said, 'You have now seen him; in fact, he is the one speaking with you.' 38 Then the man said, 'Lord, I believe,' and he worshipped him. 39 Jesus said, 'For judgment I have come into this world, so that the blind will see and those who see will become blind.'

A fulfilled prophecy that serves as an example:

Isaiah 42:1 Here is my servant, whom I uphold, my chosen one in whom I delight; I will put my Spirit on him, and he will bring justice to the nations. 2 He will not shout or cry out, or raise his voice in the streets. 3 A bruised reed he will not break, and a smoldering wick he will not snuff out. In faithfulness he will bring forth justice; 4 he will not falter or be discouraged till he establishes justice on earth.

In his teaching the islands will put their hope.' 5 This is what God the LORD says – the Creator of the heavens, who stretches them out, who spreads out the earth with all that springs from it, who gives breath to its people, and life to those who walk on it: 6 'I, the LORD, have called you in righteousness; I will take hold of your hand. I will keep you and will make you to be a covenant for the people and a light for the Gentiles, 7 to open eyes that are blind, to free captives from prison and to release from the dungeon those who sit in darkness.

Luke 2:25 Now there was a man in Jerusalem called Simeon, who was righteous and devout. He was waiting for the consolation of Israel, and the Holy Spirit was on him. 26 It had been revealed to him by the Holy Spirit that he would not die before he had seen the Lord's Messiah. 27 Moved by the Spirit, he went into the temple courts. When the parents brought in the child Jesus to do for him what the custom of the Law required, 28 Simeon took him in his arms and praised God, saying: 29 'Sovereign Lord, as you have promised, you may now dismiss your servant in peace. 30 For my eyes have seen your salvation, 31 which you have prepared in the sight of all nations: 32 a light for revelation to the Gentiles, and the glory of your people Israel.' 33 The child's father and mother marveled at what was said about him. 34 Then Simeon blessed them and said to Mary, his mother: 'This child is destined to cause the falling and rising of many in Israel, and to be a sign that will be spoken against, 35 so that the thoughts of many hearts will be revealed. And a sword will pierce your own soul too.'

John 8:12 When Jesus spoke again to the people, he said, 'I am the light of the world. Whoever follows me will never walk in darkness, but will have the light of life.' 13 The Pharisees challenged him, 'Here you are, appearing as your own witness; your testimony is not valid.' 14 Jesus answered, 'Even if I testify on my own behalf, my testimony is valid, for I know where I came from and where I am going. But you have no idea where I come from or where I am going.

Finally, if you believe in the Perfect Being, or in Good, or in Truth, or Love, you are a believer in God. That is why Christ is so interesting because precisely those are the realities manifested in him, and that is why listening to his words ignite our faith and make us go from spiritual death (egoism) to spiritual life (Love), but they will also make us go from physical death to eternal life.

1 John 3:14a We know that we have passed from death to life, because we love each other.

John 5:24 'Very truly I tell you, whoever hears my word and believes him who sent me has eternal life and will not be judged but has crossed over from death to life.

John 20:29 Then Jesus told him, 'Because you have seen me, you have believed; blessed are those who have not seen and yet have believed.'

To trust in God.

Once we have decided to believe in God, it is important to trust God. Faith will require us to trust God even in seemingly impossible situations. It is a fact that we don't know the future, but God does. We don't have all the power, but God does. We are weak, but God is not.

Matthew 19:26 Jesus looked at them and said, 'With man this is impossible, but with God all things are possible.'

To have faith in God is to trust that He has the last words; it is to rely on that no one and nothing can separate us from Him; it is to trust that all evil will one day end and that God will fulfill his promises, his justice, his mercy, and his word - to perfection.

Jeremiah 17:7 'But blessed is the one who trusts in the LORD, whose confidence is in him. 8 They will be like a tree planted by the water that sends out its roots by the stream. It does not fear when heat comes; its leaves are always green. It has no worries in a year of drought and never fails to bear fruit.'

Proverbs 3:5 Trust in the LORD with all your heart and lean not on your own understanding; 6 in all your ways submit to him, and he will make your paths straight.

We will have many moments of uncertainty and fear in life. It will be critical to stay united to Him and to trust that God is in control. In the Bible, there are several chronicles about the importance of trusting God; however, the following one is a preeminent one.

Matthew 14:22 Immediately Jesus made the disciples get into the boat and go on ahead of him to the other side, while he dismissed the crowd. 23 After he had dismissed them, he went up on a mountainside by himself to pray. Later that night, he was there alone, 24 and the boat was already a considerable distance from land, buffeted by the waves because the wind was against it. 25 Shortly before dawn Jesus went out to them, walking on the lake. 26 When the disciples saw him walking on the lake, they were terrified. 'It's a ghost,' they said, and cried out in fear. 27 But Jesus immediately said to them: 'Take courage! It is I. Don't be afraid.' 28 'Lord, if it's you,' Peter replied, 'tell me to come to you on the water.' 29 'Come,' he said. Then Peter got down out of the boat, walked on the water and came towards Jesus. 30 But when he saw the wind, he was afraid and, beginning to sink, cried out, 'Lord, save me!' 31 Immediately Jesus reached out his hand and caught him. 'You of little faith,' he said, 'why did you doubt?' 32 And when they climbed into the boat, the wind died down. 33 Then those who were in the boat worshipped him, saying, 'Truly you are the Son of God.'

When we trust God, our life literally stops sinking. Amazing things will happen if we venture on following him and fully trust Him!

To live for God.

"And you will again see the distinction between the righteous and the wicked, between those who serve God and those who do not."
Malachi 3:18

Faith is also putting God first in our life, which means serving Him and living for Him. We cannot conceive someone with the virtue of faith that places God as something secondary in his life. God cannot take a secondary place in our hearts. He must be our main motive and our main reason for living.

Galatians 1:10 Am I now trying to win the approval of human beings, or of God? Or am I trying to please people? If I were still trying to please people, I would not be a servant of Christ.

Sirach 2:15 Those who fear the Lord do not disobey his words, and those who love him keep his ways. 16 Those who fear the Lord seek to please him, and those who love him are filled with his law. 17 Those who fear the Lord prepare their hearts, and humble themselves before him. 18 Let us fall into the hands of the Lord, but not into the hands of mortals; for equal to his majesty is his mercy, and equal to his name are his works.

Living for God implies facing and defeating many evils during our lives, especially those that arise from our interior. Faith is built mainly through challenging experiences of love, and it is by overcoming them that we get to understand why being a Jesus follower feels like this...

Philippians 4:13 I can do all things through Christ who strengthens me.

To do good.

The virtue of faith always must go beyond belief; for it is only authentic when it is lived. True faith always translates the moral principles into holy deeds; it always implies transforming our human actions into miracles of divine love.

Psalm 37:3a Trust in the LORD and do good.

In a passage in the New Testament, we find a reference to a prayer that serves as a guide to continually ask God for the grace, so we can move from good desires to the works of faith.

2 Thessalonians 1:11 With this in mind, we constantly pray for you, that our God may make you worthy of his calling, and that by his power he may bring to fruition your every desire for goodness and your every deed prompted by faith. 12 We pray this so that the name of our Lord Jesus may be glorified in you, and you in him, according to the grace of our God and the Lord Jesus Christ.

In the apostles' acts, we find a story of Saint Peter that serves as an inspiration to do evangelical works.

Acts 9:36 In Joppa there was a disciple named Tabitha; she was always doing good and helping the poor. 37 About that time she became ill and died, and her body was washed and placed in an upstairs room. 38 Lydda was near Joppa; so when the disciples heard that Peter was in Lydda, they sent two men to him and urged him, 'Please come at once!' 39 Peter went with them, and when he arrived he was taken upstairs to the room. All the widows stood round him, crying and showing him the robes and other clothing that Dorcas had made while she was still with them. 40 Peter sent them all out of the room; then he got down on his knees and prayed. Turning towards the dead woman, he said, 'Tabitha, get up.' She opened her eyes, and seeing Peter she sat up. 41 He took her by the hand and helped her to her feet. Then he called for the believers, especially the widows, and presented her to them alive.

To contemplate God.

Finally, the most shocking thing about faith is that it ends on the beatific vision of God. In the story of saint Stephen, we find some of the most stunning revelations of that sacred moment.

Acts 7:55 But Stephen, full of the Holy Spirit, looked up to heaven and saw the glory of God, and Jesus standing at the right hand of God. 56 'Look,' he said, 'I see heaven open and the Son of Man standing at the right hand of God.' 57 At this they covered their ears and, yelling at the top of their voices, they all rushed at him, 58 dragged him out of the city and began to stone him. Meanwhile, the witnesses laid their coats at the feet of a young man named Saul. 59 While they were stoning him, Stephen prayed, 'Lord Jesus, receive my spirit.' 60 Then he fell on his knees and cried out, 'Lord, do not hold this sin against them.' When he had said this, he fell asleep.

"The problem of disbelieving in God is not that a man ends up believing nothing. Alas, it is much worse. He ends up believing anything." G. K. Chesterton

Not wanting to know God.

The basis of radical skepticism is incredulity, which means a willing ignorance or simply not wanting to know. What typically happens around God's knowledge is that we do not have enough interest in listening and understanding Him; therefore, we do not take the time to seek Him. Thus, this is how we waste all the little opportunities to know him.

Remembering Pascal's reasoning:

1.- The reasonable and happy. (Those who seek and have found God)

2.- The reasonable and unhappy. (Those who seek, but have not yet found God)

3.- The irrational and unhappy. (Those who neither seek nor have found God)

The third individuals have the vice of incredulity because they are indifferent to the knowledge and search for God. The primary manifestation of unbelief is closing yourself to the possibility of believing in God. If we do not seek to know and reason before believing, our incredulity on God is unjustifiable.

The next verse is revealing because it shows us that a sinful heart is consequently unbelieving. Our personal sin is what generates our unbelief, which leads us to turn away from God.

Hebrews 3:12 See to it, brothers and sisters, that none of you has a sinful, unbelieving heart that turns away from the living God.

Not to discern God.

If we place our faith in any creature, activity, or thing outside of God, it is no longer faith but idolatry. Faith corresponds only to God; it is our duty to honor that reality by giving God that priority place in our lives. In sacred scriptures, we find several passages where the idea of idolatry is clarified. The most common examples are demons or evil spirits, the idols made by humans, or anything that we place at the center of our life that is not God so as money, fame, or pleasure.

Exodus 20:3 'You shall have no other gods before me. 4 'You shall not make for yourself an image in the form of anything in heaven above or on the earth beneath or in the waters below. 5 You shall not bow down to them or worship them; for I, the LORD your God, am a jealous God, punishing the children for the sin of the parents to the third and fourth generation of those who hate me, 6 but showing love to a thousand generations of those who love me and keep my commandments.

Revelation 9:20 The rest of mankind who were not killed by these plagues still did not repent of the work of their hands; they did not stop worshipping demons, and idols of gold, silver, bronze, stone and wood – idols that cannot see or hear or walk.

1 Corinthians 10:14 Therefore, my dear friends, flee from idolatry.

Colossians 3:5 Put to death, therefore, whatever belongs to your earthly nature: sexual immorality, impurity, lust, evil desires and greed, which is idolatry. 6 Because of these, the wrath of God is coming.

The most common thing about modern atheism is to deny what it does not understands. Idolatry arises due to this irrational attitude of denying the unknown, and that's why people end up praising some ridiculous concept compared to that of God. By not discerning where we put our faith, we will choose as a priority of life or moral guide some unworthy reality such as economic prosperity, science, selfish desires, or any modern ideology (utilitarianism, nihilism, materialism). A phrase by an unknown author reflects that reality very well "He who does not know God kneels before anything".

Not to believe in God.

Not believing in God is not believing in truth and love. We usually get to that mindset because our life is not going spiritually well, and thus because we are immersed in vices.

John 3:18 Whoever believes in him is not condemned, but whoever does not believe stands condemned already because they have not believed in the name of God's one and only Son. 19 This is the verdict: light has come into the world, but people loved darkness instead of light because their deeds were evil. 20 Everyone who does evil hates the light, and will not come into the light for fear that their deeds will be exposed. 21 But whoever lives by the truth comes into the light, so that it may be seen plainly that what they have done has been done in the sight of God.

Disbelief is even more profound when we see and hear the evidence, and still, we deny it. Many times in life we are faced with certain obvious truths, whether testimonials or reasons, which are in some way irrefutable. Yet, by having free will, we have the possibility to deny even what we know to be true.

Matthew 13:13 This is why I speak to them in parables: 'Though seeing, they do not see; though hearing, they do not hear or understand. 14 In them is fulfilled the prophecy of Isaiah: '"You will be ever hearing but never understanding; you will be ever seeing but never perceiving. 15 For this people's heart has become calloused; they hardly hear with their ears, and they have closed their eyes. Otherwise they might see with their eyes, hear with their ears, understand with their hearts and turn, and I would heal them."

If we refuse to believe God after knowing the Gospels and Christ, we will be the unbelievers who remained in their vices and sins.

John 8:23 But he continued, 'You are from below; I am from above. You are of this world; I am not of this world. 24 I told you that you would die in your sins; if you do not believe that I am he, you will indeed die in your sins.'

Romans 1:18 The wrath of God is being revealed from heaven against all the godlessness and wickedness of people, who suppress the truth by their wickedness, 19 since what may be known about God is plain to them, because God has made it plain to them. 20 For since the creation of the world God's invisible qualities – his eternal power and divine nature – have been clearly seen, being understood from what has been made, so that people are without excuse. 21 For although they knew God, they neither glorified him as God nor gave thanks to him, but their thinking became futile and their foolish hearts were darkened. 22 Although they claimed to be wise, they became fools 23 and exchanged the glory of the immortal God for images made to look like a mortal human being and birds and animals and reptiles. 24 Therefore God gave them over in the sinful desires of their hearts to sexual impurity for the degrading of their bodies with one another. 25 They exchanged the truth about God for a lie, and worshipped and served created things rather than the Creator – who is for ever praised. Amen.

Finally, let's imagine that we met Jesus, that we listened to his wisdom, and that we witnessed his miracles and his goodness. And yet, we decide to close our hearts to the truth of his story. By denying the one who is genuinely good, we would be committing the greatest injustice. This incredulous and irrational mentality was precisely the reason why Jesus was crucified.

Wisdom 2:1 For they have said, reasoning with themselves, but not right: The time of our life is short and tedious, and in the end of a man there is no remedy, and no man hath been known to have returned from hell: 2 For we are born of nothing, and after this we shall be as if we had not been: for the breath in our nostrils is smoke: and speech a spark to move our heart, 3 Which being put out, our body shall be ashes, and our spirit shall be poured abroad as soft air, and our life shall pass away as the trace of a cloud, and shall be dispersed as a mist, which is driven away by the beams of the sun, and overpowered with the heat thereof: 4 And our name in time shall be forgotten, and no man shall have any remembrance of our works. 5 For our time is as the passing of a shadow, and there is no going back of our end: for it is fast sealed, and no man returned: 6 Come, therefore, and let us enjoy the good things that are present, and let us speedily use the creatures as in youth. 7 Let us fill ourselves with costly wine, and ointments: and let not the flower of the time pass by us. 8 Let us crown ourselves with roses, before they be withered: let no meadow escape our riot. 9 Let none of us go without his part in luxury: let us every where leave tokens of joy: for this is our portion, and this our lot. 10 Let us oppress the poor just man, and not spare the widow, nor honor the ancient grey hairs of the aged. 11 But let our strength be the law of justice: for that which is feeble is found to be nothing worth. 12 Let us, therefore, lie in wait for the just, because he is not for our turn, and he is contrary to our doings, and upbraided us with transgressions of the law, and divulged against us the sins of our way of life. 13 He boasted that he hath the knowledge of God, and calleth himself the son of God. 14 He is become a censurer of our thoughts. 15 He is grievous unto us, even to behold: for his life is not like other men's, and his ways are very different. 16 We are esteemed by him as triflers, and he abstained from our ways as from filthiness, and he preferred the latter end of the just, and gloried that he hath God for his father. 17 Let us see then if his words be true, and let us prove what shall happen to him, and we shall know what his end shall be. 18 For if he be the true son of God, he will defend him, and will deliver him from the hands of his enemies. 19 Let us examine him by outrages and tortures, that we may know his meekness, and try his patience. 20 Let us condemn him to a most shameful death: for there shall be respect had unto him by his words.

Mathew 26:62 Then the high priest stood up and said to Jesus, 'Are you not going to answer? What is this testimony that these men are bringing against you?' 63 But Jesus remained silent. The high priest said to him, 'I charge you under oath by the living God: Tell us if you are the Messiah, the Son of God.' 64 'You have said so,' Jesus replied. 'But I say to all of you: from now on you will see the Son of Man sitting at the right hand of the Mighty One and coming on the clouds of heaven.' 65 Then the high priest tore his clothes and said, 'He has spoken blasphemy! Why do we need any more witnesses? Look, now you have heard the blasphemy. 66 What do you think?' 'He is worthy of death,' they answered. 67 Then they spat in his face and struck him with their fists. Others slapped him 68 and said, 'Prophesy to us, Messiah. Who hit you?'

John 18:19 The high priest questioned Jesus about his disciples and about his doctrine. 20 Jesus replied, "I have spoken clearly to the world, I have always taught in the synagogue and in the Temple, where all the Jews meet, and I have not said anything in secret. 21 Why are you asking me? Ask those who heard me what I have told them about: they know what I have said. 22 As he said this, one of the servants who was there slapped Jesus, saying, "Is this how you respond to the high priest?" 23 Jesus answered, "If I have spoken evil, declare that evil; But if I'm right, why do you hit me?

Not to trust God.

The lack of faith is also shown as a lack of trust in God. There are multiple complex circumstances in life where we face doubt and uncertainty. It might seem that there is no solution to the problems we find ourselves in. Still, we must not allow ourselves to be carried away by disbelief. In the Bible, we find a story that seems prophetic; because those of us who want to follow Jesus during our lives will go through similar spiritual moments.

Mark 4:35 That day when evening came, he said to his disciples, 'Let us go over to the other side.' 36 Leaving the crowd behind, they took him along, just as he was, in the boat. There were also other boats with him. 37 A furious squall came up, and the waves broke over the boat, so that it was nearly swamped. 38 Jesus was in the stern, sleeping on a cushion. The disciples woke him and said to him, 'Teacher, don't you care if we drown?' 39 He got up, rebuked the wind and said to the waves, 'Quiet! Be still!' Then the wind died down and it was completely calm. 40 He said to his disciples, 'Why are you so afraid? Do you still have no faith?' 41 They were terrified and asked each other, 'Who is this? Even the wind and the waves obey him!'

Not to live for God.

After knowing, believing, and trusting God, faith stands at a crucial moment. At this point, there are two types of people, 1) those who believe and are at the service of God; and 2) those who believe and want God to be at their service. Indeed, a new form of incredulity manifests in those who believe that God exists but refuse to accept that God is a reality that deserves our obedience and our faithfulness. So, by rejecting that premise, they seek to use God for their benefit; hence, their belief at that moment stops being faith and turns into an amulet or talisman mentality which seeks God as a mean to an egotistical end.

Jesus speaks of this type of situation and clarifies that faith is not merely recognizing him as Lord but implies living and preferring God's will to ours in everyday life.

Mathew 7:21 'Not everyone who says to me, "Lord, Lord," will enter the kingdom of heaven, but only the one who does the will of my Father who is in heaven. 22 Many will say to me on that day, "Lord, Lord, did we not prophesy in your name and in your name drive out demons and in your name perform many miracles?" 23 Then I will tell them plainly, "I never knew you. Away from me, you evildoers!"

Luke 6:46 'Why do you call me, "Lord, Lord," and do not do what I say? 47 As for everyone who comes to me and hears my words and puts them into practice, I will show you what they are like. 48

They are like a man building a house, who dug down deep and laid the foundation on rock. When the flood came, the torrent struck that house but could not shake it, because it was well built. 49 But the one who hears my words and does not put them into practice is like a man who built a house on the ground without a foundation. The moment the torrent struck that house, it collapsed and its destruction was complete.'

Not to do good.

Faith must always be reflected in works of charity. When we profess to have faith in God but our actions indicate the contrary, we become a sham. The following Bible verses are very forceful; they give us two clear examples of the magnitude of the unity between faith and good deeds.

Titus 1:15 To the pure, all things are pure, but to those who are corrupted and do not believe, nothing is pure. In fact, both their minds and consciences are corrupted. 16 They claim to know God, but by their actions they deny him. They are detestable, disobedient and unfit for doing anything good.

James 2:14 What good is it, my brothers and sisters, if someone claims to have faith but has no deeds? Can such faith save them? 15 Suppose a brother or a sister is without clothes and daily food. 16 If one of you says to them, 'Go in peace; keep warm and well fed,' but does nothing about their physical needs, what good is it? 17 In the same way, faith by itself, if it is not accompanied by action, is dead. 18 But someone will say, 'You have faith; I have deeds.' Show me your faith without deeds, and I will show you my faith by my deeds. 19 You believe that there is one God. Good! Even the demons believe that – and shudder.

Not to contemplate God.

Finally, the worst consequence of incredulity is the loss of the contemplation of God. Suppose we deny God's goodness and close our hearts to His calling of love. In that case, we will become apostates, and we will miss the beatific vision. We must always fight the vice of incredulity with authentic virtue of faith.

Hebrews 3:7 So, as the Holy Spirit says: 'Today, if you hear his voice, 8 do not harden your hearts as you did in the rebellion, during the time of testing in the wilderness, 9 where your ancestors tested and tried me, though for forty years they saw what I did. 10 That is why I was angry with that generation; I said, "Their hearts are always going astray, and they have not known my ways." 11 So I declared on oath in my anger, "They shall never enter my rest."'12 See to it, brothers and sisters, that none of you has a sinful, unbelieving heart that turns away from the living God. 13 But encourage one another daily, as long as it is called 'Today', so that none of you may be hardened by sin's deceitfulness.

Hebrews 3:18 And to whom did God swear that they would never enter his rest if not to those who disobeyed? 19 So we see that they were not able to enter, because of their unbelief.

Hope vs. Hopelessness

Hope is...	Hopelessness is...
To place our heart in God and his love.	To place our heart outside of God and his love.
To accept the Savior and his redemption.	To reject the Savior and his redemption.
To trust in the words and promises of God.	Not to trust in the words and promises of God.
To accept that we will be judge on love.	To deny that we will be judge on love.
To rejoice in the resurrection and eternal life.	To deny to the possibility of resurrection and eternal life.

"The earth has no sadness that heaven cannot heal."
Saint Thomas Aquinas

To place our heart in God and his love.

Humans are rational beings, so we naturally look to the future generating expectations or hopes by which we guide our lives. A verse in the Bible reflects that truth, pointing out that we live by what we hope.

Matthew 6:19 'Do not store up for yourselves treasures on earth, where moths and vermin destroy, and where thieves break in and steal. 20 But store up for yourselves treasures in heaven, where moths and vermin do not destroy, and where thieves do not break in and steal. 21 For where your treasure is, there your heart will be also.

There is an abysmal difference between placing our treasure in God and placing our treasure in the world, since the totality of reality (visible and invisible) is sustained in the Trinity. It is up to us to choose what treasure we want to pursue. God is the only Being in whom we must put all our hope because there are realities that we can only expect from Him, realities that no one else can give or donate. Only in God, our expectations become hope.

Psalm 147:11 the LORD delights in those who fear him, who put their hope in his unfailing love.

Psalm 62:5 Yes, my soul, find rest in God; my hope comes from him. 6 Truly he is my rock and my salvation; he is my fortress, I shall not be shaken. 7 My salvation and my honor depend on God; he is my mighty rock, my refuge.

Psalm 33:18 But the eyes of the LORD are on those who fear him, on those whose hope is in his unfailing love, 19 to deliver them from death and keep them alive in famine. 20 We wait in hope for the LORD; he is our help and our shield. 21 In him our hearts rejoice, for we trust in his holy name. 22 May your unfailing love be with us, LORD, even as we put our hope in you.

Psalm 25:5 Guide me in your truth and teach me, for you are God my Savior, and my hope is in you all day long.

To accept the Savior and his redemption.

Thanks to Christ, we can have divine hope because He is True Man and True God. We are all called to perfection in love through Christ our Savior.

John 3:13 No one has ever gone into heaven except the one who came from heaven – the Son of Man. 14 Just as Moses lifted up the snake in the wilderness, so the Son of Man must be lifted up, 15 that everyone who believes may have eternal life in him.' 16 For God so loved the world that he gave his one and only Son, that whoever believes in him shall not perish but have eternal life. 17 For God did not send his Son into the world to condemn the world, but to save the world through him.

Hebrews 9:14 How much more, then, will the blood of Christ, who through the eternal Spirit offered himself unblemished to God, cleanse our consciences from acts that lead to death, so that we may serve the living God! 15 For this reason Christ is the mediator of a new covenant, that those who are called may receive the promised eternal inheritance – now that he has died as a ransom to set them free from the sins committed under the first covenant.

Romans 5:5 And hope does not put us to shame, because God's love has been poured out into our hearts through the Holy Spirit, who has been given to us. 6 You see, at just the right time, when we were still powerless, Christ died for the ungodly. 7 Very rarely will anyone die for a righteous person, though for a good person someone might possibly dare to die. 8 But God demonstrates his own love for us in this: while we were still sinners, Christ died for us. 9 Since we have now been justified by his blood, how much more shall we be saved from God's wrath through him! 10 For if, while we were God's enemies, we were reconciled to him through the death of his Son, how much more, having been reconciled, shall we be saved through his life! 11 Not only is this so, but we also boast in God through our Lord Jesus Christ, through whom we have now received reconciliation.

Hope seen as a virtue is like a divine force that arises from contemplating the truths that God communicated to us. It is especially important to understand that, in hope, love plays a central role. It is in the love of God (perfect and eternal), where we can know ourselves and feel loved forever. Hope is trusting that nothing can definitively separate us from the love of God.

Romans 8:38 For I am convinced that neither death nor life, neither angels nor demons, neither the present nor the future, nor any powers, 39 neither height nor depth, nor anything else in all creation, will be able to separate us from the love of God that is in Christ Jesus our Lord.

Christian hope must become evident in our lives. As the Holy Spirit guides us to a life of love, we must live displaying the light of hope through holiness and virtue so that our way of living is a concrete sign of the realities that we hope to share in eternity with God.

Philippians 2:5 In your relationships with one another, have the same mindset as Christ Jesus: 6 who, being in very nature God, did not consider equality with God something to be used to his own advantage; 7 rather, he made himself nothing by taking the very nature of a servant, being made in human likeness. 8 And being found in appearance as a man, he humbled himself by becoming obedient to death – even death on a cross! 9 Therefore God exalted him to the highest place and gave him the name that is above every name, 10 that at the name of Jesus every knee should bow, in heaven and on earth and under the earth, 11 and every tongue acknowledge that Jesus Christ is Lord, to the glory of God the Father.

Romans 15:13 May the God of hope fill you with all joy and peace as you trust in him, so that you may overflow with hope by the power of the Holy Spirit.

To trust in the words and promises of God.

It could also be said that much of hope is contained and expressed in the words and promises of God. The Holy Bible is where God reveals his will and his message of love. The better we know the sacred scriptures, the better we can understand salvific message of divine love.

Psalm 33:4 For the word of the LORD is right and true; he is faithful in all he does.

Psalm 119:114 You are my refuge and my shield; I have put my hope in your word.

Matthew 24:35 Heaven and earth will pass away, but my words will never pass away.

John 8:31 To the Jews who had believed him, Jesus said, 'If you hold to my teaching, you are really my disciples. 32 Then you will know the truth, and the truth will set you free.'

John 10:27 My sheep listen to my voice; I know them, and they follow me. 28 I give them eternal life, and they shall never perish; no one will snatch them out of my hand.

Hebrews 10:23 Let us hold unswervingly to the hope we profess, for he who promised is faithful.

One of the central promises of the gospel is the beatitude or the complete happiness of souls. God is preparing a heavenly home in which a divine family is waiting for us; there, we will eternally live full of joy and peace.

Jeremiah 29:11 I know well the plans that I have proposed for you —oracle of the Lord—: plans for peace and not for misfortune, to give you luck and hope. 12 You will call upon Me, you will come to pray to Me, and I will listen to you. 13 You will seek me and find me, if you seek me with all your heart.

John 14:1 Do not let your hearts be troubled. You believe in God; believe also in me. 2 My Father's house has many rooms; if that were not so, would I have told you that I am going there to prepare a place for you? 3 And if I go and prepare a place for you, I will come back and take you to be with me that you also may be where I am. 4 You know the way to the place where I am going.'

To accept that we will be judge on love.

Humanly we come to intuit that good will triumph over evil, and that from these two spiritual forces, only good will remain forever. But for that to happen, we need a Judge and a Divine Judgment.

Hope is very closely related to this culminating moment in the history of creation. The Holy Scriptures reveal that Christ is the Judge, and his Judgment is perfect.

Job 34:10 So listen to me, you men of understanding. Far be it from God to do evil, from the Almighty to do wrong. 11 He repays everyone for what they have done; he brings on them what their conduct deserves. 12 It is unthinkable that God would do wrong, that the Almighty would pervert justice.

2 Corinthians 5:10 For we must all appear before the judgment seat of Christ, so that each of us may receive what is due to us for the things done while in the body, whether good or bad.

Matthew 12:36 But I tell you that everyone will have to give account on the day of judgment for every empty word they have spoken. 37 For by your words you will be acquitted, and by your words you will be condemned.'

James 4:12a There is only one Lawgiver and Judge, the one who is able to save and destroy.

2 Thessalonians 1:5 All this is evidence that God's judgment is right, and as a result you will be counted worthy of the kingdom of God, for which you are suffering. 6 God is just: he will pay back trouble to those who trouble you 7 and give relief to you who are troubled, and to us as well. This will happen when the Lord Jesus is revealed from heaven in blazing fire with his powerful angels. 8 He will punish those who do not know God and do not obey the gospel of our Lord Jesus. 9 They will be punished with everlasting destruction and shut out from the presence of the Lord and from the glory of his might 10 on the day he comes to be glorified in his holy people and to be marveled at among all those who have believed. This includes you, because you believed our testimony to you.

Matthew 25:31 'When the Son of Man comes in his glory, and all the angels with him, he will sit on his glorious throne. 32 All the nations will be gathered before him, and he will separate the people one from another as a shepherd separates the sheep from the goats. 33 He will put the sheep on his right and the goats on his left. 34 'Then the King will say to those on his right, "Come, you who are blessed by my Father; take your inheritance, the kingdom prepared for you since the creation of the world. 35 For I was hungry and you gave me something to eat, I was thirsty and you gave me something to drink, I was a stranger and you invited me in, 36 I needed clothes and you clothed me, I was ill and you looked after me, I was in prison and you came to visit me." 37 'Then the righteous will answer him, "Lord, when did we see you hungry and feed you, or thirsty and give you something to drink? 38 When did we see you a stranger and invite you in, or needing clothes and clothe you? 39 When did we see you ill or in prison and go to visit you?" 40 'The King will reply, "Truly I tell you, whatever you did for one of the least of these brothers and sisters of mine, you did for me." 41 'Then he will say to those on his left, "Depart from me, you who are cursed, into the eternal fire prepared for the devil and his angels. 42 For I was hungry and you gave me nothing to eat, I was thirsty and you gave me nothing to drink, 43 I was a stranger and you did not invite me in, I needed clothes and you did not clothe me, I was ill and in prison and you did not look after me." 44 'They also will answer, "Lord, when did we see you hungry or thirsty or a stranger or needing clothes or ill or in prison, and did not help you?" 45 'He will reply, "Truly I tell you, whatever you did not do for one of the least of these, you did not do for me." 46 'Then they will go away to eternal punishment, but the righteous to eternal life.

We Christians should not be afraid towards the Judgment of God because the living of the gospel sanctifies us, leading us to entrust our destiny entirely in God's hands. It is important to emphasize that God is perfectly just and merciful. He knows perfectly what corresponds to each one of us. Hope in salvation is precisely knowing that we have received and reciprocated God's love. From that reality, a thought is born that makes us see the judgment as a glorious moment of union with God and the saints.

Sirach 34:14 The spirit of those that fear God; is sought after, and by his regard shall be blessed. 15 For their hope is on him that saved them, and the eyes of God are upon them that love him. 16 He that feared the Lord shall tremble at nothing, and shall not be afraid for he is his hope.

1 John 4:17 This is how love is made complete among us so that we will have confidence on the day of judgment: in this world we are like Jesus. 18 There is no fear in love. But perfect love drives out fear, because fear has to do with punishment. The one who fears is not made perfect in love.

It is essential to mention that God is always offering us his infinite mercy. We must never forget that He is always waiting for us. Despite our sins and failures, God has not stopped loving us but seeks to heal our hearts and transform our lives. In the Bible, we find one story that reveals this inexhaustible mercy of God.

Luke 7:36 When one of the Pharisees invited Jesus to have dinner with him, he went to the Pharisee's house and reclined at the table. 37 A woman in that town who lived a sinful life learned that Jesus was eating at the Pharisee's house, so she came there with an alabaster jar of perfume. 38 As she stood behind him at his feet weeping, she began to wet his feet with her tears. Then she wiped them with her hair, kissed them and poured perfume on them. 39 When the Pharisee who had invited him saw this, he said to himself, 'If this man were a prophet, he would know who is touching him and what kind of woman she is – that she is a sinner.' 40 Jesus answered him, 'Simon, I have something to tell you.' 'Tell me, teacher,' he said. 41 'Two people owed money to a certain money-lender. One owed him five hundred denarii, and the other fifty. 42 Neither of them had the money to pay him back, so he forgave the debts of both. Now which of them will love him more?' 43 Simon replied, 'I suppose the one who had the bigger debt forgiven.' 'You have judged correctly,' Jesus said. 44 Then he turned towards the woman and said to Simon, 'Do you see this woman? I came into your house. You did not give me any water for my feet, but she wet my feet with her tears and wiped them with her hair. 45 You did not give me a kiss, but this woman, from the time I entered, has not stopped kissing my feet. 46 You did not put oil on my head, but she has poured perfume on my feet. 47 Therefore, I tell you, her many sins have been forgiven – as her great love has shown. But whoever has been forgiven little loves little.' 48 Then Jesus said to her, 'Your sins are forgiven.' 49 The other guests began to say among themselves, 'Who is this who even forgives sins?' 50 Jesus said to the woman, 'Your faith has saved you; go in peace.'

To rejoice in the resurrection and eternal life.

All humans have a spiritual thirst: a thirst for divine life and lasting love. We want to relish with our loved ones for eternity. When hope shines within the depths of hearts, our love for God is transformed into praise. The apostle Peter in a passage of the Gospel, manifests that divine thirst. His words are an authentic proclamation of the Christian hope.

John 6:68 Simon Peter answered him, 'Lord, to whom shall we go? You have the words of eternal life. 69 We have come to believe and to know that you are the Holy One of God.'

The virtue of hope is fundamentally to live believing in the resurrection of the body and eternal life. In the book of the Maccabees, we find an archetypical story. These heroes face the unjust penalty of death, but still, they are full of hope in God.

2 Maccabees 7:9 And when he was at his last breath, he said, "You accursed wretch, you dismiss us from this present life, but the King of the universe will raise us up to an everlasting renewal of life, because we have died for his laws." 10 After him, the third was the victim of their sport. When it was demanded, he quickly put out his tongue and courageously stretched forth his hands, 11 and said nobly, "I got these from Heaven, and because of his laws I disdain them, and from him I hope to get them back again." 12 As a result the king himself and those with him were astonished at the young man's spirit, for he regarded his sufferings as nothing. 13 When he too had died, they maltreated and tortured the fourth in the same way. 14 And when he was near death, he said, "One cannot but choose to die at the hands of men and to cherish the hope that God gives of being raised again by him. But for you there will be no resurrection to life!"

2 Maccabees 15:7 But Maccabeus did not cease to trust with all confidence that he would get help from the Lord. 8 He exhorted his troops not to fear the attack of the Gentiles, but to keep in mind

the former times when help had come to them from heaven, and so to look for the victory that the Almighty would give them.

2 Maccabees 7:20 The mother was the most amazing one of them all, and she deserves a special place in our memory. Although she saw her seven sons die in a single day, she endured it with great courage because she trusted in the Lord. 21 She combined womanly emotion with manly courage and spoke words of encouragement to each of her sons in their native language. 22 I do not know how your life began in my womb, she would say, I was not the one who gave you life and breath and put together each part of your body. 23 It was God who did it, God who created the universe, the human race, and all that exists. He is merciful and he will give you back life and breath again, because you love his laws more than you love yourself.

The stories of the Maccabees are prophetic in some way, their hope is answered by the life of Christ, which opens history and humanity to the reality of the glorious resurrection.

1 Peter 1:3 Praise be to the God and Father of our LORD Jesus Christ! In his great mercy he has given us new birth into a living hope through the resurrection of Jesus Christ from the dead, 4 and into an inheritance that can never perish, spoil or fade. This inheritance is kept in heaven for you, 5 who through faith are shielded by God's power until the coming of the salvation that is ready to be revealed in the last time.

The resurrection of Christ is the fact that fills us with hope because we too are called to participate in the resurrection; so that our life reaches its ultimate end in our true home that is heaven. To live with hope is to understand that we are on a pilgrimage towards the house of God.

John 11:17 On his arrival, Jesus found that Lazarus had already been in the tomb for four days. 18 Now Bethany was less than two miles from Jerusalem, 19 and many Jews had come to Martha and Mary to comfort them in the loss of their brother. 20 When Martha heard that Jesus was coming, she went out to meet him, but Mary stayed at home. 21 'Lord,' Martha said to Jesus, 'if you had been here, my brother would not have died. 22 But I know that even now God will give you whatever you ask.' 23 Jesus said to her, 'Your brother will rise again.' 24 Martha answered, 'I know he will rise again in the resurrection at the last day.' 25 Jesus said to her, 'I am the resurrection and the life. The one who believes in me will live, even though they die; 26 and whoever lives by believing in me will never die. Do you believe this?' 27 'Yes, Lord,' she replied, 'I believe that you are the Messiah, the Son of God, who is to come into the world.'

Philippians 3:20 But our citizenship is in heaven. And we eagerly await a Savior from there, the Lord Jesus Christ, 21 who, by the power that enables him to bring everything under his control, will transform our lowly bodies so that they will be like his glorious body.

Colossians 3:1 Since, then, you have been raised with Christ, set your hearts on things above, where Christ is, seated at the right hand of God. 2 Set your minds on things above, not on earthly things. 3 For you died, and your life is now hidden with Christ in God. 4 When Christ, who is your life, appears, then you also will appear with him in glory.

Luke 20:35 But those who are considered worthy of taking part in the age to come and in the resurrection from the dead will neither marry nor be given in marriage, 36 and they can no longer die; for they are like the angels. They are God's children, since they are children of the resurrection.

1 Corinthians 15:35 But someone will ask, 'How are the dead raised? With what kind of body will they come?' 36 How foolish! What you sow does not come to life unless it dies. 37 When you sow, you do not plant the body that will be, but just a seed, perhaps of wheat or of something else. 38 But God gives it a body as he has determined, and to each kind of seed he gives its own body. 39 Not all flesh is the same: people have one kind of flesh, animals have another, birds another and fish another. 40 There are also heavenly bodies and there are earthly bodies; but the splendor of the heavenly bodies is one kind, and the splendor of the earthly bodies is another. 41 The sun has one kind of splendor, the moon another and the stars another; and star differs from star in splendor. 42 So will it be with the resurrection of the dead. The body that is sown is perishable, it

is raised imperishable; 43 it is sown in dishonor, it is raised in glory; it is sown in weakness, it is raised in power; 44 it is sown a natural body, it is raised a spiritual body. If there is a natural body, there is also a spiritual body. 45 So it is written: 'The first man Adam became a living being'; the last Adam, a life-giving spirit. 46 The spiritual did not come first, but the natural, and after that the spiritual. 47 The first man was of the dust of the earth; the second man is of heaven. 48 As was the earthly man, so are those who are of the earth; and as is the heavenly man, so also are those who are of heaven. 49 And just as we have borne the image of the earthly man, so shall weg bear the image of the heavenly man. 50 I declare to you, brothers and sisters, that flesh and blood cannot inherit the kingdom of God, nor does the perishable inherit the imperishable. 51 Listen, I tell you a mystery: we will not all sleep, but we will all be changed – 52 in a flash, in the twinkling of an eye, at the last trumpet. For the trumpet will sound, the dead will be raised imperishable, and we will be changed. 53 For the perishable must clothe itself with the imperishable, and the mortal with immortality. 54 When the perishable has been clothed with the imperishable, and the mortal with immortality, then the saying that is written will come true: 'Death has been swallowed up in victory.' 55 'Where, O death, is your victory? Where, O death, is your sting?' 56 The sting of death is sin, and the power of sin is the law. 57 But thanks be to God! He gives us the victory through our Lord Jesus Christ. 58 Therefore, my dear brothers and sisters, stand firm. Let nothing move you. Always give yourselves fully to the work of the Lord, because you know that your labor in the Lord is not in vain.

God's love reaches its fullness in the promise of the new heavens and the new earth. Through the resurrection, we will be able to obtain eternal life, which is not merely living forever but living in Love forever.

2 Peter 3:3 Above all, you must understand that in the last days scoffers will come, scoffing and following their own evil desires. 4 They will say, 'Where is this "coming" he promised? Ever since our ancestors died, everything goes on as it has since the beginning of creation.' 5 But they deliberately forget that long ago by God's word

the heavens came into being and the earth was formed out of water and by water. 6 By these waters also the world of that time was deluged and destroyed. 7 By the same word the present heavens and earth are reserved for fire, being kept for the day of judgment and destruction of the ungodly. 8 But do not forget this one thing, dear friends: with the Lord a day is like a thousand years, and a thousand years are like a day. 9 The Lord is not slow in keeping his promise, as some understand slowness. Instead he is patient with you, not wanting anyone to perish, but everyone to come to repentance. 10 But the day of the Lord will come like a thief. The heavens will disappear with a roar; the elements will be destroyed by fire, and the earth and everything done in it will be laid bare. 11 Since everything will be destroyed in this way, what kind of people ought you to be? You ought to live holy and godly lives 12 as you look forward to the day of God and speed its coming. That day will bring about the destruction of the heavens by fire, and the elements will melt in the heat. 13 But in keeping with his promise we are looking forward to a new heaven and a new earth, where righteousness dwells. 14 So then, dear friends, since you are looking forward to this, make every effort to be found spotless, blameless and at peace with him. 15 Bear in mind that our Lord's patience means salvation, just as our dear brother Paul also wrote to you with the wisdom that God gave him. 16 He writes the same way in all his letters, speaking in them of these matters. His letters contain some things that are hard to understand, which ignorant and unstable people distort, as they do the other Scriptures, to their own destruction. 17 Therefore, dear friends, since you have been forewarned, be on your guard so that you may not be carried away by the error of the lawless and fall from your secure position. 18 But grow in the grace and knowledge of our Lord and Savior Jesus Christ. To him be glory both now and for ever! Amen.

Revelation 21:1 Then I saw 'a new heaven and a new earth,' for the first heaven and the first earth had passed away, and there was no longer any sea. 2 I saw the Holy City, the new Jerusalem, coming down out of heaven from God, prepared as a bride beautifully dressed for her husband. 3 And I heard a loud voice from the throne saying, 'Look! God's dwelling-place is now among the people, and he will dwell with them. They will be his people, and God himself will be with them and be their God. 4 "He will wipe every tear from their eyes. There will be no more death" or mourning or crying or pain, for the old order of things has passed away.' 5 He who was seated on the throne said, 'I am making everything new!' Then he said, 'Write this down, for these words are trustworthy and true.' 6 He said to me: 'It is done. I am the Alpha and the Omega, the Beginning and the End. To the thirsty I will give water without cost from the spring of the water of life. 7 Those who are victorious will inherit all this, and I will be their God and they will be my children.

"To live without hope is to stop living." Dostoevsky

To place our heart outside of God and his love.

The most common reason we live disappointed, defeated, and pessimistic is because we have placed our hope in something outside of God and his love. If we are honest outside of God, our hopes are empty. The world cannot offer us eternal life nor authentic happiness. No matter how "victorious" we are in life, we will face the death of the body, a reality that without hope is clearly seen as a nightmare with a cruel ending. Sadly, we tend to put our hopes in things less than God, and hence we live with uncertainty, fear, and bitterness.

Wisdom 13:10 But unhappy are they, and their hope is among the dead, who have called gods the works of the hand of men, gold and silver, the inventions of art, and the resemblances of beasts, or an unprofitable stone the work of an ancient hand.

Job 27:8 For what is the hope of the wicked when he dies, when God takes his life from him?

Wisdom 6:14 The hope of the wicked is like dust that the wind blows away, like light frost that blows away the storm, like smoke that disperses the wind and passes as a memory of a single day's guest.

Proverbs 11:7 The hope of the wicked fades with death, and the expectation of the wicked perishes.

Philippians 3:19 Their destiny is destruction, their god is their stomach, and their glory is in their shame. Their mind is set on earthly things.

1 Timothy 6:17 Command those who are rich in this present world not to be arrogant nor to put their hope in wealth, which is so uncertain, but to put their hope in God, who richly provides us with everything for our enjoyment.

Matthew 16:26 What good will it be for someone to gain the whole world, yet forfeit their soul? Or what can anyone give in exchange for their soul?

To reject the Savior and his redemption.

By rejecting Jesus as our savior and trusting our life to any other reality, we basically condemn ourselves to live miserably. Jesus speaks very clearly that if we do not accept his offer of love and redemption, we will die without the forgiveness of our sins, and that is hopelessness.

John 8:21 Once more Jesus said to them, 'I am going away, and you will look for me, and you will die in your sin. Where I go, you cannot come.' 22 This made the Jews ask, 'Will he kill himself? Is that why he says, "Where I go, you cannot come"?' 23 But he continued, 'You are from below; I am from above. You are of this world; I am not of this world. 24 I told you that you would die in your sins; if you do not believe that I am he, you will indeed die in your sins.'

John 10:25 Jesus answered, 'I did tell you, but you do not believe. The works I do in my Father's name testify about me, 26 but you do not believe because you are not my sheep.

John 12:48 There is a judge for the one who rejects me and does not accept my words; the very words I have spoken will condemn them at the last day. 49 For I did not speak on my own, but the Father who sent me commanded me to say all that I have spoken.

1 Corinthians 15:19 If only for this life we have hope in Christ, we are of all people most to be pitied.

Not to trust in the words and promises of God.

When we do not trust God's words and promises, it is extremely easy to exchange the desires of holiness or excellence for something vain or mundane. Holiness is the universal moral duty that God requests from all humans, and by its accomplishment, God promises eternal joy.

Sometimes working on our moral development might seem like a non-essential activity, but if we think about it, it is the main goal of our life. It is precisely from the indifference towards holiness from where most injustices, sufferings, and pains emerge.

Wisdom 2:21 Thus they reasoned, but they were led astray, for their wickedness blinded them, 22 and they did not know the secret purposes of God, nor hoped for the wages of holiness, nor discerned the prize for blameless souls; 23 for God created us for incorruption, and made us in the image of his own eternity, 24 but through the devil's envy death entered the world, and those who belong to his company experience it.

1 Thessalonians 4:6 and that in this matter no one should wrong or take advantage of a brother or sister The Lord will punish all those who commit such sins, as we told you and warned you before. 7 For God did not call us to be impure, but to live a holy life. 8 Therefore, anyone who rejects this instruction does not reject a human being but God, the very God who gives you his Holy Spirit.

To deny that we will be judge on love.

It is always convenient to deny God's Judgement in order to elude the responsibility for our actions. It is true that if God does not exist, neither life after death, nor invisible realities, nor a moral law and universal judgment, then spirituality, virtue, and holiness will make no sense. Those who have committed the worst atrocities would have gotten away with it and would have oppressed the innocent definitively and irremediably. In the dialogues of the Maccabees, we can find some warnings so that can help us to understand the reality that there will be a judgment and that no one will be able to deceive God.

Maccabees 7:19 But do not think that you will go unpunished for having tried to fight against God!".

Maccabees 7:34 But you, unholy wretch, you most defiled of all men, do not be elated in vain and puffed up by uncertain hopes, when you raise your hand against the children of heaven. 35 You have not yet escaped the judgment of the almighty, all-seeing God.

If we vehemently cling to the vice of hopelessness, we will surely be reckless in acting against love and truth. It is precisely in this scenario that selfishness can deceive us towards believing that our sins are irrelevant before the eyes of God.

Sirach 5:1 Do not rely on your wealth, or say, "I have enough." 2 Do not follow your inclination and strength in pursuing the desires of your heart. 3 Do not say, "Who can have power over me?" for the Lord will surely punish you. 4 Do not say, "I sinned, yet what has happened to me?" for the Lord is slow to anger. 5 Do not be so confident of forgiveness that you add sin to sin. 6 Do not say, "His mercy is great, he will forgive the multitude of my sins," for both mercy and wrath are with him, and his anger will rest on sinners. 7 Do not delay to turn back to the Lord, and do not postpone it from day to day; for suddenly the wrath of the Lord will come upon you, and at the time of punishment you will perish.

To deny to the possibility of resurrection and eternal life.

Denying the resurrection and eternal life will cause us an existential crisis. If we truly adopt nihilistic thinking, the logical thing would be to think that our life is irrelevant. The natural thing would be to become pessimistic and selfish in order to preserve our existence. Life would be unbearable without hope because we would all be destined to die once and for all.

Acts 27:8 Why should any of you consider it incredible that God raises the dead?

Continually in the scriptures, it is spoken about the opposite reality of heaven and eternal life. In the book of Revelation, an explicit mention is made that there will be a second death, which is the condemnation of hell. These readings are complemented by what Jesus had said throughout the Gospels about the Last Judgment and the separation of the sheep from the goats and between good and evil.

Revelation 20:14 Then death and Hades were thrown into the lake of fire. The lake of fire is the second death. 15 Anyone whose name was not found written in the book of life was thrown into the lake of fire.

Revelation 21:8 But the cowardly, the unbelieving, the vile, the murderers, the sexually immoral, those who practice magic arts, the idolaters and all liars – they will be consigned to the fiery lake of burning sulfur. This is the second death.'

Chapter 7: A Good Heart

"Let us love, since that is what our hearts were made for."
Saint Therese of Lisieux

In this section we will analyze the most common and visible virtues and vices in the world, consequently, they are the meeting point in a multiplicity of philosophies, cultures, and religions.

These are the virtues to which we all have access through our nature, they do not require a special revelation like the previous virtues, but they are understood with exceptional depth through the teachings of Christianity.

The virtues represented with the heart are associated mainly with the goodness of the souls. These virtues are the most accepted and recognized heroic traits in most of the transcendental stories about love.

The vices in this section, in contrast, are the most destructive; they are the most common and dangerous manifestations of egoism.

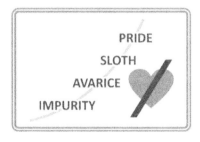

Humility vs. Pride

Humility is...	Pride is...
To recognize our identity as creatures and children of God.	Denying our identity as creatures and children of God.
To accept that we are sinners and that we need God.	Denying that we are sinners and that we need God.
To acknowledge that we have received everything.	To deny that we have received everything.
To accept God's holly will.	To reject God's holly will.
To serve and to treat others well.	Not serving and mistreating others.

"There are only two kinds of men: the righteous who think they are sinners and the sinners who think they are righteous."
Blaise Pascal

To recognize our identity as creatures and children of God.

The first thing is to understand that Christian humility is the fruit of our identity as human beings. We must realize that humility is based on valuing ourselves as children of God and accepting the truth that we were created out of love and for love. How many things would we do differently in our lives if only we could live in the humility that that identity implies!

Genesis 1:27 So God created mankind in his own image, in the image of God he created them; male and female he created them.

Genesis 1:31 God saw all that he had made, and it was very good. And there was evening, and there was morning – the sixth day.

Galatians 4:4 But when the set time had fully come, God sent his Son, born of a woman, born under the law, 5 to redeem those under the law, that we might receive adoption to sonship. 6 Because you are his sons, God sent the Spirit of his Son into our hearts, the Spirit who calls out, 'Abba, Father.' 7 So you are no longer a slave, but God's child; and since you are his child, God has made you also an heir.

Isaiah 19:15 'Can a mother forget the baby at her breast and have no compassion on the child she has borne? Though she may forget, I will not forget you!

1 John 3:9 No one who is born of God will continue to sin, because God's seed remains in them; they cannot go on sinning, because they have been born of God. 10 This is how we know who the children of God are and who the children of the devil are: anyone who does not do what is right is not God's child, nor is anyone who does not love their brother and sister.

By recognizing the dignity of other people, who are also creatures and children of God, we open ourselves to the possibility of seeing and treating ourselves as brothers. Humility enables us to recognize the value of our neighbor and act accordingly.

1 Peter 3:8 Finally, all of you, be like-minded, be sympathetic, love one another, be compassionate and humble.

To accept that we are sinners and that we need God.

Being humble is neither belittling nor devaluing ourselves but acknowledging our weakness and the fact that we have committed sins. That capacity to see our misery, is the maturity of humility. Without that ability to recognize our evil, we cannot grow nor achieve personal fulfillment. When we shut ourselves off from acknowledging that we are acting morally wrong, we automatically stagnate and block our ability to love. In the parable of the prodigal son, we find a phrase that shows that knowing one's evil is a great step in the right direction.

Luke 15:18 I will set out and go back to my father and say to him: Father, I have sinned against heaven and against you. 19 I am no longer worthy to be called your son; make me like one of your hired servants."

The other part of the human experience of humility, in general, is to recognize that many times we want to do things right, but we end up doing them wrong. When we want to be virtuous but end up being vicious, we experience human weakness and limitation at its best. Saint Paul shows this inner struggle that we all live in many moments of our lives, from the simplest to the most complex situations.

Romans 7:15 I do not understand what I do. For what I want to do I do not do, but what I hate I do. 16 And if I do what I do not want to do, I agree that the law is good. 17 As it is, it is no longer I myself who do it, but it is sin living in me. 18 For I know that good itself does not dwell in me, that is, in my sinful nature. For I have the desire to do what is good, but I cannot carry it out. 19 For I do not do the good I want to do, but the evil I do not want to do – this I keep on doing. 20 Now if I do what I do not want to do, it is no longer I who do it, but it is sin living in me that does it. 21 So I find this law at work: although I want to do good, evil is right there with me. 22 For in my inner being I delight in God's law; 23 but I see another law at work in me, waging war against the law of my mind and making me a prisoner of the law of sin at work within me. 24 What a wretched man I am! Who will rescue me from this body that is subject to death? 25 Thanks be to God, who delivers me through Jesus Christ our Lord! So then, I myself in my mind am a slave to God's law, but in my sinful natured a slave to the law of sin.

Interestingly, humility comes many times through interior humiliation, which arises due to our vices and sins. We have all experienced how painful it is to accept that we are the wrong ones and that we are the ones who must change, but; on the other hand, if we do not recognize it, we will drag the consequences of vice throughout our lives; and that is undoubtedly going to be way much more painful. If something is impressive about humility, is that it helps us avoid thousands of unnecessary sufferings and sorrows. In a Biblical passage, Jesus speaks to us directly about this fundamental virtue.

Matthew 11:28 'Come to me, all you who are weary and burdened, and I will give you rest. 29 Take my yoke upon you and learn from me, for I am gentle and humble in heart, and you will find rest for your souls. 30 For my yoke is easy and my burden is light.'

It is crucial to recognize that we cannot be good without God and that we need his grace to live well. The following passage serves to avoid believing that we are the sole authors of the good we do. It can help us understand that we are dependent on God to exist and to love.

Luke 17:10 So you also, when you have done everything you were told to do, should say, "We are unworthy servants; we have only done our duty."

To acknowledge that we have received everything.

Humility is based on gratitude to divine providence, which provides all the goods and particular graces. It is essential to delve into two phases of this providence, on the one hand, the unique faculties and talents with which we are born, and, on the other hand, the particular opportunities of our life.

In the first place, our faculties and talents in life were given by God. To boast of our abilities as if they were our merit will always be a mistake. We indeed have the responsibility and duty to develop our capacities, but that development will always be relative to what we initially receive from God.

Secondly, the particular opportunities we receive from life. For example, the family we have, the place where we were born, the people we meet. These circumstantial opportunities are unmerited realities, and we have the freedom to take of advantage of them or waste them. Saint Paul speaks precisely about this thought that has greatly influenced the understanding of humility in Christianity.

1 Corinthians 4:7 For who sees anything different in you? What do you have that you did not receive? And if you received it, why do you boast as if it were not a gift?

This virtue allows us to be happy with what we have, be it a lot or be it a little. We simply cannot imagine a humble person who is not grateful. Often the reason we are not happy is that we are not thankful enough to God and to the people around us.

1 Chronicles 16:34 Give thanks to the Lord, for he is good, for his mercy endures forever.

Psalm 92:2 It is good to give thanks to the Lord and to sing psalms to your Name, O Most High!

1 Thessalonians 5:18 give thanks in all circumstances; for this is God's will for you in Christ Jesus.

To accept God's holy will.

"If you truly love God and His will, then doing what you will, will, in fact, be doing what God wills." Peter Kreeft

The humble person makes his faculties, his talents, and his time available to God because he knows that God is the one who can best guide him on the path of life. The humble person knows that God loves him and that whatever God wants for him; is the best.

Psalm 25:8 Good and upright is the LORD; therefore he instructs sinners in his ways. 9 He guides the humble in what is right and teaches them his way. 10 All the ways of the LORD are loving and faithful towards those who keep the demands of his covenant.

Isaiah 55:8 'For my thoughts are not your thoughts, neither are your ways my ways,' declares the LORD.

Before God, humility is to recognize his greatness and to dispose ourselves to his will with simplicity and faith. God is asking us for humility to carry out his divine works in/and with us. By being meek and docile, we can receive grace, which means living in his ways of holiness.

James 4:6b 'God opposes the proud but shows favor to the humble.'

Psalm 138:6 Though the LORD is exalted, he looks kindly on the lowly; though lofty, he sees them from afar.

Being humble means knowing that we can always learn from God, and within all that we can learn from God, intellectually speaking, wisdom is the most extraordinary thing. Without humility, we would irrationally assume that we have nothing left to learn. It is fascinating that one must be humble to acquire wisdom, and one must be wise to value humility.

Proverbs 11:2 When pride comes, then comes disgrace, but with humility comes wisdom.

We can find an archetypical example of humility in the Fiat of Mary, the mother of Jesus. In a simple yet magnificent story, she shows all of humanity what it means to have a humble heart; she allows God's will to be fulfilled in her life. And that is the main meaning of being humble.

Luke 1:26 In the sixth month of Elizabeth's pregnancy, God sent the angel Gabriel to Nazareth, a town in Galilee, 27 to a virgin pledged to be married to a man named Joseph, a descendant of David. The virgin's name was Mary. 28 The angel went to her and said, 'Greetings, you who are highly favored! The Lord is with you.' 29 Mary was greatly troubled at his words and wondered what kind of greeting this might be. 30 But the angel said to her, 'Do not be afraid,

Mary, you have found favor with God. 31 You will conceive and give birth to a son, and you are to call him Jesus. 32 He will be great and will be called the Son of the Most High. The Lord God will give him the throne of his father David, 33 and he will reign over Jacob's descendants for ever; his kingdom will never end.' 34 'How will this be,' Mary asked the angel, 'since I am a virgin?' 35 The angel answered, 'The Holy Spirit will come on you, and the power of the Most High will overshadow you. So the holy one to be born will be called the Son of God. 36 Even Elizabeth your relative is going to have a child in her old age, and she who was said to be unable to conceive is in her sixth month. 37 For no word from God will ever fail.' 38 'I am the Lord's servant,' Mary answered. 'May your word to me be fulfilled.' Then the angel left her.

To serve and to treat others well.

This exceptional virtue only develops through serving and helping others; and is very frequently perceived by noble and amiable expressions and behaviors. The Bible continually invites us to value and to serve others just as Jesus did.

Philippians 2:3b Rather, in humility value others above yourselves, 4 not looking to your own interests but each of you to the interests of the others. 5 In your relationships with one another, have the same mindset as Christ Jesus: 6 who, being in very nature God, did not consider equality with God something to be used to his own advantage; 7 rather, he made himself nothing by taking the very nature of a servant, being made in human likeness.

Humility has a special light when we become virtuous and successful; because despite achieving many good things in life, it allows us to voluntarily become the last in order to give a complete testimony of love. How often many people, after the accomplishment of great things, lose their humility and begin to feel superior, more worthy, or better than others simply because they do not recognize that their achievements are based on God's gifts.

Sirach 3:17 My child, perform your tasks with humility then you will be loved by those whom God accepts. 18 The greater you are, the more you must humble yourself; so you will find favor in the sight of the Lord. 20 For great is the might of the Lord; but by the humble he is glorified.

The humble will always be counted as the worthiest of honor. This reasoning is contrary to the thinking of the world, but it will always be the truth. In the end, there is no human greatness without that concrete love that characterizes the humble.

Matthew 20:25 But Jesus called them to him and said, "You know that the rulers of the Gentiles lord it over them, and their great ones are tyrants over them. 26 It will not be so among you; but whoever wishes to be great among you must be your servant, 27 and whoever wishes to be first among you must be your slave; 28 just as the Son of Man came not to be served but to serve, and to give his life a ransom for many."

Matthew 23:11 The greatest among you will be your servant. 12 For those who exalt themselves will be humbled, and those who humble themselves will be exalted.

"It was pride that changed angels into devils; it is humility that makes men as angels." Saint Augustine

Denying our identity as creatures and children of God.

Pride, like humility, is born mainly from an identity that we assume. If we deny that we are creatures and children of God, we nullify our worth and that of our neighbor. Rejecting the true God and believing that we are our own God is the foundation of pride. In the Bible, we find a reading that refers to Satan's desire to be equal to God.

Isaiah 14:13 You said in your heart, 'I will ascend to the heavens; I will raise my throne above the stars of God; I will sit enthroned on the mount of assembly, on the utmost heights of Mount Zaphon. 14 I will ascend above the tops of the clouds; I will make myself like the Most High.'

Pride is a transgression of the first commandment. By failing to give God his place and priority in our lives, we will eventually become arrogant. Prideful people are mainly those who willfully ignore the Divine Moral Laws and recklessly commit sins or injustices.

Sirach 10:14 The beginning of the pride of man, is to fall off from God: 15 Because his heart is departed from him that made him: for pride is the beginning of all sin: he that holds it, shall be filled with maledictions, and it shall ruin him in the end.

Sirach 10:7 Pride is hateful before God and men: and all iniquity of nations is execrable.

Psalm 119:21 You rebuke the arrogant, who are accursed, those who stray from your commands.

Nehemiah 9:16 'But they, our ancestors, became arrogant and stiff-necked, and they did not obey your commands.

Psalm 52:1 Why do you boast of evil, you mighty hero? Why do you boast all day long, you who are a disgrace in the eyes of God? 2 You who practice deceit, your tongue plots destruction; it is like a sharpened razor. 3 You love evil rather than good, falsehood rather than speaking the truth. 4 You love every harmful word, you deceitful tongue! 5 Surely God will bring you down to everlasting ruin: he will snatch you up and pluck you from your tent; he will uproot you from the land of the living. 6 The righteous will see and fear; they will laugh at you, saying, 7 'Here now is the man who did not make God his stronghold but trusted in his great wealth and grew strong by destroying others!'

Jeremiah 9:23 This is what the LORD says: 'Let not the wise boast of their wisdom or the strong boast of their strength or the rich boast of their riches, 24 but let the one who boasts boast about this: that they have the understanding to know me, that I am the LORD, who exercises kindness, justice and righteousness on earth, for in these I delight,' declares the LORD.

Denying that we are sinners and that we need God.

Pride or self-glorification is also the illusion of believing that we are perfect an that there is no sin or vice in us. It blinds us to see the evils that we commit, and therefore, it means closing the door to the grace and mercy of God.

1 John 1:8 If we claim to be without sin, we deceive ourselves and the truth is not in us.

1 John 1:6 If we claim to have fellowship with him and yet walk in the darkness, we lie and do not live out the truth.

John 15:1 'I am the true vine, and my Father is the gardener. 2 He cuts off every branch in me that bears no fruit, while every branch that does bear fruit he prunes so that it will be even more fruitful. 3 You are already clean because of the word I have spoken to you. 4 Remain in me, as I also remain in you. No branch can bear fruit by itself; it must remain in the vine. Neither can you bear fruit unless you remain in me. 5 'I am the vine; you are the branches. If you remain in me and I in you, you will bear much fruit; apart from me you can do nothing. 6 If you do not remain in me, you are like a branch that is thrown away and withers; such branches are picked up, thrown into the fire and burned.

To deny that we have received everything.

Pride is usually rooted in the denial of certain fundamental truths. To believe that we do not owe everything to God is a great lie, which leads us to develop a kind of absurd arrogance. As we saw before, the truth is that we have always been, are, and will always be dependent on divine providence.

Being ungrateful before God and before the people around us will lead to a kind of unhappiness and continuous frustration. Nelson Medina wisely said, "He who thinks that he deserves everything, appreciates nothing." If we focus on the evil things in life without first acknowledging the good, we will end up being unbearable prideful people.

God is always at work in our lives; it is up to us to thank him for his grace and his love. In the Gospel, we find a story that describes the encounter of some lepers with Jesus. In this story, we have the opportunity to discover that we have also been ungrateful on many occasions.

Luke 17:11 Now on his way to Jerusalem, Jesus travelled along the border between Samaria and Galilee. 12 As he was going into a village, ten men who had leprosy met him. They stood at a distance 13 and called out in a loud voice, 'Jesus, Master, have pity on us!' 14 When he saw them, he said, 'Go, show yourselves to the priests.' And as they went, they were cleansed. 15 One of them, when he saw he was healed, came back, praising God in a loud voice. 16 He threw himself at Jesus' feet and thanked him – and he was a Samaritan. 17 Jesus asked, 'Were not all ten cleansed? Where are the other nine? 18 Has no one returned to give praise to God except this foreigner?' 19 Then he said to him, 'Rise and go; your faith has made you well.'

To reject God's holly will.

If we separate ourselves from the will of God, then we will not be able to do anything useful or valuable in life. Pride drives us to commit all kinds of evil, violence, and abuse, which leads us to an eventual fall or ruin, which manifests itself in all sorts of negative experiences.

Proverbs 16:18 Pride goes before destruction, a haughty spirit before a fall.

In the book of Deuteronomy, we find a passage that precisely speaks of this self-sufficient and arrogant attitude towards God. It is Him who tells us not to trust or magnify ourselves for our achievements, for they are all gifts from God.

Deuteronomy 8:11 Be careful that you do not forget the LORD your God, failing to observe his commands, his laws and his decrees that I am giving you this day. 12 Otherwise, when you eat and are satisfied, when you build fine houses and settle down, 13 and when your herds and flocks grow large and your silver and gold increase and all you have is multiplied, 14 then your heart will become proud and you will forget the LORD your God. ----- 17 You may say to yourself, 'My power and the strength of my hands have produced this wealth for me.' 18 But remember the LORD your God, for it is he who gives you the ability to produce wealth, and so confirms his covenant, which he swore to your ancestors, as it is today.

Not serving or treating others well.

This vice is similar to narcissism, where the important thing is my ego even at others' expense. With this mentality, we deceive ourselves with false ideas of superiority and greatness. This conceit leads us to always seek the best for ourselves and leave the worst for others. In the following passage, Jesus gives a warning of this choice of life.

Luke 11:43 'Woe to you Pharisees, because you love the most important seats in the synagogues and respectful greetings in the market-places.

The prideful person forgets that we all have the same dignity; he feels and thinks of himself as superior, and he judges others as his inferiors. Consequently, he becomes unable to help, and instead of serving people, he uses them. The conceited incapacitate themselves from showing charity and mercy. They tend to end up alone because no one can put up with being with them because of their cruelty and mistreatment of others.

Romans 12:16b Do not be proud, but be willing to associate with people of low position. Do not be conceited.

Tobit 4:14 Never suffer pride to reign in thy mind, or in thy words: for from it all perdition took its beginning.

Sirach 13:24 And as humility is an abomination to the proud: so also the rich man abhorred the poor.

Psalm 10:4 In his pride the wicked man does not seek him; in all his thoughts there is no room for God. 5 His ways are always prosperous; your laws are rejected by him; he sneers at all his enemies. 6 He says to himself, 'Nothing will ever shake me.' He swears, 'No one will ever do me harm.' 7 His mouth is full of lies and threats; trouble and evil are under his tongue.

Perseverance vs. Sloth

Perseverance is...	Sloth is...
Striving to do things well.	Not striving to do things well.
Diligence in the pursuit of moral excellence.	Negligence in the pursuit of moral excellence.
Constancy in the fulfillment of the commandments.	Inconsistency in the fulfillment of the commandments.
Self-discipline and commitment.	Lacking self-discipline and commitment.

"Beginning is for everyone; persevering is for saints."
Saint José María Escrivá de Balaguer

Striving to do things well.

The virtue of perseverance stands on value of human effort. By common sense, we realize that all good things require work, dedication, and sacrifice. Consequently, we naturally give credit or honor to those who have achieved difficult things in life through their continual effort, those who have spent their lives going through many moments of fatigue in the search of an ideal.

Ecclesiastes 1:8a All things are full of labor.

If we really want something, we must be willing to strive for it, be it ideals, dreams, or whatever reality we wish to fulfill; we will always require discipline. We will only succeed if we are determined to dedicate body and soul to those goals. This truth that we know by common sense is also expressed in the Bible.

Proverbs 12:27b Diligence is one's most important possession.

Proverbs 14:23 All hard work brings a profit, but mere talk leads only to poverty.

In the parable of the good sower, Saint Luke teaches us that a good and perseverant heart is the basis for bearing good fruits.

Luke 8:4 While a large crowd was gathering and people were coming to Jesus from town after town, he told this parable: 5 'A farmer went out to sow his seed. As he was scattering the seed, some fell along the path; it was trampled on, and the birds ate it up. 6 Some fell on rocky ground, and when it came up, the plants withered because they had no moisture. 7 Other seed fell among thorns, which grew up with it and choked the plants. 8 Still other seed fell on good soil. It came up and yielded a crop, a hundred times more than was sown.' When he said this, he called out, 'Whoever has ears to hear, let them hear.' 9 His disciples asked him what this parable meant. 10 He said, 'The knowledge of the secrets of the kingdom of God has been given to you, but to others I speak in parables, so that, ' "though seeing, they may not see; though hearing, they may not understand." 11 'This is the meaning of the parable: the seed is the word of God. 12 Those along the path are the ones who hear, and then the devil comes and takes away the word from their hearts, so that they may not believe and be saved. 13 Those on the rocky ground are the ones who receive the word with joy when they hear it, but they have no root. They believe for a while, but in the time of testing they fall away. 14 The seed that fell among thorns stands for those who hear, but as they go on their way they are choked by life's worries, riches and pleasures, and they do not mature. 15 But the seed on good soil stands for those with a noble and good heart, who hear the word, retain it, and by persevering produce a crop.

Complementing, in the same parable, but according to Saint Mark, it is explained to us that according to God's order, the fruits will be given in abundance at 30, 60, or 100 to 1.

Mark 4:20 Others, like seed sown on good soil, hear the word, accept it, and produce a crop – some thirty, some sixty, some a hundred times what was sown.'

Diligence in the pursuit of moral excellence.

But persevering is not just to strive; but to strive for the good, for our duty, and for love. No one can persevere on egoism or evil; one can only persist on it, because in the end, vices do not add anything of positive value. Jesus invites us to strive for holiness to achieve salvation, which is the primary purpose of every Christian life. Becoming a virtuous person or achieving moral excellence is not easy; it requires a continuous battle against our ego that will last a lifetime.

Luke 13:22 Then Jesus went through the towns and villages, teaching as he made his way to Jerusalem. 23 Someone asked him, 'Lord, are only a few people going to be saved?' He said to them, 24 'Make every effort to enter through the narrow door, because many, I tell you, will try to enter and will not be able to.

In the spiritual realm, God offers us his help and promises that he will respond generously to our efforts.

Perseverance has something fascinating because as we grow in our virtues, what previously was difficult and took much effort, with time and dedication, becomes something almost easy and natural. Like any human process, our moral or spiritual excellence takes time and practice to be perfected. It is essential to recognize that this virtue implies not giving up and starting over again; It means trying again and again to do the right thing despite all the difficulties.

Constancy in the fulfillment of the commandments.

Biblically speaking, the word perseverance is always accompanied by a moral-ethical sense. In the Old Testament, it is directly related to the fulfillment and living of the Ten Commandments. In the New Testament, this criterion is complemented by the application of the Christian virtues.

Deuteronomy 5:29 Oh, that their hearts would be inclined to fear me and keep all my commands always, so that it might go well with them and their children for ever!

1 Chronicles 28:7 I will establish his kingdom for ever if he is unswerving in carrying out my commands and laws, as is being done at this time."

James 1:25 But whoever looks intently into the perfect law that gives freedom and continues in it – not forgetting what they have heard but doing it – they will be blessed in what they do.

Hebrews 6:11 We want each of you to show this same diligence to the very end, so that what you hope for may be fully realized.

Persevering will require effort throughout our entire lives, the good news is that we can be sure that God will be with us every day until the end of the world.

Matthew 28:20 and teaching them to obey everything I have commanded you. And surely I am with you always, to the very end of the age.'

Self-discipline and commitment.

One of the overwhelming signs of someone who has this virtue is his capacity to fulfill his commitments. By committing ourselves, we decide on a goal and endeavor until the end to achieve its accomplishment. People who value commitment know that starting something and bringing it to fruition is not easy. They know that they will have to overcome a series of situations and adversities to achieve their goals. They know that the road will be full of those little moments where they will have to give everything and fight with their soul to persevere, and when they do, it will be a glorious moment. In his letter, Saint Paul demonstrates to us the level of commitment that his journey required.

1 Corinthians 4:11 To this very hour we go hungry and thirsty, we are in rags, we are brutally treated, we are homeless. 12 We work hard with our own hands. When we are cursed, we bless; when we are persecuted, we endure it; 13 when we are slandered, we answer kindly. We have become the scum of the earth, the garbage of the world – right up to this moment.

"I don't understand how you can call yourself a Christian and lead such an idle, useless life. Have you forgotten Christ's life of toil?"
Saint Jose Maria Escriva de Balaguer

Not striving to do things well.

In life, there is an immensity of goods in which we play a unique role. Laziness begins in rejecting that personal duty to do things well. In the order that God established, each one of us has a particular responsibility, which must be fulfilled through effort and personal dedication in favor of the common good and in function to the Kingdom of Heaven. God gave each one of us an important script in the play of life; it is our freedom to choose between a mentality of hard work or a mentality of minimal effort. To strive or not will always be a decisive action with contrasting consequences.

Proverbs 13:4 A sluggard's appetite is never filled, but the desires of the diligent are fully satisfied.

Tobit 4:13c In idleness there is loss and dire poverty, because idleness is the mother of famine.

Proverbs 15:19 The way of the sluggard is blocked with thorns, but the path of the upright is a highway.

If we are honest, what would the value of our achievements if they came without effort? This vice is like a kind of cowardice that leads us to failure before even trying. There is no bigger loser than the lazy person, for such a person hates to participate in life through his efforts. The lazy person typically tends to minimize and deny his personal and social responsibilities, and tragically he ends up living a mediocre life.

The sloth's tragedy is that the more he hides in his famous "comfort zone" or in its superficial comforts, the weaker and useless he becomes. The lazy person tends to have a sterile mentality by looking for that which does not challenge him or removes his fake tranquility fruit of his complacency. The lazy person prefers the easier and more pleasurable activities, which leads him to become weak.

The people that lack the self-discipline to work and to study for doing something good are a burden. What can we expect from such behavior? In the following biblical passages, we will see some thoughts that reflect the Christian rejection of laziness and idleness.

Proverbs 6:6 Go to the ant, you sluggard; consider its ways and be wise! 7 It has no commander, no overseer or ruler, 8 yet it stores its provisions in summer and gathers its food at harvest. 9 How long will you lie there, you sluggard? When will you get up from your sleep? 10 A little sleep, a little slumber, a little folding of the hands to rest – 11 and poverty will come on you like a thief and scarcity like an armed man.

2 Thessalonians 3:6 In the name of the Lord Jesus Christ, we command you, brothers and sisters, to keep away from every believer who is idle and disruptive and does not live according to the teaching you received from us. 7 For you yourselves know how you ought to follow our example. We were not idle when we were with you, 8 nor did we eat anyone's food without paying for it. On the contrary, we worked night and day, laboring and toiling so that we would not be a burden to any of you. 9 We did this, not because we do not have the right to such help, but in order to offer ourselves as

a model for you to imitate. 10 For even when we were with you, we gave you this rule: 'The one who is unwilling to work shall not eat.' 11 We hear that some among you are idle and disruptive. They are not busy; they are busybodies. 12 Such people we command and urge in the Lord Jesus Christ to settle down and earn the food they eat. 13 And as for you, brothers and sisters, never tire of doing what is good. 14 Take special note of anyone who does not obey our instruction in this letter. Do not associate with them, in order that they may feel ashamed. 15 Yet do not regard them as an enemy, but warn them as you would a fellow believer.

Negligence in the pursuit of moral excellence.

"The person who commits the sin of laziness may not be doing anything visibly wrong. Yet he is rejecting the presence of God, rejecting the joy of love." Peter Kreeft

Developing and perfecting our moral life is an exciting duty to God. People who have this vice, by rejecting that duty, end up living monotonous and empty lives even when they have money and material goods. Laziness far from developing our capacities towards excellence leads us to become dull and boring. In the following verses, we will look at some biblical proverbs that unveil the reality of lazy behavior.

Proverbs 10:26 As vinegar to the teeth and smoke to the eyes, so are sluggards to those who send them.

Proverbs 21:25 The craving of a sluggard will be the death of him, because his hands refuse to work.

Proverbs 26:14 As a door turns on its hinges, so a sluggard turns on his bed. 15 A sluggard buries his hand in the dish; he is too lazy to bring it back to his mouth. 16 A sluggard is wiser in his own eyes than seven people who answer discreetly.

Inconsistency in the fulfillment of the commandments.

It is important to mention that laziness is the omission of the fulfill-ment of Divine Moral Law, that is, of loving God and our neighbor through our behavior. Precisely the acts based on this vice are con-sidered evil because they are a transgression of the moral command-ments. It might even be thought that our lack of love is more common due to our omission of good works than to our evil deeds. Christianity clearly sustains that we are bound by life not to be car-ried away by laziness.

James 4:17 If anyone, then, knows the good they ought to do and doesn't do it, it is sin for them.

In some way, failing to persevere, is to stop working for the good, which means letting ourselves be carried away by egoism and its vices. It is evident that to persevere it is necessary to remain on the right path until the end of our days.

Ezekiel 18:24 'But if a righteous person turns from their right-eousness and commits sin and does the same detestable things the wicked person does, will they live? None of the righteous things that person has done will be remembered. Because of the unfaithfulness they are guilty of and because of the sins they have committed, they will die.

Lacking self-discipline and commitment.

The idle because of his lack of love grows weaker; and when he achieves what is enough for his selfishness, he thinks that he has al-ready fulfilled his duties in life. The lazy person avoids committing himself to life and does not like the idea of having to work for the good of others; and hence, he does not engage with others in a col-lective effort towards the common good.

The person with this vice typically willingly ignores that his lack of self-discipline and commitment has negative consequences for oth-ers. Perhaps the part of the scripture where sloth is most clearly con-demned is the parable of the talents, where Jesus teaches us that the only way to bear fruit and glorify God is by putting into practice all the gifts that He has given us.

Matthew 25:14 -The parable of the bags of gold- 'Again, it will be like a man going on a journey, who called his servants and entrusted his wealth to them. 15 To one he gave five bags of gold, to another two bags, and to another one bag, each according to his ability. Then he went on his journey. 16 The man who had received five bags of gold went at once and put his money to work and gained five bags more. 17 So also, the one with two bags of gold gained two more. 18 But the man who had received one bag went off, dug a hole in the ground and hid his master's money. 19 'After a long time the master of those servants returned and settled accounts with them. 20 The man who had received five bags of gold brought the other five. "Master," he said, "you entrusted me with five bags of gold. See, I have gained five more." 21 'His master replied, "Well done, good and faithful servant! You have been faithful with a few things; I will put you in charge of many things. Come and share your master's happiness!" 22 'The man with two bags of gold also came. "Master," he said, "you entrusted me with two bags of gold: see, I have gained two more." 23 'His master replied, "Well done, good and faithful servant! You have been faithful with a few things; I will put you in charge of many things. Come and share your master's happiness!" 24 'Then the man who had received one bag of gold came. "Master," he said, "I knew that you are a hard man, harvesting where you have not sown and gathering where you have not scattered seed. 25 So I was afraid and went out and hid your gold in the ground. See, here is what belongs to you." 26 'His master replied, "You wicked, lazy servant! So you knew that I harvest where I have not sown and gather where I have not scattered seed? 27 Well then, you should have put my money on deposit with the bankers, so that when I returned I would have received it back with interest. 28 ' "So take the bag of gold from him and give it to the one who has ten bags. 29 For whoever has will be given more, and they will have an abundance. Whoever does not have, even what they have will be taken from them. 30 And throw that worthless servant outside, into the darkness, where there will be weeping and gnashing of teeth."

Matthew 7:19 Every tree that does not bear good fruit is cut down and thrown into the fire.

God did not create us to become useless because of our laziness. God has given us many goods in life, and we must respond by making a firm commitment to bear fruit for his divine kingdom. It is wise to recognize that the lack of moral self-discipline and commitment in the present will become a cause of misery in the future.

We cannot afford the egoistical luxury of burying the gifts, talents and opportunities that God has given us. A passage from the book of Revelation, although it may sound strong, confirms God's position in the face of this sin.

Revelation 3:15 I know your deeds, that you are neither cold nor hot. I wish you were either one or the other! 16 So, because you are lukewarm – neither hot nor cold – I am about to spit you out of my mouth.

Generosity vs. Avarice

Generosity is...	Avarice is...
To receive the gifts from God.	Rejecting the gifts from God.
Sharing who we are and what we have.	Refusing to share who we are and what we have.
Having empathy and solidarity.	Lacking empathy and solidarity.
In giving, to prioritize good itself.	In giving, to prioritize our personal gain.
The path to abundance and friendship.	The path to scarcity and loneliness.

"Love is an exchange of gifts." Saint Ignatius

To receive the gifts from God.

"Blessed are those who give without remembering and those who receive without forgetting." Saint Teresa of Calcutta

God has arranged everything through his goodness and wisdom; He freely disposes himself to give us every good, both natural and supernatural. To be generous is to participate in the flow of divine generosity. Only God can grant life's maximum goods, such as existence, love, truth, fullness, and eternal life. Therefore, no one can be more generous than God. To be generous in our donation, it is necessary first to receive from his providence.

James 1:17 Every good and perfect gift is from above, coming down from the Father of the heavenly lights, who does not change like shifting shadows.

We will have countless opportunities to be generous during our lives, but to give, we must first receive, since no one gives what he does not have.

1 Chronicles 29:14 'But who am I, and who are my people, that we should be able to give as generously as this? Everything comes from you, and we have given you only what comes from your hand.

God's wealth is absolute, he has everything, and he lacks nothing. God is magnanimous because He will give us the most valuable wealth: The Holy Spirit. God gives himself, and he is the highest good, so to receive God is to receive the highest good in life.

John 14:26 But the Advocate, the Holy Spirit, whom the Father will send in my name, will teach you all things and will remind you of everything I have said to you.

Acts 1:8 But you will receive power when the Holy Spirit comes on you; and you will be my witnesses in Jerusalem, and in all Judea and Samaria, and to the ends of the earth.'

Philippians 4:19 And my God will meet all your needs according to the riches of his glory in Christ Jesus.

Sharing who we are and what we have.

Giving is not merely a material concern, but mainly a spiritual and personal issue exhibited in human behavior. To be generous is primarily to be willing to donate ourselves for the good of others; it is finding the great joy of sharing life; and it is focusing more on giving than in receiving.

Sirach 14:16 Give and take, and justify thy soul.

Luke 6:38a Give, and it will be given to you.

Acts 20:35b The Lord Jesus himself said: "It is more blessed to give than to receive."

Generosity is mainly managing our personal-spiritual-material goods for the benefit of others. The example of fathers and mothers is helpful because they usually want to give the best to their children. Parents, on the spiritual side, use their virtues to help their children mature. Complementarily, on the material side, they also seek to provide for the practical things so their children can grow in a healthy manner. In a more general sense, the Bible teaches us that we ought to care for each other as humans. We ought to manage and share the things we own in function for the greater good.

Proverbs 3:27 Do not withhold good from those to whom it is due, when it is in your power to act.

Proverbs 19:17 Whoever is kind to the poor lends to the LORD, and he will reward them for what they have done.

Sirach 29:8 Nevertheless, be understanding with those who are poor. Don't keep them waiting for your generosity. 9 The Lord has commanded us to help the poor; don't refuse them the help they need. 10 It is better to lose your money by helping a relative or a friend than to lose it by letting it rust away under a rock somewhere.

Deuteronomy 15:7 If anyone is poor among your fellow Israelites in any of the towns of the land that the LORD your God is giving you, do not be hard-hearted or tight-fisted towards them. 8 Rather, be open-handed and freely lend them whatever they need. 9 Be careful not to harbor this wicked thought: 'The seventh year, the year for cancelling debts, is near,' so that you do not show ill will towards the needy among your fellow Israelites and give them nothing. They may then appeal to the LORD against you, and you will be found guilty of sin. 10 Give generously to them and do so without a grudging heart; then because of this the LORD your God will bless you in all your work and in everything you put your hand to.

Romans 12:13 Share with the Lord's people who are in need. Practice hospitality.

In the parable of the poor widow, Jesus shows us that virtue, and especially generosity, is always proportional to who we are and what we have; it is in that wisdom where we discover that to be generous, we do not need to be rich or have many things; we simply must be willing to give the best of who we are and of what have.

Luke 21:1 As Jesus looked up, he saw the rich putting their gifts into the temple treasury. 2 He also saw a poor widow put in two very small copper coins. 3 'Truly I tell you,' he said, 'this poor widow has put in more than all the others. 4 All these people gave their gifts out of their wealth; but she out of her poverty put in all she had to live on.'

Having empathy and solidarity.

Generous people show a genuine interest in the good of others. They are frequently looking to use their talents and goods to benefit others. Due to their great empathy, such people are realistic towards the needs of their neighbors. In the Bible, we find the epic story of the good Samaritan. A man who on his walk discovers a stranger who has gone through an unfortunate situation and is needy and desolate. The Good Samaritan has the compassion to fix his eyes on the tragic reality, and, allowing himself to be carried away by his generosity, he takes responsibility and action towards the solution of a problem that was not even his.

Luke 10:30 In reply Jesus said: 'A man was going down from Jerusalem to Jericho, when he was attacked by robbers. They stripped him of his clothes, beat him and went away, leaving him half-dead. 31 A priest happened to be going down the same road, and when he saw the man, he passed by on the other side. 32 So too, a Levite, when he came to the place and saw him, passed by on the other side. 33 But a Samaritan, as he travelled, came where the man was; and when he saw him, he took pity on him. 34 He went to him and bandaged his wounds, pouring on oil and wine. Then he put the man on his own donkey, brought him to an inn and took care of him. 35 The next day he took out two denarii and gave them to the inn-keeper. "Look after him," he said, "and when I return, I will reimburse you for any extra expense you may have."

In giving, to prioritize on good itself.

True generosity is silent; its objective is neither the recognition nor the reciprocity of the others. The basis of this virtue is simply doing good because it is the fair thing to do; this intention means that one seeks to give freely out of love. Jesus clarifies this principle in the following passage.

Matthew 6:1 Be careful not to practice your righteousness in front of others to be seen by them. If you do, you will have no reward from your Father in heaven. 2 'So when you give to the needy, do not announce it with trumpets, as the hypocrites do in the synagogues and on the streets, to be honored by others. Truly I tell you, they have received their reward in full. 3 But when you give to the needy, do not let your left hand know what your right hand is doing, 4 so that your giving may be in secret. Then your Father, who sees what is done in secret, will reward you.

Jesus also teaches us that generosity is especially valuable before God when no personal gain is sought and when we are capable of taking the risk to share with those who cannot compensate or repay us.

Luke 14:12 Then Jesus said to his host, 'When you give a luncheon or dinner, do not invite your friends, your brothers or sisters, your relatives, or your rich neighbors; if you do, they may invite you back and so you will be repaid. 13 But when you give a banquet, invite the poor, the crippled, the lame, the blind, 14 and you will be blessed. Although they cannot repay you, you will be repaid at the resurrection of the righteous.'

The path to abundance and friendship.

Finally, if we were all wisely generous with our many goods and possessions, the world would become a prosperous place. Whether material or spiritual, abundance has a direct cause in the generosity and reciprocity by which we live. Initiative is needed to start the cycle, and solidarity is needed to maintain it.

Proverbs 11:25 A generous person will prosper; whoever refreshes others will be refreshed.

Sirach 31:8 Blessed is the rich man that is found without blemish: and that hath not gone after gold, nor put his trust in money nor in treasures. 9 Who is he, and we will praise him? for he hath done wonderful things in his life. 10 Who hath been tried thereby, and made perfect, he shall have glory everlasting. He that could have transgressed, and hath not transgressed: and could do evil things, and hath not done them: 11 Therefore are his goods established in the Lord, and all the church of the saints shall declare his alms.

2 Corinthians 9:6 Remember this: whoever sows sparingly will also reap sparingly, and whoever sows generously will also reap generously. 7 Each of you should give what you have decided in your heart to give, not reluctantly or under compulsion, for God loves a cheerful giver. 8 And God is able to bless you abundantly, so that in all things at all times, having all that you need, you will abound in every good work. 9 As it is written: 'They have freely scattered their gifts to the poor; their righteousness endures for ever.'

"Then he said to them, 'Watch out! Be on your guard against all kinds of greed; life does not consist in an abundance of possessions." Jesus - Luke 12:15

To reject the gifts from God.

Greed is when we become obsessed with desires of power and wealth, leaving aside the transcendent goods and duties that come from God. This mentality implies rejecting God's natural and super-natural gifts and graces and searching for everlasting or permanent happiness on transient and limited realities. By altering the hierarchy of values and turning God, virtue, and love into something trivial, we are heading to an abyss that never reaches satisfaction.

This vice is prominently evident in the ultimate goals or ends we are freely choosing to pursue in life. This idea is embodied throughout many Biblical stories, and Jesus himself is the one who clarifies this dilemma for us.

Luke 16:13 'No one can serve two masters. Either you will hate the one and love the other, or you will be devoted to the one and despise the other. You cannot serve both God and Money.'

Thinking that getting rich is the purpose of our life is the sin of avarice. Well, how can we be spiritually generous when our ambition is egoistic, and our main wish is to get rich? The Bible inspires us to understand that success in life is not about becoming rich in a bank account since we can take nothing to the afterlife. Life will always be about being, not about having.

Ecclesiastes 5:15 Everyone comes naked from their mother's womb, and as everyone comes, so they depart. They take nothing from their toil that they can carry in their hands.

1 Timothy 6:7 For we brought nothing into the world, and we can take nothing out of it. 8 But if we have food and clothing, we will be content with that. 9 Those who want to get rich fall into temptation and a trap and into many foolish and harmful desires that plunge people into ruin and destruction. 10 For the love of money is a root of all kinds of evil. Some people, eager for money, have wandered from the faith and pierced themselves with many griefs.

If we think about it, we find an egotistical desire for power and/or pleasure in all types of greed. We normally do not want money in itself, but by the possibilities or opportunities it brings. Superficially speaking, money is the key to having what we want; but spiritually speaking, it is not. In the end, no money can buy spiritual goods. That is why "loving" money or putting money in the first place of our lives is something evil.

Sirach 31:3 Rich people work hard to make a lot of money; then they can sit back and live in luxury. 4 Poor people work hard and have nothing to show for it, and when they rest, they are still poor. 5 No one who loves money can be judged innocent; his efforts to get rich have led him into sin. 6 Many people have been ruined because of money, brought face-to-face with disaster. 7 Money is a trap for those who are fascinated by it, a trap that every fool falls into.

Ecclesiastes 5:9 A covetous man shall not be satisfied with money: and he that loveth riches shall reap no fruit from them: so this also is vanity.

Refusing to share who we are and what we have.

From a spiritual perspective, the greedy is rarely interested in sharing his personal gifts and abilities since he detests the idea of using his talents in favor of others and only uses them for himself. This vice becomes evident when someone voluntarily ignores giving and focuses interestedly on receiving.

From a more general and practical perspective, the main economic problem is not a lack of resources or money. The problem is that most of the resources are distributed and managed wrongly because of the selfish, vain, and greedy mentality of people.

If there is something absurd and illogical about greed, it's the unbridled desire to accumulate things we do not need nor use. Knowing that we are pilgrims in this world, we understand that accumulating material things does not make sense and that the possessions we have should be optimally used for good ends.

Sirach 14:3 It isn't right for someone who is selfish to be rich. What use is money to a stingy person? 4 If you deny yourself in order to accumulate wealth, you are only accumulating it for someone else. Others will use your riches to live in luxury. 5 How can you be generous with others if you are stingy with yourself, if you are not willing to enjoy your own wealth? 6 No one is worse off than someone who is stingy with himself; it is a sin that brings its own punishment. 7 When such a person does something good, it is only by accident; his selfishness will sooner or later be evident. 8 A selfish person is evil; he turns his back on people's needs 9 and is never satisfied with what he has. Greed will shrivel up a person's soul. 10 Some people are too stingy to put bread on their own table.

Lacking empathy and solidarity.

Greed increases by forgetting that everything we have comes from God and that our possessions are to be used and shared with prudence for our neighbors' good. In the Gospel, according to Saint Luke, we find a story that manifests that mentality, where, out of greed, we limit ourselves to thinking only of our egoism in how to be more comfortable and secure. That is the major mistake of trusting our life on material wealth.

Luke 12:15 Then he said to them, 'Watch out! Be on your guard against all kinds of greed; life does not consist in an abundance of possessions.' 16 And he told them this parable: 'The ground of a certain rich man yielded an abundant harvest. 17 He thought to himself, "What shall I do? I have no place to store my crops." 18 'Then he said, "This is what I'll do. I will tear down my barns and build bigger ones, and there I will store my surplus grain. 19 And I'll say to myself, 'You have plenty of grain laid up for many years. Take life easy; eat, drink and be merry.' " 20 'But God said to him, "You fool! This very night your life will be demanded from you. Then who will get what you have prepared for yourself?" 21 'This is how it will be with whoever stores up things for themselves but is not rich towards God.'

Greed blinds us to the point of considering our luxuries preferable to giving a hand to those who truly needy; it is a kind of blindness to realities and needs that are not ours. At first sight, it implies a grievous scene for the poor, but in the final picture, it means a tragic end for the greedy.

Luke 16:19 'There was a rich man who was dressed in purple and fine linen and lived in luxury every day. 20 At his gate was laid a beggar named Lazarus, covered with sores 21 and longing to eat what fell from the rich man's table. Even the dogs came and licked his sores. 22 'The time came when the beggar died and the angels carried him to Abraham's side. The rich man also died and was buried. 23In Hades, where he was in torment, he looked up and saw Abraham far away, with Lazarus by his side. 24 So he called to him, "Father Abraham, have pity on me and send Lazarus to dip the tip of his finger in water and cool my tongue, because I am in agony in this fire." 25 'But Abraham replied, "Son, remember that in your lifetime you received your good things, while Lazarus received bad things, but now he is comforted here and you are in agony. 26 And besides all this, between us and you a great chasm has been set in place, so that those who want to go from here to you cannot, nor can anyone cross over from there to us." 27 'He answered, "Then I beg you, father, send Lazarus to my family, 28 for I have five brothers. Let him warn them, so that they will not also come to this place of torment." 29 'Abraham replied, "They have Moses and the Prophets; let them listen to them." 30 ' "No, father Abraham," he said, "but if someone from the dead goes to them, they will repent." 31 'He said to him, "If they do not listen to Moses and the Prophets, they will not be convinced even if someone rises from the dead." '

1 John 3:17 If anyone has material possessions and sees a brother or sister in need but has no pity on them, how can the love of God be in that person?

In giving, to prioritize our personal gain.

We have all witnessed people who appear to be generous, but in reality, they act out of convenience or personal interest. Its main objective is not to do good but to obtain benefits, reputation, or power. Such people are not really interested in the good of others; they simply want to use them. It is common for them to deceive people in fragile circumstances through false gestures of philanthropy or hospitality. This behavior is what we call false generosity, which is actually greed.

As a result of always thinking about our personal convenience envy arises, and this complementary vice is like a manifestation of greed and selfishness but applied to the goods of others. Envy is also contrary to generosity. It appears as a negative sentiment triggered by a twisted reasoning. When an envious man meets someone more virtuous, instead of learning from him, he criticizes him; and instead of recognizing the good in him, he slanders him. Somehow, faced with the same fact (the good of another), the generous rejoices, while the envious becomes bitter.

James 3:16 For where you have envy and selfish ambition, there you find disorder and every evil practice.

Galatians 5:26 Let us not become conceited, provoking and envying each other.

If we were all greedy and envious, no good would give us satisfaction; shockingly, we would be miserable even in prosperity. We must stop comparing our egos. The idea is simply to strive to achieve our personal best without demeaning the good qualities of others.

It is interesting to note two important things about envy. First, the Bible tells us that sin and death entered the world because of the devil's envy. Second, that Christ was persecuted and crucified out of the jealousy of certain Jews with religious authority. Two critical events show how harmful envy can be.

Wisdom 2:24 But by the envy of the devil, death came into the world: 25 And they follow him that are of his side.

Mark 15:1 Very early in the morning, the chief priests, with the elders, the teachers of the law and the whole Sanhedrin, made their plans. So they bound Jesus, led him away and handed him over to Pilate. 2 'Are you the king of the Jews?' asked Pilate. 'You have said so,' Jesus replied. 3 The chief priests accused him of many things. 4 So again Pilate asked him, 'Aren't you going to answer? See how many things they are accusing you of.' 5 But Jesus still made no reply, and Pilate was amazed. 6 Now it was the custom at the festival to release a prisoner whom the people requested. 7 A man called Barabbas was in prison with the rebels who had committed murder in the uprising. 8 The crowd came up and asked Pilate to do for them what he usually did. 9 'Do you want me to release to you the king of the Jews?' asked Pilate, 10 For he realized it was out of jealousy that the chief priests had handed Jesus over.

The path to scarcity and loneliness.

Part of the Christian philosophy is to cooperate to solve spiritual and material evils; that is why greed on either of these two levels is a sin, because, through the lack of virtue and concrete aid, we resolve nothing. If we have good things to offer and we do not donate them, we become uncaring and heartless. Interestingly, great philosophers and religious people have chosen material poverty to seek spiritual abundance; they stop focusing on money to focus on virtue.

Think about it; if we all acted greedily, the world would plunge into scarcity, filled with even more miserable situations. From a material perspective, people would be interested in using their resources only on themselves. On a personal level, they would always be waiting to receive instead of giving. It does not surprise the loneliness of those who lack this great virtue. In the end, you cannot reap in abundance when you sowed ungenerously.

Sirach 4:31 Do not let your hand be stretched out to receive and closed when it is time to give.

Purity vs. Impurity

Purity is...	Impurity is...
Reflection of goodness.	Reflection of malice.
To renounce sin and vice.	Not to renounce sin and vice.
Honesty before the truth.	Falsity before the truth.
To preserve the divine dignity of our being.	To degenerate the divine dignity of our being.
To clearly see God in life.	Not to clearly see God in life.

"He who loves with purity considers not the gift of the lover, but the love of the giver." Thomas of Kempis

Reflection of goodness.

The first thing we can know about this virtue is that all human beings are created with certain goodness; it is a grace that God gives us when he calls us into existence. We can intuit a pure person as someone who will not do evil to his neighbor. It is interesting that we generally observe that young children are more authentic than adults because we know that they are often less contaminated by the evil in the world. In the first meditation on this virtue, Christ calls us to be like children in the sense of living with purity in order to enter the Divine Kingdom.

Matthew 18:1 At that time the disciples came to Jesus and asked, 'Who, then, is the greatest in the kingdom of heaven?' 2 He called a little child to him, and placed the child among them. 3 And he said: 'Truly I tell you, unless you change and become like little children, you will never enter the kingdom of heaven. 4 Therefore, whoever takes the lowly position of this child is the greatest in the kingdom of heaven.

To renounce sin and vice.

In the Old Testament, purity was directly related to the obedience of the divine commandments, which direct us to live in friendship with God.

Psalm 18:21 For I have kept the ways of the LORD; I am not guilty of turning from my God. 22 All his laws are before me; I have not turned away from his decrees. 23 I have been blameless before him and have kept myself from sin. 24 The LORD has rewarded me according to my righteousness, according to the cleanness of my hands in his sight. 25 To the faithful you show yourself faithful, to the blameless you show yourself blameless, 26 to the pure you show yourself pure, but to the devious you show yourself shrewd.

It is up to us to attempt to be pure by not falling into sin. The good news is that even if we fall into sin, we can repent and heal because God is merciful and forgives. Christ came to give us the strength to regain the purity and kindness of our hearts. We find some biblical accounts about the purification we seek only through God.

1 John 3:3 All who have this hope in him purify themselves, just as he is pure.

2 Chronicles 30:18 Although most of the many people who came from Ephraim, Manasseh, Issachar and Zebulun had not purified themselves, yet they ate the Passover, contrary to what was written. But Hezekiah prayed for them, saying, 'May the LORD, who is good, pardon everyone 19 who sets their heart on seeking God – the LORD, the God of their ancestors – even if they are not clean according to the rules of the sanctuary.' 20 And the LORD heard Hezekiah and healed the people. 21 The Israelites who were present in Jerusalem celebrated the Festival of Unleavened Bread for seven days with great rejoicing, while the Levites and priests praised the LORD every day with resounding instruments dedicated to the LORD.

Ezekiel 36:25 I will sprinkle clean water on you, and you will be clean; I will cleanse you from all your impurities and from all your idols. 26 I will give you a new heart and put a new spirit in you; I will remove from you your heart of stone and give you a heart of flesh. 27 And I will put my Spirit in you and move you to follow my decrees and be careful to keep my laws. 28 Then you will live in the land I gave your ancestors; you will be my people, and I will be your God.

Honesty before the truth.

Another characteristic related to purity is honesty, the simple fact of always speaking prioritizing the truth. Purity allows us to see reality clearly; when something is pure, there is no room for confusion and doubts. An honest person does not have double intentions, nor does he live with a double standard; he simply values the truth and is coherent with it. The Bible is full of teachings about honesty. Jesus himself speaks clearly about the importance of always seeking the truth, to the point that he declares that the children of God live according to the truth, while the children of the devil live according to lies.

John 8:40 As it is, you are looking for a way to kill me, a man who has told you the truth that I heard from God. Abraham did not do such things. 41 You are doing the works of your own father.' 'We are not illegitimate children,' they protested. 'The only Father we have is God himself.' 42 Jesus said to them, 'If God were your Father, you would love me, for I have come here from God. I have not come on my own; God sent me. 43 Why is my language not clear to you? Because you are unable to hear what I say. 44 You belong to your father, the devil, and you want to carry out your father's desires. He was a murderer from the beginning, not holding to the truth, for there is no truth in him. When he lies, he speaks his native language, for he is a liar and the father of lies. 45 Yet because I tell the truth, you do not believe me! 46 Can any of you prove me guilty of sin? If I am telling the truth, why don't you believe me? 47 Whoever belongs to God hears what God says. The reason you do not hear is that you do not belong to God.'

Being honest implies detesting lies; we cannot be faithful to the truth and falsehood simultaneously; our heart will eventually prefer one or the other. We find a biblical passage that manifests this thought.

Proverbs 13:5 The righteous hate what is false, but the wicked make themselves obnoxious and bring shame on themselves.

To preserve the divine dignity of our being.

Purity is also related to human sexuality in the form of chastity; this virtue guides the sexuality to the original and perfect design/plan for which God created it (love, goodness, truth, faithfulness, fertility, matrimony, lasting joy, and pleasure).

Genesis 2:24 That is why a man leaves his father and mother and is united to his wife, and they become one flesh.

Mathew 19:4 'Haven't you read,' he replied, 'that at the beginning the Creator "made them male and female," 5 and said, "For this reason a man will leave his father and mother and be united to his wife, and the two will become one flesh"? 6 So they are no longer two, but one flesh. Therefore what God has joined together, let no one separate.'

The problem is that impurity, in the form of lust, degenerates that same design/plan except for the pleasure part. It is crucial to understand that we must fight against our lustful thoughts and desires, which are the ones that drive us to see the other person as an object of pleasure, which is unmistakably evil.

Matthew 5:27 'You have heard that it was said, "You shall not commit adultery." 28 But I tell you that anyone who looks at a woman lustfully has already committed adultery with her in his heart.

One of the most prominent Christian beliefs is that the human body is a temple of the Holy Spirit, and therefore, we must take care of it by conserving its complete purity; we must not corrupt or degrade it by lustful acts. We Christians must respect and care for our bodies and our souls, because both have a sacred purpose. The following passage clarifies that God gave divine dignity to the human body.

1 Corinthians 6:19 Do you not know that your bodies are temples of the Holy Spirit, who is in you, whom you have received from God? You are not your own; 20 you were bought at a price. Therefore honor God with your bodies.

The most beautiful and hopeful thing about this virtue is understanding that we can always return to the path to God if we have fallen into sin; it is necessary to ask for forgiveness and to have a real commitment to sin no more. To conclude, we find one of the strongest and deepest stories in the gospel. This story manifests the value of forgiveness and the opportunity for a new beginning. God is always willing to help us start over in the struggle to regain purity. Recovering our purity is not easy, but there is no doubt that it is one of the greatest joys that we can experience in life.

John 8:1 But Jesus went to the Mount of Olives. 2 At dawn he appeared again in the temple courts, where all the people gathered round him, and he sat down to teach them. 3 The teachers of the law and the Pharisees brought in a woman caught in adultery. They made her stand before the group 4 and said to Jesus, 'Teacher, this woman was caught in the act of adultery. 5 In the Law Moses commanded us to stone such women. Now what do you say?' 6 They were using this question as a trap, in order to have a basis for accusing him. But Jesus bent down and started to write on the ground with his finger. 7 When they kept on questioning him, he straightened up and said to them, 'Let any one of you who is without sin be the first to throw a stone at her.' 8 Again he stooped down and wrote on the ground. 9 At this, those who heard began to go away one at a time, the older ones first, until only Jesus was left, with the woman still standing there. 10 Jesus straightened up and asked her, 'Woman, where are they? Has no one condemned you?' 11 'No one, sir,' she said. 'Then neither do I condemn you,' Jesus declared. 'Go now and leave your life of sin.'

To clearly see God in life.

Perhaps this is the most transcendent outcome of living with this virtue since, as we purify our hearts, we will be able to see God's messages clearly in our lives. Whatever reality we live in, whatever challenge we face, with purity, we will be able to understand God's will in it. The key to live an authentic life is to stop living in relation to the seductions of the world, to live in function of our friendship with the Lord.

Matthew 5:8 Blessed are the pure in heart, for they will see God.

Deception

Falsehood   Dishonesty

IMPURITY

Immodesty   Infidelity

Lust

"Lust indulged became habit, and habit unresisted became necessity." Saint Augustine

Reflection of malice.

We begin by clarifying that the vice of impurity reflects certain malice; since we are impure to the extent that we consent to evil, sin, or egoism. For it is an empirical truth that those who indulge in immoralities lose their innocence. And by doing so, they go against the teaching of Jesus to become like children. Typically, someone who portrays this vice tends to repudiate others' purity or integrity; indeed, only someone malicious does evil to those who are innocent. Perhaps a representative story around the loss of purity is the story of Cain and Abel, where Cain, by consenting temptation, abandoned his goodness and acted maliciously.

Genesis 4:3 In the course of time Cain brought some of the fruits of the soil as an offering to the LORD. 4 But Abel also brought an offering – fat portions from some of the firstborn of his flock. The LORD looked with favor on Abel and his offering, 5 but on Cain and his offering he did not look with favor. So Cain was very angry, and his face was downcast. 6 Then the LORD said to Cain, 'Why are you angry? Why is your face downcast? 7 If you do what is right, will you not be accepted? But if you do not do what is right, sin is crouching at your door; it desires to have you, but you must rule over it.' 8 Now Cain said to his brother Abel, 'Let's go out to the field.' While they were in the field, Cain attacked his brother Abel and killed him. 9 Then the LORD said to Cain, 'Where is your brother Abel?' 'I don't know,' he replied. 'Am I my brother's keeper?' 10 The LORD said, 'What have you done? Listen! Your brother's blood cries out to me from the ground.

Something remarkably interesting is what God says to Cain. He explains that the reason why he does not walk with his head held high; is because he has done wrong and has consented sin. And, like all vices, impurity has negative effects on the human psyche, and its outcome will always end up being a profound unhappiness or an existential emptiness. In a complementary teaching, Jesus affirms that it is not the external realities that make us impure, but the internal ones founded on evil.

Mark 7:15 Nothing outside a person can defile them by going into them. Rather, it is what comes out of a person that defiles them.'

Mark 7:20 He went on: 'What comes out of a person is what defiles them. 21 For it is from within, out of a person's heart, that evil thoughts come – sexual immorality, theft, murder, 22 adultery, greed, malice, deceit, lewdness, envy, slander, arrogance and folly. 23 All these evils come from inside and defile a person.'

Not to renounce sin and vice.

Christianity teaches us that, to maintain our purity given by God, we must avoid all kinds of sins since they damage the soul and generate guilt. We believe that God can forgive us everything, but what usually happens is that we do not want to repent, which is even more severe than the sin committed; because we understand that the lack of repentance towards one's vice is what we name as a sin against the Holy Spirit.

Matthew 12:31 And so I tell you, every kind of sin and slander can be forgiven, but blasphemy against the Spirit will not be forgiven.

If we think about it, denying the purity and mercy of God is the great injustice. It is a matter of common sense to understand that only the one who repents achieves forgiveness, while the one who does not renounce his sin retains his guilt. Well, who is more impure than the one who denies his sin based on his own ego? Understandably, a person who does not seek to clean the stains from his soul assumes himself as superior to the God.

Falsity before the truth.

An impure heart can use all kinds of lies to manipulate people in order to achieve his goals. The liar often deceits to gain advantages, even if it harms the dignity of others. The liar despises the truth and betrays his moral duty to satisfy his selfish desires. In the Bible, we find several verses that can help us glimpse how wicked lying is.

Proverbs 12:22 The LORD detests lying lips, but he delights in people who are trustworthy.

Psalm 101:7 No one who practices deceit will dwell in my house; no one who speaks falsely will stand in my presence.

Psalm 59:12 For the sins of their mouths, for the words of their lips, let them be caught in their pride. For the curses and lies they utter.

Psalm 26:4 I do not sit with the deceitful, nor do I associate with hypocrites.

Proverbs 12:19 Truthful lips endure for ever, but a lying tongue lasts only a moment.

Proverbs 26:24 Enemies disguise themselves with their lips, but in their hearts they harbor deceit.

Sirach 7:13 Devise not a lie against thy brother: neither do the like against thy friend. 14 Be not willing to make any manner of lie: for the custom thereof is not good.

Sirach 20:26 A lie is a foul blot in a man, and yet it will be continually in the mouth of men without discipline. 27 A thief is better than a man that is always lying: but both of them shall inherit destruction. 28 The manners of lying men are without honor: and their confusion is with them without ceasing.

Proverbs 24:28 Do not testify against your neighbor without cause – would you use your lips to mislead?

Ephesians 4:25 Therefore each of you must put off falsehood and speak truthfully to your neighbor, for we are all members of one body.

By lying, we seek to deceive others; we typically combine false and confusing ideas with a valid reasoning to create fallacies. But before God, there is no deception, so eventually, everything will come to light, and the only thing we will have achieved will be self-deception. By lying, we are merely deceiving ourselves and damaging our friendship with God.

Job 13:7 Will you speak wickedly on God's behalf? Will you speak deceitfully for him? 8 Will you show him partiality? Will you argue the case for God? 9 Would it turn out well if he examined you? Could you deceive him as you might deceive a mortal?

Being impure also means being a hypocrite, which is totally abominable to God because we betray the ethical and moral principles that we understand and expect from others. In a speech, Saint Paul joins the teachings of Jesus and calls us to avoid hypocritical behavior, which is a betrayal of God.

Romans 2:21 You, then, who teach others, do you not teach yourself? You who preach against stealing, do you steal? 22 You who say that people should not commit adultery, do you commit adultery? You who abhor idols, do you rob temples? 23 You who boast in the law, do you dishonor God by breaking the law? 24 As it is written: 'God's name is blasphemed among the Gentiles because of you.'

Mark 7:6 He replied, 'Isaiah was right when he prophesied about you hypocrites; as it is written: ' "These people honor me with their lips, but their hearts are far from me. 7 They worship me in vain;

their teachings are merely human rules." 8 You have let go of the commands of God and are holding on to human traditions.'

Disregard the divine dignity of our soul and our body.

Part of impurity is what we know as lust, which arises from minimizing the divinity and sacredness of our beings, which were created in God's image and likeness. In the Bible, we find many examples that indicate that consenting disordered sexual desires, or any form of sexual perversion (masturbation, fornication, adultery, homosexual acts), is immoral, unnatural, and selfish.

Tobias 4:12a Beware, my son, of every kind of fornication.

Galatians 5:19 The acts of the flesh are obvious: sexual immorality, impurity and debauchery.

Leviticus 18:22 Do not have sexual relations with a man as one does with a woman; that is detestable.

Jude 1:7 In a similar way, Sodom and Gomorrah and the surrounding towns gave themselves up to sexual immorality and perversion. They serve as an example of those who suffer the punishment of eternal fire.

Ephesians 5:3 But among you there must not be even a hint of sexual immorality, or of any kind of impurity, or of greed, because these are improper for God's holy people. 4 Nor should there be obscenity, foolish talk or coarse joking, which are out of place, but rather thanksgiving. 5 For of this you can be sure: no immoral, impure or greedy person – such a person is an idolater – has any inheritance in the kingdom of Christ and of God.

1 Thessalonians 4:3 It is God's will that you should be sanctified: that you should avoid sexual immorality; 4 that each of you should learn to control your own body in a way that is holy and honorable, 5 not in passionate lust like the pagans, who do not know God; 6 and that in this matter no one should wrong or take advantage of a brother or sister. The Lord will punish all those who commit such sins, as we told you and warned you before. 7 For God did not call us to be impure, but to live a holy life. 8 Therefore,

anyone who rejects this instruction does not reject a human being but God, the very God who gives you his Holy Spirit.

By being selfish and arrogant in rejecting God's design/plan for human sexuality, all we do is destroy our opportunity to live it fully. Believing that we can achieve true happiness being single or married without giving up lust is a great lie; simple physical pleasure cannot give the Spirit's lasting happiness. In a biblical passage, we are warned not to corrupt our bodies through impure acts.

1 Corinthians 6:13b The body, however, is not meant for sexual immorality but for the Lord, and the Lord for the body.

1 Corinthians 6:15 Do you not know that your bodies are members of Christ himself? Shall I then take the members of Christ and unite them with a prostitute? Never! 16 Do you not know that he who unites himself with a prostitute is one with her in body? For it is said, 'The two will become one flesh.' 17 But whoever is united with the Lord is one with him in spirit. 18 Flee from sexual immorality. All other sins a person commits are outside the body, but whoever sins sexually, sins against their own body.

How much joy disappears when purity and chastity are lost? If we knew how many problems, how much suffering, how many matrimonies and families impurity has destroyed, we would unquestionably realize how destructive and harmful this vice is. That's why we find a serious warning in one of the Catholic letters that alert us about the false teachers that will arise. They will be depraved people who promote impure ideas that challenge the value and beauty of purity.

2 Peter 2:1 But there were also false prophets among the people, just as there will be false teachers among you. They will secretly introduce destructive heresies, even denying the sovereign Lord who bought them – bringing swift destruction on themselves. 2 Many will follow their depraved conduct and will bring the way of truth into disrepute. 3 In their greed these teachers will exploit you with fabricated stories. Their condemnation has long been hanging over them, and their destruction has not been sleeping. 4 For if God did not spare angels when they sinned, but sent them to hell, putting them in chains of darkness to be held for judgment; 5 if he did not

spare the ancient world when he brought the flood on its ungodly people, but protected Noah, a preacher of righteousness, and seven others; 6 if he condemned the cities of Sodom and Gomorrah by burning them to ashes, and made them an example of what is going to happen to the ungodly; 7 and if he rescued Lot, a righteous man, who was distressed by the depraved conduct of the lawless 8 (for that righteous man, living among them day after day, was tormented in his righteous soul by the lawless deeds he saw and heard) – 9 if this is so, then the Lord knows how to rescue the godly from trials and to hold the unrighteous for punishment on the day of judgment. 10 This is especially true of those who follow the corrupt desire of the flesh and despise authority. Bold and arrogant, they are not afraid to heap abuse on celestial beings; 11 yet even angels, although they are stronger and more powerful, do not heap abuse on such beings when bringing judgment on them from the Lord. 12 But these people blaspheme in matters they do not understand. They are like unreasoning animals, creatures of instinct, born only to be caught and destroyed, and like animals they too will perish. 13 They will be paid back with harm for the harm they have done. Their idea of pleasure is to carouse in broad daylight. They are blots and blemishes, reveling in their pleasures while they feast with you. 14 With eyes full of adultery, they never stop sinning; they seduce the unstable; they are experts in greed – an accursed brood! 15 They have left the straight way and wandered off to follow the way of Balaam son of Bezer, who loved the wages of wickedness. 16 But he was rebuked for his wrongdoing by a donkey – an animal without speech – who spoke with a human voice and restrained the prophet's madness. 17 These people are springs without water and mists driven by a storm. Blackest darkness is reserved for them. 18 For they mouth empty, boastful words and, by appealing to the lustful desires of the flesh, they entice people who are just escaping from those who live in error. 19 They promise them freedom, while they themselves are slaves of depravity – for 'people are slaves to whatever has mastered them.' 20 If they have escaped the corruption of the world by knowing our Lord and Savior Jesus Christ and are again entangled in it and are overcome, they are worse off at the end than they were at the beginning. 21 It would have been better for them not to have known the way of righteousness, than to have known it and then to turn their backs on the sacred command that was passed on to them. 22 Of them the proverbs are true: 'A dog returns to its vomit,' and, 'A sow that is washed returns to her wallowing in the mud.'

Not to clearly see God in life.

Finally, an impure heart is unable to see God's will. Doing lustful actions eventually causes spiritual blindness. That is why living with impurity is living blinded to love and truth because it deprives us of seeing God in reality. In Ezekiel's book, we find a passage that highlights the fact of not differentiating between good and evil as a concrete sign of the vice of impurity. To confuse these realities, having known them, will always be an injustice before God.

Ezekiel 22:26 His priests have violated my Law and have profaned my sanctuary. They have not made a distinction between the holy and the profane, they have not taught to distinguish between the pure and the impure.

This idea is complemented by one of the most profound and practical yet overlooked lessons of the gospel. Jesus explains that the presence or absence of God manifests itself in our eyes; as incredible as it may seem, we reflect the spiritual state of our conscience in our gaze.

Luke 11:34 Your eye is the lamp of your body. When your eyes are healthy, your whole body also is full of light. But when they are unhealthy, your body also is full of darkness. 35 See to it, then, that the light within you is not darkness. 36 Therefore, if your whole body is full of light, and no part of it dark, it will be just as full of light as when a lamp shines its light on you.'

Matthew 6:22 'The eye is the lamp of the body. If your eyes are healthy, your whole body will be full of light. 23 But if your eyes are unhealthy, your whole body will be full of darkness. If then the light within you is darkness, how great is that darkness!

Chapter 8: A Brilliant Mind

"Now in matters of action the reason directs all things in view of the end." Saint Thomas Aquinas

Because we act according to what we understand, it can be assured that our intelligence guides our will through thoughts and reasons. In Christianity, reason is not despised; on the contrary, it is considered fundamental to live well; to love.

The virtues and vices represented with the mind are mainly associated with the truth so that they are closely related to our criterion or our knowledge about reality.

Sirach 37:16 Reason is the beginning of every work, and counsel precedes every undertaking.

1 Corinthians 14:20 Brothers and sisters, stop thinking like children. In regard to evil be infants, but in your thinking be adults.

This book segment will analyze the two principal virtues related to the intellect: wisdom and prudence. Indeed, these virtues stand their ground first and foremost in the great virtue of love. So, its primary meaning is about focusing our intellectual powers on understanding and living according to the Divine Moral Law.

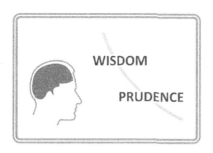
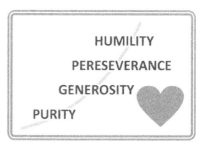

It is fascinating that the four virtues mentioned above: humility, generosity, perseverance, and purity; in some way, they are directed and potentiated by the intellectual virtues, so developing our mind will help us to love in a more complete or perfect form. One might think that wisdom is about correctly discerning between good and evil, while prudence is about choosing and applying what is best according to our circumstances.

Romans 12:2 Do not be conformed to this world, but be transformed by the renewing of your minds, so that you may discern what is the will of God—what is good and acceptable and perfect.

In contrast, we will also reflect on the two primary vices related to the intellect: vanity and foolishness. We will be able to reason and discover the connection that these two vices have with those previously mentioned: pride, avarice, laziness, and impurity, and how our intellectual capacity and our thoughts also potentiate them. The darkening of our minds will lead us to experience a more destructive and dangerous egoism.

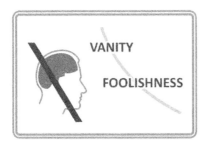 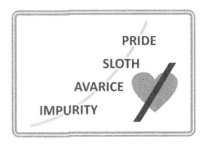

"Those who do not want to be defeated by the truth, are defeated by error." Saint Augustine

Wisdom vs. Vanity

Wisdom is...	*Vanity is...*
To continually seek the truth.	*Not to continually seek the truth.*
To know Christ profoundly.	*To willfully ignore Christ.*
To have a holy criterion, to understand and value life in unity with God.	*To have a selfish criterion, to understand and value life in disunity with God.*
To live enlightened and inspired by the Holy Spirit.	*To live without being enlightened and inspired by the Holy Spirit.*
Spiritual or moral knowledge.	*Spiritual or moral ignorance.*

"Wisdom teaches her children and gives help to those who seek her. Whoever loves her loves life, and those who seek her from early morning are filled with joy." Sirach 4:11-12

To continually seek the truth.

The first step in finding wisdom is seeking the truth wholeheartedly. Through the writings of the book of Sirach, we find some practical ideas that can give some insights into this continual quest.

Sirach 6:18 -Blessings of Wisdom- My son, from thy youth up receive instruction, and even to thy grey hairs thou shalt find wisdom. 19 Come to her as one that ploughed, and soweth, and wait for her good fruits: 20 For in working about her thou shalt labor a little, and shalt quickly eat of her fruits. 21 How very unpleasant is wisdom to the unlearned, and the unwise will not continue with her. 22 She shall be to them as a mighty stone of trial, and they will cast her from them before it be long. 23 For the wisdom of doctrine is according to her name, and she is not manifest unto many, but with them to whom she is known, she continued even to the sight of God.

Sirach 6:28 Search for her, and she shall be made known to thee, and when thou hast gotten her, let her not go: 29 For in the latter end thou shalt find rest in her, and she shall be turned to thy joy.

Sirach 6:33 My son, if thou wilt attend to me, thou shalt learn: and if thou wilt apply thy mind, thou shalt be wise. 34 If thou wilt incline thy ear, thou shalt receive instruction: and if thou love to hear, thou shalt be wise. 35 Stand in the multitude of ancients that are wise, and join thyself from thy heart to their wisdom, that thou mayst hear every discourse of God, and the sayings of praise may not escape thee.

Sirach 6:37 Let thy thoughts be upon the precepts of God, and meditate continually on his commandments: and he will give thee a heart, and the desire of wisdom shall be given to thee.

Sirach 1:33 Son, if thou desire wisdom, keep justice, and God will give her to thee.

When we think of wise people, we should not look only at the individuals' intellectual capacity. Wisdom first requires a good heart or the virtues described before. To become wise, we must behave according to God's commandments; therefore, this virtue can only be discovered and observed in those who fulfill the Divine Moral Law.

To imagine a genuinely wise person living a life full of vices is absurd. We can be sure that God's wisdom manifests itself in the humble, generous, pure, and persevering souls.

Psalm 37:30 The mouths of the righteous utter wisdom, and their tongues speak what is just. 31 The law of their God is in their hearts; their feet do not slip.

Proverbs 11:2 When pride comes, then comes disgrace, but with humility comes wisdom.

Wisdom 1:1 Love justice, you that are the judges of the earth. Think of the Lord in goodness, and seek him in simplicity of heart: 2 For he is found by them that tempt him not: and he showed himself to them that have faith in him. 3 For perverse thoughts separate from God: and his power, when it is tried, reproved the unwise: 4 For wisdom will not enter into a malicious soul, nor dwell in a body subject to sins. 5 For the Holy Spirit of discipline will flee from the deceitful, and will withdraw himself from thoughts that are without understanding, and he shall not abide when iniquity cometh in.

Sirach 3:31 The heart of the wise is understood in wisdom, and a good ear will hear wisdom with all desire. 32 A wise heart, and which hath understanding, will abstain from sins, and in the works of justice shall have success.

Proverbs 18:15 The heart of the discerning acquires knowledge, for the ears of the wise seek it out.

Daniel 12:3 Those who are wise will shine like the brightness of the heavens, and those who lead many to righteousness, like the stars for ever and ever.

  Finally, we find a poem that illustrates us about the search for wisdom, a search that is not only done with our mind, but also with our heart.

Sirach 51:18 When I was yet young, before I wandered about, I sought for wisdom openly in my prayer. 19 I prayed for her before the temple, and unto the very end I will seek after her, and she flourished as a grape soon ripe. 20 My heart delighted in her, my foot walked in the right way, from my youth up I sought after her. 21 I bowed down my ear a little, and received her. 22 I found much wisdom in myself, and profited much therein. 23 To him that giveth me wisdom, will I give glory. 24 For I have determined to follow her: I have had a zeal for good, and shall not be confounded. 25 My soul hath wrestled for her, and in doing it I have been confirmed. 26 I stretched forth my hands on high, and I bewailed my ignorance of her. 27 I directed my soul to her, and in knowledge I found her. 28 I possessed my heart with her from the beginning: therefore I shall not be forsaken. 29 My entrails were troubled in seeking her: therefore shall I possess a good possession. 30 The Lord hath given me a tongue for my reward: and with it I will praise him.

To know Christ profoundly.

Sacred Scripture is the most reflected and studied book in the history of mankind. Countless people in different times have sought the truth and wisdom in its words. In its content, we find stories and meditations with great depth and significance for human life. Within the Bible, the New Testament stands out for the clarity and beauty of its message; by reading it, we get to know Jesus Christ, who is the wisest and most influential person in the history of mankind, we can affirm that his words and his wisdom have transformed the world forever.

At the first instance, it's good to reflect on his mysterious identity because when He talked people were shocked by how a person without an intellectual preparation could be so wise, they did not understand where his wisdom was coming from. Jesus leaves us in awe because of the depth of his thoughts and ideas; his life perspective continues to be, and will continue to be a source of divine wisdom. By the expressions described in the following verses of the Gospel, we can see the amazement Jesus caused. In current times, the same splendor can be born in our hearts just by reading his stories and by getting to know Him.

Luke 2:46 After three days they found him in the temple courts, sitting among the teachers, listening to them and asking them questions. 47 Everyone who heard him was amazed at his understanding and his answers.

Mathew 13:53 When Jesus had finished these parables, he moved on from there. 54 Coming to his home town, he began teaching the people in their synagogue, and they were amazed. 'Where did this man get this wisdom and these miraculous powers?' they asked. 55 'Isn't this the carpenter's son? Isn't his mother's name Mary, and aren't his brothers James, Joseph, Simon and Judas? 56 Aren't all his sisters with us? Where then did this man get all these things?'

When reading the gospels, we can discover that the main character shows impeccable morality since all his faculties are directed to the Good. Certainly, Jesus shows incomparable holiness because He reveals the meaning of love through his being. As a wise master, he leads us towards the way of justice; he preaches things previously unknown and gives an example full of virtue.

His public life is a series of stories and lessons full of wisdom that have the power to transform our lives, but beyond his lessons, we can see that the knowledge of Jesus himself is the greatest truth that we can aspire to know. In the Bible, Jesus proclaimed to be the Truth that always existed, that knows everything. To know Christ is to know the Truth, and therefore, to become wise.

John 1:1 -The Word became flesh- In the beginning was the Word, and the Word was with God, and the Word was God. 2 He was with God in the beginning.

John 1:11 He came to that which was his own, but his own did not receive him. 12 Yet to all who did receive him, to those who believed in his name, he gave the right to become children of God – 13 children born not of natural descent, nor of human decision or a husband's will, but born of God. 14 The Word became flesh and made his dwelling among us. We have seen his glory, the glory of the one and only Son, who came from the Father, full of grace and truth.

John 14:6 Jesus answered, 'I am the way and the truth and the life. No one comes to the Father except through me. 7 If you really know me, you will know my Father as well. From now on, you do know him and have seen him.'

1 John 5:20 We know also that the Son of God has come and has given us understanding, so that we may know him who is true. And we are in him who is true by being in his Son Jesus Christ. He is the true God and eternal life.

When we acknowledge Him, we realize that his person is the most valuable and wondrous thing we can desire to comprehend, since knowing the Truth does not mean knowing a theory or a principle, but a person.

Philippians 3:8 What is more, I consider everything a loss because of the surpassing worth of knowing Christ Jesus my Lord, for whose sake I have lost all things. I consider them garbage, that I may gain Christ.

Ephesians 3:17 So that Christ may dwell in your hearts through faith. And I pray that you, being rooted and established in love, 18 may have power, together with all the Lord's holy people, to grasp how wide and long and high and deep is the love of Christ, 19 and to know this love that surpasses knowledge – that you may be filled to the measure of all the fullness of God.

By understanding that Jesus is the Truth, we should intuit that what He says is extremely important, because God's perfect thoughts and feelings are being revealed through his words. That's why his messages take on an incredible force; they are always full of wisdom, love, and justice; they carry outstanding clarity to inspire for good and warn from evil.

Sirach 1:5 The word of God on high is the fountain of wisdom, and her ways are everlasting commandments.

Hebrews 4:12 For the word of God is alive and active. Sharper than any double-edged sword, it penetrates even to dividing soul and spirit, joints and marrow; it judges the thoughts and attitudes of the heart.

We indeed become wise as we grow in our understanding of Christ; his light and his words illuminate the form we intelligize life, that is, our way of perceiving, thinking, evaluating, and judging the realities of life. The expressions of Christ are wise because they open to us the possibility of understanding and living the spiritual life, allowing us to see the essences behind superficiality so that, in effect, we can discover the truth.

John 6:63 The Spirit gives life; the flesh counts for nothing. The words I have spoken to you – they are full of the Spirit and life.

His words unquestionably have continued to transform humanity ever since. In the Bible, we find a passage that illustrates this priority of being close to Christ and listening to him, for true wisdom arises from that experience. If we could spend more time reading the sacred writings and deepening into his words, without a doubt, our wisdom would increase, our love would grow, and therefore our life would improve.

Luke 10:38 - At the home of Martha and Mary- As Jesus and his disciples were on their way, he came to a village where a woman named Martha opened her home to him. 39 She had a sister called Mary, who sat at the Lord's feet listening to what he said. 40 But Martha was distracted by all the preparations that had to be made. She came to him and asked, 'Lord, don't you care that my sister has left me to do the work by myself? Tell her to help me!' 41 'Martha, Martha,' the Lord answered, 'you are worried and upset about many things, 42 but few things are needed – or indeed only one. Mary has chosen what is better, and it will not be taken away from her.'

To have a holy criterion, to understand and value life in unity with God.

Wisdom is also intended to modify and perfect what we think about creation. In a biblical passage, we learn that God impressed this virtue into his works. That is why the realities of life are intelligible.

Sirach 1:9 The Lord himself created wisdom; he saw her and apportioned her, he poured her out upon all his works. 10 She dwells with all flesh according to his gift, and he supplied her to those who love him.

Think about it, every area of study aims to find a criterion capable of understanding a specific part of God's creation or reality with certainty. Interestingly, in the ethical realm, we all naturally develop some criteria; we all try to distinguish between good and evil, between virtue and vice, and between truth and lies. These mental distinctions reflect our philosophy of life; when they are right, we call it wisdom, while when they are wrong, we call it vanity. That is why Christianity strives to reveal the truth through its various writings so that we pass from vanity to wisdom.

2 Peter 3:1 Dear friends, this is now my second letter to you. I have written both of them as reminders to stimulate you to wholesome thinking. 2 I want you to recall the words spoken in the past by the holy prophets and the command given by our Lord and Savior through your apostles.

A moral criterion is composed of two intellectual moves:

1.- Understanding life in union with God.

2.- Valuing life in union with God.

The moral criterion directs our desires for good; it governs and guides our decisions and, therefore, our lives. The moral criterion is wise insofar as it is ordered and compatible with the Divine Moral Law and its hierarchy of goods. The moral criterion is vain insofar as it disorders and contradicts the Divine Moral Law in its hierarchy of goods.

Psalm 119:33 Teach me, LORD, the way of your decrees, that I may follow it to the end. 34 Give me understanding, so that I may keep your law and obey it with all my heart. 35 Direct me in the path of your commands, for there I find delight. 36 Turn my heart towards your statutes and not towards selfish gain. 37 Turn my eyes away from worthless things; preserve my life according to your word. 38 Fulfil your promise to your servant, so that you may be feared. 39 Take away the disgrace I dread, for your laws are good. 40 How I long for your precepts! In your righteousness preserve my life.

Philippians 1:9 And this is my prayer: that your love may abound more and more in knowledge and depth of insight, 10 so that you may be able to discern what is best and may be pure and blameless for the day of Christ, 11 filled with the fruit of righteousness that comes through Jesus Christ – to the glory and praise of God.

Wisdom results in a scale of priorities that reflect our knowledge of what we consider to be the most valuable and most important goods in life. Divine revelation shows that we should always put God and the Kingdom of Heaven in the first place.

Matthew 10:37 'Anyone who loves their father or mother more than me is not worthy of me; anyone who loves their son or daughter more than me is not worthy of me.'

Matthew 6:31 So do not worry, saying, "What shall we eat?" or "What shall we drink?" or "What shall we wear?" 32 For the pagans run after all these things, and your heavenly Father knows that you need them. 33 But seek first his kingdom and his righteousness, and all these things will be given to you as well.

In the Old Testament, there appears a personage who will mark and develop knowledge about this virtue, Solomon, who, within all that he could ask of God, prioritized in praying for wisdom.

2 Chronicles 1:7 That night God appeared to Solomon and said to him, 'Ask for whatever you want me to give you.' 8 Solomon answered God, 'You have shown great kindness to David my father and have made me king in his place. 9 Now, LORD God, let your promise to my father David be confirmed, for you have made me king over a people who are as numerous as the dust of the earth. 10 Give me wisdom and knowledge, that I may lead this people, for who is able to govern this great people of yours?' 11 God said to Solomon, 'Since this is your heart's desire and you have not asked for wealth, possessions or honor, nor for the death of your enemies, and since you have not asked for a long life but for wisdom and knowledge to govern my people over whom I have made you king, 12 therefore wisdom and knowledge will be given you. And I will also give you wealth, possessions and honor, such as no king who was before you ever had and none after you will have.'

Wisdom and knowledge are not only useful to govern people, but they are mainly useful to govern our actions, our habits, and our lives. If we reflect, our life is governed precisely by the criterion of the daily priorities. It is important to note that we must seek wisdom naturally through the study of the sacred scriptures, but at the same time by asking God for it. We can be sure that He is happy with this request, and that, due to his generosity, he will also grant us many other graces. Wisdom will always move us to the path of holiness and lead us to a life of virtue.

To live enlightened and inspired by the Holy Spirit.

In the Old Testament, in the book of Wisdom, we find a text that explicitly tells us that wisdom is the presence of the Divine Spirit, and this really changes everything because wisdom goes beyond simple reasoning or a set of knowledge as is often believed, we now understand that wisdom is the same Spirit of God acting within us. God himself is the one who inspires us to live loving according to the truth in every moment of our lives. It is thanks to his mystical presence in our souls that we can become wise.

Wisdom 7:22 For in her there is a spirit that is intelligent, holy, unique, manifold, subtle, mobile, clear, unpolluted, distinct, invulnerable, loving the good, keen, irresistible, 23 beneficent, humane, steadfast, sure, free from anxiety, all-powerful, overseeing all, and penetrating through all spirits that are intelligent and pure and most subtle. 24 For wisdom is more mobile than any motion; because of her pureness she pervades and penetrates all things. 25 For she is a breath of the power of God, and a pure emanation of the glory of the Almighty; therefore nothing defiled gains entrance into her. 26 For she is a reflection of eternal light, a spotless mirror of the working of God, and an image of his goodness. 27 Though she is but one, she can do all things, and while remaining in herself, she renews all things; in every generation she passes into holy souls and makes them friends of God, and prophets; 28 for God loves nothing so much as the man who lives with wisdom. 29 For she is more beautiful than the sun, and excels every constellation of the stars. Compared with the light she is found to be superior, 30 for it is succeeded by the night, but against wisdom evil does not prevail.

Wisdom 6:12 Wisdom is radiant and unfading, and she is easily discerned by those who love her, and is found by those who seek her. 13 She hastens to make herself known to those who desire her.

14 He who rises early to seek her will have no difficulty, for he will find her sitting at his gates. 15 To fix one's thought on her is perfect understanding, and he who is vigilant on her account will soon be free from care, 16 because she goes about seeking those worthy of her, and she graciously appears to them in their paths, and meets them in every thought. 17 The beginning of wisdom is the most sincere desire for instruction, and concern for instruction is love of her, 18 and love of her is the keeping of her laws, and giving heed to her laws is assurance of immortality, 19 and immortality brings one near to God; 20 so the desire for wisdom leads to a kingdom.

The fact that wisdom is imperishable means that wisdom does not change; it does not essentially depend on an era; it does not go out of style or become useless with time. Wisdom is the true knowledge we have about God, which is the most valuable knowledge at all times and in all places. As we grow in our understanding of God/Love truths, we become wiser. Being wise in a nutshell means being led by the Holy Spirit, and when He guides us, we love and fulfill his Divine Law.

In the New Testament, we can see that the wisdom described by Saint Paul is similar to what Solomon described. It is important to note that being wise implies the knowledge of spiritual realities, before which, without the Holy Spirit, we remain ignorant, not because we do not understand anything about reality, but because those spiritual realities simply surpass us.

1 Corinthians 2:6 We do, however, speak a message of wisdom among the mature, but not the wisdom of this age or of the rulers of this age, who are coming to nothing. 7 No, we declare God's wisdom, a mystery that has been hidden and that God destined for our glory before time began. 8 None of the rulers of this age understood it, for if they had, they would not have crucified the Lord of glory. 9 However, as it is written: 'What no eye has seen, what no ear has heard, and what no human mind has conceived' – the things God has prepared for those who love him – 10 these are the things God has revealed to us by his Spirit. The Spirit searches all things, even the deep things of God. 11 For who knows a person's thoughts except their own spirit within them? In the same way no one knows the

thoughts of God except the Spirit of God. 12 What we have received is not the spirit of the world, but the Spirit who is from God, so that we may understand what God has freely given us. 13 This is what we speak, not in words taught us by human wisdom but in words taught by the Spirit, explaining spiritual realities with Spirit-taught words. 14 The person without the Spirit does not accept the things that come from the Spirit of God but considers them foolishness, and cannot understand them because they are discerned only through the Spirit. 15 The person with the Spirit makes judgments about all things, but such a person is not subject to merely human judgments, 16 for, 'Who has known the mind of the Lord so as to instruct him?' But we have the mind of Christ.

Spiritual or moral knowledge.

Wisdom will always be related to spiritual knowledge, and perhaps this is the easiest way to discern between true sages and worldly charlatans. The Apostle James writes precisely about the difference between human "wisdom" and divine wisdom. He explains that true wisdom is not just an abstract mindset or theory but that this virtue's identity is directly revealed through a good human behavior. James follows the line of Jesus, saying that wisdom produces good fruits and it is a source of peace and justice.

James 3:13 -Two kinds of wisdom- Who is wise and understanding among you? Let them show it by their good life, by deeds done in the humility that comes from wisdom. 14 But if you harbor bitter envy and selfish ambition in your hearts, do not boast about it or deny the truth. 15 Such 'wisdom' does not come down from heaven but is earthly, unspiritual, demonic. 16 For where you have envy and selfish ambition, there you find disorder and every evil practice. 17 But the wisdom that comes from heaven is first of all pure; then peace-loving, considerate, submissive, full of mercy and good fruit, impartial and sincere. 18 Peacemakers who sow in peace reap a harvest of righteousness.

We end with a prayer to ask God for this virtue. Just as Solomon prayed for wisdom, the apostle James tells us that we must also ask God for it with faith.

James 1:5 If any of you lacks wisdom, you should ask God, who gives generously to all without finding fault, and it will be given to you. 6 But when you ask, you must believe and not doubt, because the one who doubts is like a wave of the sea, blown and tossed by the wind. 7 That person should not expect to receive anything from the Lord. 8 Such a person is double-minded and unstable in all they do.

Wisdom 9: "O God of my fathers and Lord of mercy, who hast made all things by thy word, 2 and by thy wisdom hast formed man, to have dominion over the creatures thou hast made, 3 and rule the world in holiness and righteousness, and pronounce judgment in up-rightness of soul, 4 give me the wisdom that sits by thy throne, and do not reject me from among thy servants. 5 For I am thy slave and the son of thy maidservant, a man who is weak and short-lived, with little understanding of judgment and laws; 6 for even if one is perfect among the sons of men, yet without the wisdom that comes from thee he will be regarded as nothing. 7 Thou hast chosen me to be king of thy people and to be judge over thy sons and daughters. 8 Thou hast given command to build a temple on thy holy mountain, and an altar in the city of thy habitation, a copy of the holy tent which thou didst prepare from the beginning. 9 With thee is wisdom, who knows thy works and was present when thou didst make the world, and who understand what is pleasing in thy sight and what is right according to thy commandments. 10 Send her forth from the holy heavens, and from the throne of thy glory send her, that she may be with me and toil, and that I may learn what is pleasing to thee. 11 For she knows and understands all things, and she will guide me wisely in my actions and guard me with her glory.

"Vanity not only alienates us from God: it makes us look ridiculous."
Pope Francis I

Not to continually seek the truth.

We must recognize that humans naturally have a hunger to know the truth, whether in our friendships, in our profession, in our family, or in our faith. The truth is, and always will be, the meeting point of all human beings. That is why indifference to it is the starting point towards vanity. The apostle Paul warns us that this vice is born from voluntarily ignoring and despising God's knowledge.

Romans 3:11 There is no one who understands; there is no one who seeks God. 12 All have turned away, they have together become worthless; there is no one who does good, not even one.' 13 'Their throats are open graves; their tongues practice deceit.' 'The poison of vipers is on their lips.' 14 'Their mouths are full of cursing and bitterness.' 15 'Their feet are swift to shed blood; 16 ruin and misery mark their ways, 17 and the way of peace they do not know.' 18 'There is no fear of God before their eyes.'

By undervaluing ideas or truths related to God, like the Trinity, Divine Law, Good, Love, Truth, Happiness, or virtue, our sense of responsibility loses its meaning; our intellect darkens, and our life ruins. When our thoughts are not rooted in the transcendental, what remains is the superficial.

Wisdom 10:8a For regarding not wisdom, they did not only slip in this, that they were ignorant of good things-

Wisdom 3:11 for those who despise wisdom and instruction are miserable. Their hope is vain, their labors are unprofitable, and their works are useless.

To willfully ignore Christ.

The vanity regarding the knowledge of Christ is mainly to ignore his person and his words willfully. Saint Jerome's phrase brilliantly illustrates this reality: "To ignore the Scriptures is to ignore Christ." We cannot attain true wisdom without deepening our knowledge of Christ, which is why, arguably, we will have many superficial insights into life until we find the wisdom of his words.

In the following story, we encounter a person who gives God a secondary place, so his priorities are vain or disordered before the Divine Moral Law. It is the story of someone unwilling to prefer the greater good (God) to the lesser good (wealth); it is an example that shows us what happens when we value other things more than God himself, the long-term consequence will be either happiness or sadness. The shocking thing is that we will also face similar moments or decisions, and we will also have to choose what we put on first place.

Mark 10:21 Jesus looked at him and loved him. 'One thing you lack,' he said. 'Go, sell everything you have and give to the poor, and you will have treasure in heaven. Then come, follow me.' 22 At this the man's face fell. He went away sad, because he had great wealth. 23 Jesus looked round and said to his disciples, 'How hard it is for the rich to enter the kingdom of God!' 24 The disciples were amazed at his words. But Jesus said again, 'Children, how hard it is to enter the kingdom of God! 25 It is easier for a camel to go through the eye of a needle than for someone who is rich to enter the kingdom of God.'

26 The disciples were even more amazed, and said to each other, 'Who then can be saved?' 27 Jesus looked at them and said, 'With man this is impossible, but not with God; all things are possible with God.'

It is a fact that morals and ethics guide all human behavior, so what knowledge is more valuable than that? That is why the teachings or doctrine of Christ are not opposed to the other human sciences; on the contrary, it is what allows us to direct and guide all human sciences. That is why the knowledge of Jesus is like his person, a cornerstone because it orders and gives meaning to all other knowledge. In the end, who understands good and evil better than Christ? That is the problem with rejecting Christ because, in a sense, it means despising the Master of love and wisdom.

Colossians 2:9 For in Christ all the fullness of the Deity lives in bodily form, 10 and in Christ you have been brought to fullness. He is the head over every power and authority.

1 Peter 2:6 For in Scripture it says: 'See, I lay a stone in Zion, a chosen and precious cornerstone, and the one who trusts in him will never be put to shame.' 7 Now to you who believe, this stone is precious. But to those who do not believe, 'The stone the builders rejected has become the cornerstone,' 8 and, 'A stone that causes people to stumble and a rock that makes them fall.' They stumble because they disobey the message – which is also what they were destined for.

Mathew 12:30 'Whoever is not with me is against me, and whoever does not gather with me scatters.

To have a selfish criterion, to understand and value life in disunity with God.

Vanity is related to intellectual superficiality, which, as we saw previously, is reflected in our way of understanding and valuing life. It is a knowledge that remains in appearances or on the surface of reality; it does not get to know what things are in themselves due to the disunity with God. The criterion that separates itself from Divine Moral

Law is based on egotistical reasoning that seeks to distort or twist the truth through fallacies.

Colossians 2:8 See to it that no one takes you captive through hollow and deceptive philosophy, which depends on human tradition and the elemental spiritual forces of this world rather than on Christ.

Throughout the Bible, we notice a clear differentiation between first-order goods (eternal-transcendental), which are directly related to the Kingdom of God; and second-order goods (temporal-worldly), which are indirectly related to the Kingdom of God. Vanity means focusing our thoughts mainly on the secondary goods of life. The superficial mentality pursues secondary or nonessential goods as if they were primary or necessary ones, and so, it develops a chaotic criterion or an empty philosophy of life. The most common examples are preferring power, wealth, fame, and pleasure, over truth, love, virtue, and friendship.

Psalm 119:37 Turn my eyes away from worthless things; preserve my life according to your word.

Luke 6:22 Then Jesus said to his disciples: 'Therefore I tell you, do not worry about your life, what you will eat; or about your body, what you will wear. 23 For life is more than food, and the body more than clothes. 24 Consider the ravens: they do not sow or reap, they have no storeroom or barn; yet God feeds them. And how much more valuable you are than birds! 25 Who of you by worrying can add a single hour to your life? 26 Since you cannot do this very little thing, why do you worry about the rest? 27 'Consider how the wild flowers grow. They do not labor or spin. Yet I tell you, not even Solomon in all his splendor was dressed like one of these. 28 If that is how God clothes the grass of the field, which is here today, and tomorrow is thrown into the fire, how much more will he clothe you – you of little faith! 29 And do not set your heart on what you will eat or drink; do not worry about it. 30 For the pagan world runs after all such things, and your Father knows that you need them. 31 But seek his kingdom, and these things will be given to you as well.

To live without being enlightened and inspired by the Holy Spirit.

Ultimately, vanity is not allowing ourselves to be enlightened and inspired by the Spirit of God; it is to believe that we are the absolute owners and authors of the truth; it is to guide ourselves by human truths and renounce divine truths; it is rejecting the explicit messages that the Holy Spirit is continually giving us to live better, and it is to measure our life by selfish standards; not recognizing that only God is wise or imagining that we are just as sage as God is vanity.

Proverbs 26:12 Do you see a person wise in their own eyes? There is more hope for a fool than for them.

1 Corinthians 3:18 Do not deceive yourselves. If any of you think you are wise by the standards of this age, you should become 'fools' so that you may become wise. 19 For the wisdom of this world is foolishness in God's sight. As it is written: 'He catches the wise in their craftiness'; 20 and again, 'The Lord knows that the thoughts of the wise are futile.'

Spiritual or moral ignorance.

The most obvious sign of vanity is the difficulty to recognize spiritual realities, which, in everyday life, leads us to value or denigrate people with worldly and unfair criteria. The most common examples we find are the following:

In the first place, utilitarianism/materialism. This mentality implies valuing or estimating someone in relation to the utility or benefit that they can mean to us. Here we refer to all kinds of judgments and preferences based on selfish interests or personal convenience, mainly related to economic reality. A biblical passage makes a simple yet strong representation of this well-known situation.

Sirach 13:25 When a rich man is shaken, he is kept up by his friends: but when a poor man is fallen down, he is thrust away even by his acquaintance. 26 When a rich man hath been deceived, he hath many helpers: he hath spoken proud things, and they have justified him. 27 The poor man was deceived, and he is rebuked also: he hath spoken wisely, and could have no place. 28 The rich man spoke, and all held their peace, and what he said they extol even to the clouds. 29 The poor man spoke, and they say: Who is this? and if he stumble, they will overthrow him. 30 Riches are good to him that hath no sin in his conscience: and poverty is very wicked in the mouth of the ungodly.

Second, racism/classism. This vain mentality implies estimating or valuing someone in relation to the skin color, ethnic group, or any other superficial quality that fixes the person's dignity on the circumstantial, irrelevant, or unmerited characteristics. Martin Luther King said, "Judge a man not by the color of his skin but by the content of his character." His phrase did not say judge a man by their personal preferences or his subjective assumptions; he said by his character, which in some sense represent the moral virtues.

These vain or superficial mentalities are part of what is known as partiality, which is precisely the action of favoring or benefiting some people more than others for some particular unfair reason, which means valuing or devaluing someone for something that is neither their dignity nor their morality. The Bible teaches us in different texts that partiality or favoritism is unfair and evil.

Deuteronomy 1:16 And I charged your judges at that time, 'Hear the disputes between your people and judge fairly, whether the case is between two Israelites or between an Israelite and a foreigner residing among you. 17 Do not show partiality in judging; hear both small and great alike. Do not be afraid of anyone, for judgment belongs to God. Bring me any case too hard for you, and I will hear it.'

Deuteronomy 10:17 For the LORD your God is God of gods and Lord of lords, the great God, mighty and awesome, who shows no partiality and accepts no bribes. 18 He defends the cause of the fatherless and the widow, and loves the foreigner residing among you, giving them food and clothing. 19 And you are to love those who are foreigners, for you yourselves were foreigners in Egypt.

Deuteronomy 16:18 Appoint judges and officials for each of your tribes in every town the LORD your God is giving you, and they shall judge the people fairly. 19 Do not pervert justice or show partiality. Do not accept a bribe, for a bribe blinds the eyes of the wise and twists the words of the innocent. 20 Follow justice and justice alone, so that you may live and possess the land the LORD your God is giving you.

Proverbs 24:23 These also are sayings of the wise: To show partiality in judging is not good: 24 whoever says to the guilty, 'You are innocent,' will be cursed by peoples and denounced by nations.

Sirach 4:27 Do not subject yourself to a foolish fellow, nor show partiality to a ruler.

Acts 10:34 Then Peter began to speak: 'I now realize how true it is that God does not show favoritism 35 but accepts from every nation the one who fears him and does what is right.

Colossians 3:25 Anyone who does wrong will be repaid for their wrongs, and there is no favoritism.

Mark 12:14a They came to him and said, 'Teacher, we know that you are a man of integrity. You aren't swayed by others, because you pay no attention to who they are; but you teach the way of God in accordance with the truth.

Sirach 4:22 Do not show partiality, to your own harm, or deference, to your downfall.

James 2:1 -Favoritism forbidden- My brothers and sisters, believers in our glorious Lord Jesus Christ must not show favoritism. 2 Suppose a man comes into your meeting wearing a gold ring and fine clothes, and a poor man in filthy old clothes also comes in. 3 If you show special attention to the man wearing fine clothes and say, 'Here's a good seat for you,' but say to the poor man, 'You stand there' or 'Sit on the floor by my feet,' 4 have you not discriminated among yourselves and become judges with evil thoughts? 5 Listen, my dear brothers and sisters: has not God chosen those who are poor in the eyes of the world to be rich in faith and to inherit the kingdom he promised those who love him? 6 But you have dishonored the poor. Is it not the rich who are exploiting you? Are they not the ones who are dragging you into court? 7 Are they not the ones who are blaspheming the noble name of him to whom you belong?

8 If you really keep the royal law found in Scripture, 'Love your neighbor as yourself,' you are doing right. 9 But if you show favoritism, you sin and are convicted by the law as law-breakers. 10 For whoever keeps the whole law and yet stumbles at just one point is guilty of breaking all of it. 11 For he who said, 'You shall not commit adultery,' also said, 'You shall not murder.' If you do not commit adultery but do commit murder, you have become a law-breaker. 12 Speak and act as those who are going to be judged by the law that gives freedom, 13 because judgment without mercy will be shown to anyone who has not been merciful. Mercy triumphs over judgment.

Finally, we must not forget that only God saves us and rescues us from vanity, only for the love of God can we be wise and enjoy a holy criterion.

1 Peter 1:17 Since you call on a Father who judges each person's work impartially, live out your time as foreigners here in reverent fear.

1 Samuel 16:7b The LORD does not look at the things people look at. People look at the outward appearance, but the LORD looks at the heart.'

John 7:24 Stop judging by mere appearances, but instead judge correctly.'

Ephesians 4:17 This then I say and testify in the Lord: That henceforward you walk not as also the Gentiles walk in the vanity of their mind, 18 Having their understanding darkened, being alienated from the life of God through the ignorance that is in them, because of the blindness of their hearts.

Prudence vs. Foolishness

Prudence is...	Foolishness is...
To assume the God-given moral and practical responsibilities.	To reject the God-given moral and practical responsibilities.
To focus our thoughts on the transcendental.	To focus our thoughts on the temporal.
To discern the paths and circumstances of life.	Not to discern the paths and circumstances of life.
To prepare ourselves for the challenges and hardships of life.	Not to prepare ourselves for the challenges and hardships of life.
To exploit the opportunities of the present moment.	To waste the opportunities of the present moment.

"Prudence is about discovering how things can be done better."
Fr. Nelson Medina

To assume the God-given moral and practical responsibilities.

God, through the Divine Moral Law, transmits to each one of us an individual personal responsibility. His authority is the authority of love, which requires us to behave according to its standards of good through virtue. The fascinating thing is that what we judge as particularly good is always based on something universally good. Thus, wisdom is our path to what is universally good, while prudence is our path to what is particularly good. That is why the words of Jesus are so important, since they cement what we do in love, and what is done out of love will have its reward and will last forever.

Matthew 7:24 'Therefore everyone who hears these words of mine and puts them into practice is like a wise man who built his house on the rock. 25 The rain came down, the streams rose, and the winds blew and beat against that house; yet it did not fall, because it had its foundation on the rock.

This is where prudence astonishes because each of us admittedly has different capabilities or abilities by which we face life. Each of us encounters a unique set of circumstances and problems in which we have particular responsibilities or roles. Yet, the moral challenges within those scenarios are universal and remarkably similar. Whether it is a role within a family, within a job, or within any type of community, we must always respond to those responsibilities as wise and prudent people, that is, with our thoughts focused on the greater and common good or in the glory of God.

Galatians 6:5 For each one should carry their own load.

Luke 12:48b From everyone who has been given much, much will be demanded; and from the one who has been entrusted with much, much more will be asked.

Not surprisingly, if we behave and respond in a spiritually mature way to those duties, He will trust us even more valuable things to manage and control. This insight is an empirical truth; we see it all the time; most of those who take their responsibility seriously can also carry an extra load to help or potentiate others' virtues in efficient and effective manners.

Luke 16:10 'Whoever can be trusted with very little can also be trusted with much, and whoever is dishonest with very little will also be dishonest with much. 11 So if you have not been trustworthy in handling worldly wealth, who will trust you with true riches? 12 And if you have not been trustworthy with someone else's property, who will give you property of your own?

Galatians 6:2 Carry each other's burdens, and in this way you will fulfil the law of Christ.

To focus our thoughts on the transcendental.

Prudence is closely related to the creativity to live wisely; it turns our moral knowledge into divine experiences. The prudent person is always vigilant and focused on doing his best; in being excellent. Prudence inclines our thinking towards acting; it is the virtue that helps us move from theory to practice. To be prudent is to allow ourselves to be guided by the signs and signals of the Holy Spirit; He is always communicating with us through reality. We are prudent when we are able to see the demand and the opportunity for love in our circumstances. Prudence is what keeps us from all vices and sins, alerts us of evil paths, and directs us to the good and the truth. In the Old Testament, we find the first passage that can help us understand this virtue.

Proverbs 2:1 My son, if thou wilt receive my words, and wilt hide my commandments with thee, 2 That thy ear may hearken to wisdom: incline thy heart to know prudence. 3 For if thou shalt call for wisdom, and incline thy heart to prudence: 4 If thou shalt seek her as money, and shalt dig for her as for a treasure: 5 Then shalt thou understand the fear of the Lord, and shalt find the knowledge of God: 6 Because the Lord giveth wisdom: and out of his mouth cometh prudence and knowledge. 7 He wilt keep the salvation of the righteous, and protect them that walk in simplicity, 8 Keeping the paths of justice, and guarding the ways of saints. 9 Then shalt thou understand justice, and judgment, and equity, and every good path. 10 If wisdom shall enter into thy heart, and knowledge please thy soul: 11 Counsel shall keep thee, and prudence shall preserve thee,

12 That thou mayst be delivered from the evil way, and from the man that speaks perverse things.

Prudence glows through the thoughts or inspirations that incline us to act in the best possible way. That's why being prudent means not blurring ourselves from spiritual or transcendental realities because they convey the moral meaning or the purpose of life. In the following passage from the book Sirach, we are reminded that life is a pilgrimage and that we are called to carry out works of justice and mercy guided by wisdom and prudence.

Sirach 16:15 All mercy shall make a place for every man according to the merit of his works, and according to the wisdom of his sojournment.

Sirach 3:32 A wise heart, and which hath understanding, will abstain from sins, and in the works of justice shall have success.

To discern the paths and circumstances of life.

"Prudence disposes the practical reason to discern, in every circumstance, our true good and to choose the right means for achieving it." CCC 1835

Wisdom is crucial to make a good discernment to differentiate with certainty the ways of love (difficult) and the ways of egoism (easy). This book precisely intends to clarify the moral ideas, yet, in practical terms, applying those ideas is an art because everyone has a unique scenario in which to experiment them for themselves. But that is the beauty of discernment, that we all must seek somehow to discern our concrete circumstances and duties with God.

Hosea 14:9 Who is wise? Let them realize these things. Who is discerning? Let them understand. The ways of the LORD are right; the righteous walk in them, but the rebellious stumble in them.

Proverbs 16:17 The highway of the upright avoids evil; those who guard their ways preserve their lives.

Matthew 7:13 'Enter through the narrow gate. For wide is the gate and broad is the road that leads to destruction, and many enter through it. 14 But small is the gate and narrow the road that leads to life, and only a few find it.

Proverbs 2:20 Thus you will walk in the ways of the good and keep to the paths of the righteous.

Spiritual discernment consists fundamentally in knowing if a given reality has its origin and end in God. There will always be paths that seem to be good in life, but in fact, they are not, and that is why it is important to discern.

1 Thessalonians 5:21 But prove all things; hold fast that which is good 22 From all appearance of evil refrain yourselves.

Proverbs 16:25 There is a way that appears to be right, but in the end it leads to death.

Spiritual discernment is mainly made up of two questions:

1.- Why?

The question of origin or source helps us distinguish and clarify where our thoughts, attitudes, decisions, words, and actions are coming from. This basically means to reflect on whether something has its beginning in God or in that which is contrary to God; in good or evil; in love or in egoism.

2.- What for?

The question of the end or the goal helps us distinguish and clarify where our thoughts, attitudes, decisions, words, and actions are taking us. This fundamentally means to reflect on whether something has its purpose in God or in that which is contrary to God; in good or evil; love or egoism.

The prudent person, precisely by asking those questions that are in some way existential, develops the ability to foresee and distinguish between the good and the evil paths. It is advantageous to take the time to think and anticipate the possible positive or negative consequences of the actions we are taking and the paths we are choosing.

To prepare ourselves for the challenges and hardships of life.

There is a Christian teaching that describes the contradiction between prudence and foolishness; it is the parable of the foolish and prudent virgins. This parable helps us understand that being prudent means living according to those realities we comprehend as good and valuable. Life brings opportunities that will pass in front of us, but if we do not prepare, even if they are many, we will not bear any fruit. On the other hand, if we prepare, even with very few opportunities, we will bear much fruit, which will be something admirable and heroic.

Matthew 25:1 At that time the kingdom of heaven will be like ten virgins who took their lamps and went out to meet the bridegroom. 2 Five of them were foolish and five were wise. 3 The foolish ones took their lamps but did not take any oil with them. 4 The wise ones, however, took oil in jars along with their lamps. 5 The bridegroom was a long time in coming, and they all became drowsy and fell asleep. 6 'At midnight the cry rang out: "Here's the bridegroom! Come out to meet him!" 7 'Then all the virgins woke up and trimmed their lamps. 8The foolish ones said to the wise, "Give us some of your oil; our lamps are going out." 9 ' "No," they replied, "there may not be enough for both us and you. Instead, go to those who sell oil and buy some for yourselves." 10 'But while they were on their way to buy the oil, the bridegroom arrived. The virgins who were ready went in with him to the wedding banquet. And the door was shut. 11 'Later the others also came. "Lord, Lord," they said, "open the door for us!" 12 'But he replied, "Truly I tell you, I don't know you." 13 'Therefore keep watch, because you do not know the day or the hour.

To exploit the opportunities of the present moment.

"Prudence is not an absence of action; rather it is "timing", it waits on the right time to act, for the right principles and in the right way." Fulton Sheen

Being prudent is also understanding that there is no time to lose and that we must thrive in the present moment; it means taking advantage of each day of our lives through positive and productive habits. Almost all daily activities are a chance to become more humble, generous, persevering, pure, wise, and prudent persons. If we reflect on it, there is no time to waste following our selfishness, since being arrogant, greedy, lazy, impure, vain, and foolish is, in the end, wasting our time and our life.

Mathew 10:16 Therefore be as shrewd as snakes and as innocent as doves.

The life we have is one, and Jesus is calling us to give everything to do things excellently. It is vitally important to remember that no one knows the day or the hour. Life is a magnificent gift, and we must make the most of it. We should not save our energies or forces for later; on the contrary, we must continually employ them in good things. We must be faithful to God, who provides us the present so that we can own it through virtue.

Luke 12:35 'Be dressed ready for service and keep your lamps burning, 36 like servants waiting for their master to return from a wedding banquet, so that when he comes and knocks they can immediately open the door for him. 37 It will be good for those servants whose master finds them watching when he comes. Truly I tell you, he will dress himself to serve, will make them recline at the table and will come and wait on them. 38 It will be good for those servants whose master finds them ready, even if he comes in the middle of the night or towards daybreak. 39 But understand this: if the owner of the house had known at what hour the thief was coming, he would not have let his house be broken into. 40 You also must be ready, because the Son of Man will come at an hour when you do not expect him.' 41 Peter asked, 'Lord, are you telling this parable to us, or to everyone?' 42 The Lord answered, 'Who then is the faithful and wise manager, whom the master puts in charge of his servants to give them their food allowance at the proper time? 43 It will be good for that servant whom the master finds doing so when he returns. 44 Truly I tell you, he will put him in charge of all his possessions.

Prudence gives us the holy order for living each moment, each step, and each stage of life, in harmony and conformity with God. It is true that many things are lost by not giving each thing its due time and care; this is a simple yet hard truth to overcome; especially in these modern times where wasting time or avoiding reality through distractions is as easy as it has not been before.

It is real that we could be getting more out of the reality in which we find ourselves. It is crucial not to get stuck in the past neither to fear the future; if we lived each day more present, more aware, and more attentive to what life is communicating to us, truly we could grow and enjoy so much more.

Matthew 6:34 Therefore, do not worry about tomorrow, because tomorrow will bring its own worry. Every day his annoyance is enough.

In the end, the truth is the way to good, so when we are wise and prudent, we focus our minds on the kingdom of God, and consequently we achieve joy, peace, and happiness. The famous maxim "Ora et labora" or "pray and work" of Saint Benedict illustrates a clear image of these virtues because praying is more about knowing what is good while working is about applying what is right. The combination of both activities opens the possibility of receiving, accepting, and enjoying the exquisite graces of God.

Hebrews 4:16 Let us then approach God's throne of grace with confidence, so that we may receive mercy and find grace to help us in our time of need.

"Sin darkens the intellect and makes us fools."
Saint Thomas Aquinas

To reject the God-given moral and practical responsibilities.

By rejecting our God-given moral responsibility, we end up foolishly following men-created deficient-insufficient standards of morality, hence provoking a disaster in our practical duties or in our particular roles.

This might seem commonsensical, yet so many times, we end up claiming some type of independence, creativity, and originality in terms of morality only to discover that our ideas of morality are biased by our own form of ego.

In the outstanding book *Intellectuals*, Paul Johnson brilliantly describes this scenario of men inventing and twisting ethics in modern times; it would be really foolish to follow their moral ideologies after knowing about their personal lives.

That is why the Bible clearly claims that we ought to obey God rather than man. Only in Him will our lives have a divine foundation that will allow us to overcome every type of adversity.

Acts 5:29 Peter and the other apostles replied: 'We must obey God rather than human beings!

Acts 5:38b For if their purpose or activity is of human origin, it will fail. 39 But if it is from God, you will not be able to stop these men; you will only find yourselves fighting against God.'

Matthew 7:26 But everyone who hears these words of mine and does not put them into practice is like a foolish man who built his house on sand. 27 The rain came down, the streams rose, and the winds blew and beat against that house, and it fell with a great crash.' 28 When Jesus had finished saying these things, the crowds were amazed at his teaching, 29 because he taught as one who had authority, and not as their teachers of the law.

To focus our thoughts on the temporal.

The next thought related to this vice is realizing that foolishness is to put vanity into practice, which means rejecting wisdom and preferring lesser goods over greater ones, which is illogical and ridiculous. Complementarily, in the following biblical passages, it is mentioned that the act of disobeying God's precepts is an act proper to a fool since acting against God's will is irrational because only He is supremely good and his will is our holiness.

Jeremiah 4:22 'My people are fools; they do not know me. They are senseless children; they have no understanding. They are skilled in doing evil; they know not how to do good.'

Psalm 53:1 The fool says in his heart, 'There is no God.' They are corrupt, and their ways are vile; there is no one who does good.

1 Samuel 13:13 'You have done a foolish thing,' Samuel said. 'You have not kept the command the LORD your God gave you; if you had, he would have established your kingdom over Israel for all time.

Proverbs 10:8 The wise in heart accept commands, but a chattering fool comes to ruin.

Proverbs 14:16 The wise fear the LORD and shun evil, but a fool is hotheaded and yet feels secure.

Proverbs 13:19 A longing fulfilled is sweet to the soul, but fools detest turning from evil.

Interestingly, as we become vainer and more foolish, the more we hate wisdom and prudence, and as we grow wiser and more prudent, the more we hate vanity and foolishness. In the following Old Testament passages, we can find different aphorisms that speak about this contradiction. These phrases are philosophical treasures from the Bible that can help us form a clear image of what it means to be foolish or to act foolishly.

Proverbs 14:3 A fool's mouth lashes out with pride, but the lips of the wise protect them.

Proverbs 1:22 How long will mockers delight in mockery and fools hate knowledge?

Proverbs 10:23 A fool finds pleasure in wicked schemes, but a person of understanding delights in wisdom.

Proverbs 15:14 The discerning heart seeks knowledge, but the mouth of a fool feeds on folly.

Proverbs 15:2 The tongue of the wise adorns knowledge, but the mouth of the fool gushes folly.

Sirach 21:28 The lips of the unwise will be telling foolish things but the words of the wise shall be weighed in a balance.

Proverbs 14:33 Wisdom is at home in the mind of one who has understanding, but it is not known in the heart of fools.

Proverbs 10:14 The wise store up knowledge, but the mouth of a fool invites ruin.

Proverbs 13:16 All who are prudent act with knowledge, but fools expose their folly.

Proverbs 14:17 A quick-tempered person does foolish things, and the one who devises evil schemes is hated.

Sirach 33:5 The heart of a fool is as a wheel of a cart: and his thoughts are like a rolling axletree.

Ecclesiastes 10:12 The words of the mouth of a wise man are grace: but the lips of a fool shall throw him down headlong. 13 The beginning of his words is folly, and the end of his talk is a mischievous error.

Proverbs 10:21 The lips of the righteous nourish many, but fools die for lack of sense.

Sirach 4:23 Do not refrain from speaking at the crucial time, and do not hide your wisdom. 24 For wisdom is known through speech, and education through the words of the tongue.

Not to discern the paths and circumstances of life.

Fools do not like to ponder and discern their ways; they do not want to analyze their decisions wisely and are not interested in knowing their possible destinations. This lack of reasonableness or sanity usually leads them to places and situations of much unnecessary suffering and affliction, which could have been avoided with the proper discernment.

Proverbs 12:15 The way of fools seems right to them, but the wise listen to advice. 16 Fools show their annoyance at once, but the prudent overlook an insult.

Proverbs 14:8 The wisdom of the prudent is to give thought to their ways, but the folly of fools is deception. 9 Fools mock at making amends for sin, but goodwill is found among the upright.

Psalm 107:17 Some became fools through their rebellious ways and suffered affliction because of their iniquities.

Ephesians 5:15 Be very careful, then, how you live – not as unwise but as wise, 16 making the most of every opportunity, because the days are evil. 17 Therefore do not be foolish, but understand what the Lord's will is.

Not to prepare ourselves for the challenges and hardships of life.

The fool usually manifests an excess of confidence in himself; consequently, he does not worry about preparing himself for the challenges and hardships of life, but he underestimates or minimizes them like in the parable of the foolish and wise virgins. Imprudence from a pragmatic perspective also means closing ourselves off to recognize that we did something wrong and that we can and should do things better; with this mentality, we have nothing to grow or improve. We know that maturing implies constantly correcting the course towards a better way of living, towards virtue. The opportunity for correction will frequently come from the wise people around us; it is critical to accept their help, mostly when their advice is based on truth and reason. If we allow ourselves to be corrected and taught, we could grow and mature in a few months that which normally would take us years.

Ecclesiastes 7:5 It is better to be rebuked by a wise man, than to be deceived by the flattery of fools.

Proverbs 15:32 Those who ignore instruction despise themselves, but those who heed admonition gain understanding.

Proverbs 10:17 Whoever heeds instruction is on the path to life, but one who rejects a rebuke goes astray.

To waste the opportunities of the present moment.

We know that time is a divine gift and that before God, it is a duty to take advantage of it by living excellently. If we are fair and reasonable, we will understand that we do not have time to waste focusing on vain things; our gaze should be fixed on the works of love and away from the selfish deeds. One of the typical manifestations of this vice is living in the past, either recriminating ourselves or yearning for the "good" old memories. Jesus denounces this mentality as infertile and useless for the Kingdom of God.

Luke 9:62 Jesus replied, 'No one who puts a hand to the plough and looks back is fit for service in the kingdom of God.'

Living in the past is not a smart option; life requires us to move forwards with the confidence that reality and its times are entirely in the hands of God. When we are careless or foolish, we forget that only by living each moment in the fullest union with God; we can build a better future and overcome the evils of the past.

Chapter 9: The Value of Sacrifice

"There are no short and easy paths to a long and lasting happiness."
Nick Vujicic

To love, or to live the virtues mentioned before-

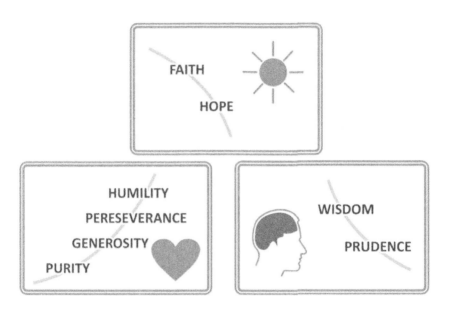

-involves both enjoying positive experiences and suffering negative experiences, which means that sometimes people will reciprocate, and circumstances will be favorable, but not always. The greatness of our virtue, our love, or our behavior will be directly related to our ability to go through both situations with moral excellence.

Sirach 2:1 My son, if you come forward to serve the Lord, prepare yourself for temptation. 2 Set your heart right and be steadfast, and do not be hasty in time of calamity. 3 Cleave to him and do not depart, that you may be honored at the end of your life. 4 Accept whatever is brought upon you, and in changes that humble you be patient. 5 For gold is tested in the fire, and acceptable men in the furnace of humiliation. 6 Trust in him, and he will help you; make your ways straight, and hope in him. 7 You who fear the Lord, wait for his mercy; and turn not aside, lest you fall. 8 You who fear the Lord, trust in him, and your reward will not fail; 9 you who fear the Lord, hope for good things, for everlasting joy and mercy.

Matthew 16:24 Then Jesus said to his disciples, 'Whoever wants to be my disciple must deny themselves and take up their cross and follow me. 25 For whoever wants to save their life will lose it, but whoever loses their life for me will find it.

1 Corinthians 1:18 For the message of the cross is foolishness to those who are perishing, but to us who are being saved it is the power of God.

2 Corinthians 4:17 For our light and momentary troubles are achieving for us an eternal glory that far outweighs them all. 18 So we fix our eyes not on what is seen, but on what is unseen, since what is seen is temporary, but what is unseen is eternal.

The virtues represented by the cross are related to our ability to sacrifice ourselves for love. Temperance is linked to the suffering that arises from voluntarily depriving ourselves of a lesser good to achieve a greater good, while patience is related to the undeserved suffering that we experience caused by the evils that happen to us when acting out of charity.

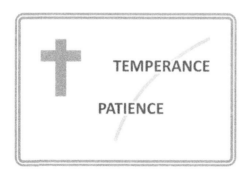

"Human progress is neither automatic nor inevitable... Every step toward the goal of justice requires sacrifice, suffering, and struggle; the tireless exertions and passionate concern of dedicated individuals." Martin Luther King Jr.

"There is no place for selfishness or fear! Do not fear when love demands you. Do not be afraid when love requires sacrifice."
Saint John Paul II

The truth is that no person finds it easy to live with patience and temperance. Indeed, for everyone involves a great sacrifice to achieve such excellence, but with God's grace, what seems impossible is, in fact, possible.

The vices in this section are the most common weaknesses humans face; they are a sign of spiritual immaturity. Overcoming and defeating these vices is a universal challenge, and perhaps, to overcome our egoism, it will be our final battle.

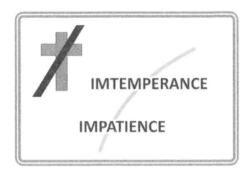

"If you don't want to suffer, don't love, but if you don't love, what do you want to live for?" Saint Augustine

Temperance vs. Intemperance

Temperance is...	Intemperance is...
Finding pleasure in good.	Finding pleasure in evil.
To moderate our pleasures in function of the greater good.	To act impulsively in our pleasures in function of the lesser goods.
To dominate or control our passions or emotions.	Not to dominate or control our passions or emotions.

"Those who belong to Christ Jesus have crucified the flesh with its passions and desires." Galatians 5:24

Finding pleasure in good.

"If human actions can be noble, shameful, or indifferent, so are the corresponding pleasures. There are pleasures derived from noble activities, and others of shameful origin." Aristotle

We must learn to find delight in the realities that please God. We must discover spiritual pleasures, to which we arrive through the experience of virtues and love. Thomas Aquinas said that a person's morality or spirituality is reflected in the pleasures he pursues or in the realities in which he is delighted, so if we find pleasure in good activities, we are good, and if we find pleasure in evil activities, we are evil.

Psalm 1:1 Blessed is the one who does not walk in step with the wicked or stand in the way that sinners take or sit in the company of mockers, 2 but whose delight is in the law of the LORD, and who meditates on his law day and night. 3 That person is like a tree planted by streams of water, which yields its fruit in season and whose leaf does not wither – whatever they do prospers.

Psalm 112:1 Blessed are those who fear the LORD, who find great delight in his commands.

Romans 7:22 For in my inner being I delight in God's law.

Psalm 16:11 You make known to me the path of life; you will fill me with joy in your presence, with eternal pleasures at your right hand.

Psalm 37:4 Take delight in the LORD, and he will give you the desires of your heart. 5 Commit your way to the LORD; trust in him and he will do this: 6 he will make your righteous reward shine like the dawn, your vindication like the noonday sun.

Psalm 111:2 Great are the works of the LORD; they are pondered by all who delight in them.

Psalm 35:9 Then my soul will rejoice in the LORD and delight in his salvation.

Isaiah 61:10a I delight greatly in the LORD; my soul rejoices in my God. For he has clothed me with garments of salvation and arrayed me in a robe of his righteousness.

Psalm 43:4 Then I will go to the altar of God, to God, my joy and my delight. I will praise you with the lyre, O God, my God.

To moderate our pleasures in function of the greater good.

There is an immensity of goods and pleasures that we can want or desire, which, ordered according to the Truth, we can enjoy in total freedom. Temperance implies precisely having the ability to control our desires for pleasure, and the reason for doing so is to direct our lives to the goods of greatest value and importance, which are inspired by wisdom and prudence. In a sentence, it could be said that we should direct our desires for pleasure and not that our desires for pleasure direct us; this, as simple as it may seem, is actually really difficult, as it involves many personal sacrifices or renunciations. In the Bible, it is clear that this virtue is a sign of the Spirit given by God.

2 timothy 1:7 for God did not give us a spirit of timidity but a spirit of power and love and self-control.

Many of the opportunities to sin appear in a persuasive manner, either because they carry a particular pleasure or because they are motivated by passions, and that is why knowing how to say ¡no! is crucial to maintain an exceptional and irreproachable behavior. Only by living a life with moderation and self-control can we achieve lasting affective stability. It is interesting that temperance seen in the short-term may seem like a sacrifice and suffering, but seen in the long-term, it is key to living in freedom and happiness.

Self-control precisely means the ability to avoid the pleasure trap of the lesser goods (purely physical) even when they are good, because, within the hierarchy of goods, we can easily intuit that there are ones more valuable than others (moral), and to obtain them, we ought to make sacrifices.

Many psychologists have recently discovered and demonstrated the power of this virtue. There is a very known social experiment of some kids who are given the option of choosing between one marsh-mallow, which they can eat instantly, or two if they wait and delay their gratification. This simple experiment is also applicable to adults; the only thing that changes is the type of reward. On many occasions, even lots of adults behave like kids in terms of delaying gratification, and in so, they fail to obtain the greater goods.

Younger generations face an even more challenging reality because, with technology, we are prone to choose goods of immediate grati-fication, which are not carrying genuine in the long run. Familiar ex-amples are choosing between doing exercise or watching some vain TV program, or between reading or playing video games, or between praying or having superficial conversations. All these types of choices reflect the presence or the lack of this virtue.

Complementing this thought of managing our desires for pleasure, we find the idea of mortification, which is a process that we establish mainly to control our instincts. Mortifications are practices we use to prevent carnal desires from dominating us; the most common word associated with mortification is abstinence. A good example is that of a diet, in which we decide to abstain from certain foods leaving the taste in the background because we prioritize on a reality of higher value, such as health.

1 Corinthians 9:27 but I punish my body and enslave it, so that after proclaiming to others I myself should not be disqualified.

Fasting is the most common practice of submitting the body to the servitude of the spirit. It is a tradition shared by the three prominent monotheistic religions. The most conventional view is praying and only eating bread and water throughout various days.

Ezra 8:23 So we fasted and petitioned our God about this, and he answered our prayer.

Matthew 6:16 'When you fast, do not look sombre as the hyp-ocrites do, for they disfigure their faces to show others they are fast-ing. Truly I tell you, they have received their reward in full. 17 But when you fast, put oil on your head and wash your face, 18 so that it will not be obvious to others that you are fasting, but only to your Father, who is unseen; and your Father, who sees what is done in secret, will reward you.

To dominate or control our passions or emotions.

"Who dominates his passions is master of the world. Whoever does not dominate them becomes their slave." Saint Dominic

When we speak of the passions, we refer to the emotional realities, which we must order and direct through intelligence according to the will of God. The Catholic Church's Catechism speaks very clearly about the role of the passions and their union with the moral or spiritual life.

CCC 1763 The term "passions" belongs to the Christian patrimony. Feelings or passions are emotions or movements of the sensitive appetite that incline us to act or not to act in regard to something felt or imagined to be good or evil.

CCC 1767 In themselves passions are neither good nor evil. They are morally qualified only to the extent that they effectively engage reason and will. Passions are said to be voluntary, "either because they are commanded by the will or because the will does not place obstacles in their way." It belongs to the perfection of the moral or human good that the passions be governed by reason.

Hippocrates, one of the most influential Greek philosophers and physicians, discovered and identified the four temperaments that influenced human behavior. The combination of these temperaments determines our personality type based on our dominant traits.

In Christian philosophy, Saint Thomas Aquinas took up part of this theory and developed it based on human knowledge from the Judeo-Christian perspective. In the following scheme, we will analyze how emotions, attitudes, and sentiments make up the human affectivity.

It's amazing how accurate these affective descriptions are. The temperaments are organized from the most extroverted to the most introverted S-C-P-M.

Negative Tendency Non-moral -	Emotions - Reactive feelings	Positive Tendency Non-moral +
Agitation	Sanguine	Enthusiasm
Anger	Choleric	Confidence
Fear	Phlegmatic	Calmness
Sadness	Melancholic	Tenderness

*This part of our affectivity is mostly reactive and uncontrollable.

*These emotions are amoral in themselves, they become moral when they relate to the free will.

Negative Tendency Intemperance -	Attitudes Moral feelings	Positive Tendency Temperance +
Impetuous - Careless	Sanguine	Friendly - Humorous
Hostile - Domineering	Choleric	Assertive - Trustable
Dependent - Susceptible	Phlegmatic	Respectful - Welcoming
Pessimistic - Antisocial	Melancholic	Empathetic - Caring

*This part of our affectivity is mostly controllable and therefore mainly moral.

*There are more attitudes than the mention above, these were selected to make it simpler.

Negative Tendency Misery or Emptiness -	Sentiments Moral fruits	Positive Tendency Beatitude or Bliss +
Anxiety	Sanguine	Joy
Irritability	Choleric	Fortitude
Insecurity	Phlegmatic	Peace
Depression	Melancholic	Kindness

*This part of our affectivity are the consequences or fruits of egoism (vices) or love (virtues), either if they are of our own or of others.

*Misery or emptiness is like the sum of negative sentiments, while beatitude or bliss is the sum of positive sentiments.

By common sense, we can assume that it would be natural to feel negative emotions when we experience some sort of evil and to feel positive emotions when we experience some sort of good. If we were only animals, the explanation of our happiness would be rooted mainly in wild causes, but we are not. We have a more complex form of conscience, and although we share natural emotions to some extent with animals, you do not see them going in the quest of truth and virtue. And hence, happiness is not exactly the same for us as it is for them. The enigma is that we often try to achieve happiness as if we were mere animals, which is obviously insufficient given our higher form of conscience. We must respond to life in a good moral-spiritual way since that is our nature; our higher form of happiness (beatitude) or unhappiness (misery) depends mainly on that.

Saint Thomas Aquinas said, "He who is not angry when there is just cause for anger is immoral. Why? Because anger looks to the good of justice. And if you can live amid injustice without anger, you are immoral as well as unjust." His argument can exemplify how we relate our emotions to our higher faculties of the intellect and will. It is a good sign to feel negative emotions for evil moral causes and to feel positive emotions for good moral causes.

There are two Bible verses related to these realities that can help us understand a Christian perspective towards these affective realities.

Ephesians 4:26 'In your anger do not sin': do not let the sun go down while you are still angry.

2 Corinthians 7:10 Godly sorrow brings repentance that leads to salvation and leaves no regret, but worldly sorrow brings death.

The signs of the virtue of temperance are remarkably visible and evident, especially when a person manages to control his temperament's usual downside and exploit his upside in function of the greater good. When we align our conscience and our behavior to God by living with love or virtue, we move towards experiencing the divine sentiments or bliss, which are fruits from being in unity with God.

Psalm 34:4 I sought the LORD, and he answered me; he delivered me from all my fears.

Psalm 94:19 When anxiety was great within me, your consolation brought me joy.

Acts 2:28 You have made known to me the paths of life; you will fill me with joy in your presence.

Luke 12:32 'Do not be afraid, little flock, for your Father has been pleased to give you the kingdom.

Romans 14:17 For the kingdom of God is not a matter of eating and drinking, but of righteousness, peace and joy in the Holy Spirit.

Romans 15:13 May the God of hope fill you with all joy and peace as you trust in him, so that you may overflow with hope by the power of the Holy Spirit.

2 Thessalonians 3:16 Now may the Lord of peace himself give you peace at all times and in every way. The Lord be with all of you.

Philippians 4:4 Rejoice in the Lord always. I will say it again: rejoice! 5 Let your gentleness be evident to all. The Lord is near. 6 Do not be anxious about anything, but in every situation, by prayer and petition, with thanksgiving, present your requests to God. 7 And the peace of God, which transcends all understanding, will guard your hearts and your minds in Christ Jesus.

John 14:27 Peace I leave with you; my peace I give you. I do not give to you as the world gives. Do not let your hearts be troubled and do not be afraid.

John 15:11 I have told you this so that my joy may be in you and that your joy may be complete.

Lack of self-control in emotions and pleasures

INTEMPERANCE

Addictions   Excesses

Impulsiveness

"Boundless intemperance in nature is a tyranny. It hath been the'
untimely emptying of the happy throne and fall of many kings."
William Shakespeare

Finding pleasure in evil.

The most harmful thing about intemperance is when we find pleasure in evil, that is, in sin or vice. That, without a doubt, is the biggest problem related to pleasure. Our God is Good, and we can be sure He takes no delight in evil things, and so should we.

Psalm 5:4 For you are not a God who is pleased with wickedness; with you, evil people are not welcome. 5 The arrogant cannot stand in your presence. You hate all who do wrong; 6 you destroy those who tell lies. The bloodthirsty and deceitful you, LORD, detest.

Sirach 12:16 Error and darkness have been with sinners from the beginning, and those who enjoy evil will have it with them into their old age.

Isaiah 66:3e They have chosen their own ways, and they delight in their abominations.

Proverbs 2:14 Who are glad when they have done evil, and rejoice in the most wicked things.

Sirach 19:5 One who rejoices in wickedness will be condemned.

2 Thessalonians 2:12 and so that all will be condemned who have not believed the truth but have delighted in wickedness.

Delighting ourselves or indulging in evil was what we saw in the first part as living according to the flesh. Taking satisfaction in virtue or sin will have eternally contrasting consequences.

To act impulsively in our pleasures in function of the lesser goods.

"When a person cannot find the deep meaning of his life, he is distracted by pleasure." Viktor Frankl

The ego's principal manifestation concerning pleasure is known philosophically as hedonism, which primarily implies acting and living according to physical pleasures, leaving good and truth (God) in a vague background. The simple act of making decisions putting physical pleasure before God is the beginning of existential disorder and chaos.

Titus 3:3 At one time we too were foolish, disobedient, deceived and enslaved by all kinds of passions and pleasures. We lived in malice and envy, being hated and hating one another.

2 Timothy 3:4 treacherous, rash, conceited, lovers of pleasure rather than lovers of God.

As the result of a hedonistic mentality about life, all kinds of addictions and excesses are born, which damage our dignity and lock us in vicious or selfish circles. It is to be expected that when our life is directed by the search for ephemeral pleasures, it will be extremely difficult for us to let ourselves be guided by God and, therefore, to love.

It is particularly interesting that in addictions, a paradoxical phenomenon can be observed, for the more pleasure we obtain, the more void we feel. The answer is that God created us for something more significant, and by not living to his standard, we lose the meaning of our life. If we do not seek the transcendental realities, we can get trapped in insignificant desires. Moderating our pleasures means staying out of addictions and excesses since these keep us enslaved to ephemeral goods, which is why, on many occasions, we lose the opportunity of enjoying the eternal goods. This idea is clearly expressed throughout the Bible.

Luke 8:14 The seed that fell among thorns stands for those who hear, but as they go on their way they are choked by life's worries, riches and pleasures, and they do not mature.

Not to dominate or control our passions or emotions.

On the other hand, intemperance related to passions means getting out of control and impulsively letting ourselves be carried away by our lower passions, by reacting in an irrational and malignant way. The Bible gives uses anger as an example, but we can also apply it to the other basic emotions.

Psalm 37:8 Refrain from anger and turn from wrath; do not fret – it leads only to evil.

Proverbs 16:32 One who is slow to anger is better than the mighty, and one whose temper is controlled than one who captures a city.

Proverbs 25:28 Like a city whose walls are broken through is a person who lacks self-control.

Positive sentiments such as joy, peace, fortitude, and benevolence serve as signals to know that we in fact living well or with virtue. Negative sentiments can serve as a guide to understand that something is not right and that something must change in our behavior at a moral level.

Often, the hard thing is to be realistic with our negative sentiments because they can hide truths that could be uncomfortable, painful, and challenging. It is vital to go beyond feelings towards the truth, that is, that we must go through our sentimental sufferings to face our spiritual or moral evils. We must always remember that the Truth is what sets us free.

The most common symptom of the lack of temperance, or the presence of intemperance, is a continuous instability in our emotional-sentimental life. Given that we know that there are different temperaments, this affective instability manifests itself in various ways. We could think that if our negative traits dominate us in a very pragmatic view, then our ego is still influencing or dominating our affective life.

It is actually very difficult for each temperament to battle its own negative tendency especially in the attitudes realm; in the end, this virtue it's all about dominating our impulses via our higher faculties and the infinite grace of God.

Sanguines: should not become impetuous, careless, and anxious.

Cholerics: should not become hostile, domineering, and irritable.

Phlegmatics: should not become dependent, susceptible, and insecure.

Melancholics: should not become pessimistic, antisocial, and depressive.

Negative Tendency Non-moral -	Emotions Reactive feelings	Positive Tendency Non-moral +
Agitation	Sanguine	Enthusiasm
Anger	Choleric	Confidence
Fear	Phlegmatic	Calmness
Sadness	Melancholic	Tenderness

*This part of our affectivity is mostly reactive and uncontrollable.

*These emotions are amoral in themselves, they become moral when they relate to the free will.

Negative Tendency Intemperance -	Attitudes Moral feelings	Positive Tendency Temperance +
Impetuous - Careless	Sanguine	Friendly - Humorous
Hostile - Domineering	Choleric	Assertive - Trustable
Dependent - Susceptible	Phlegmatic	Respectful - Welcoming
Pessimistic - Antisocial	Melancholic	Empathetic - Caring

*This part of our affectivity is mostly controllable and therefore mainly moral.

*There are more attitudes than the mention above, these were selected to make it simpler.

Negative Tendency Misery or Emptiness -	Sentiments Moral fruits	Positive Tendency Beatitude or Bliss +
Anxiety	Sanguine	Joy
Irritability	Choleric	Fortitude
Insecurity	Phlegmatic	Peace
Depression	Melancholic	Kindness

*This part of our affectivity are the consequences or fruits of egoism (vices) or love (virtues), either if they are of our own or of others.

*Misery or emptiness is like the sum of negative sentiments, while beatitude or bliss is the sum of positive sentiments.

Patience vs. Impatience

Patience is...	Impatience is...
The ability to confront evil through love and virtue.	*The inability to confront evil through love and virtue.*
To overcome the adversities and sufferings of this life.	*To be consumed by the adversities and sufferings of this life.*
To have mercy and to forgive continuously.	*To lose mercy and to stop forgiving.*
The choice of personal sacrifice out of love.	*The choice to avoid sacrifice out of egoism.*

"To reach God, Christ is the way; but Christ is on the Cross, and to ascend to the Cross one must have a free heart, detached from the things of the earth." Saint José María Escrivá de Balaguer

The ability to confront evil through love and virtue.

The main problem in the world is evil; we can all agree on that by common sense. The challenging thing is how we can battle evil and overcome the seemingly overwhelming darkness in the world. It is not a symmetrical fight because we cannot fight evil by doing evil, and this is striking for most of us yet, Jesus continually claimed that kind of action to be insufficient and sterile.

Luke 6:29 If someone slaps you on one cheek, turn to them the other also. If someone takes your coat, do not withhold your shirt from them.

Mathew 26:52 'Put your sword back in its place,' Jesus said to him, 'for all who draw the sword will die by the sword. 53 Do you think I cannot call on my Father, and he will at once put at my disposal more than twelve legions of angels?

Real changes for a better life always come through the force of love. It is logical and functional first to fight the evils we have inside so we can after face those of the world. We fight egoism through love, incredulity through faith, hopelessness through hope, pride through humility, avarice through generosity, sloth through perseverance, impurity through purity, vanity through wisdom, foolishness through prudence and intemperance through temperance. Jesus is our teacher into the virtuous life; as Christians we are destined to become like Him.

Mathew 23:8 'But you are not to be called "Rabbi", for you have one Teacher, and you are all brothers.

Luke 6:40 The student is not above the teacher, but everyone who is fully trained will be like their teacher.

We can be sure that we should stand with courage and integrity for the kingdom of God. For if we are with God in this battle then who is against us? We should not fear even death if we are truly united with the loving God.

Hebrews 13:6 So we say with confidence, 'The LORD is my helper; I will not be afraid. What can mere mortals do to me?'

Joshua 1:9 Have I not commanded you? Be strong and courageous. Do not be afraid; do not be discouraged, for the LORD your God will be with you wherever you go.'

1 Corinthians 15:58 Therefore, my dear brothers and sisters, stand firm. Let nothing move you. Always give yourselves fully to the work of the Lord, because you know that your labour in the Lord is not in vain.

Romans 8:31 What, then, shall we say in response to these things? If God is for us, who can be against us? 32 He who did not spare his own Son, but gave him up for us all – how will he not also, along with him, graciously give us all things? 33 Who will bring any charge against those whom God has chosen? It is God who justifies. 34 Who then is the one who condemns? No one. Christ Jesus who died – more than that, who was raised to life – is at the right hand of God and is also interceding for us. 35 Who shall separate us from the love of Christ? Shall trouble or hardship or persecution or famine or nakedness or danger or sword? 36 As it is written: 'For your sake we face death all day long; we are considered as sheep to be slaughtered.' 37 No, in all these things we are more than conquerors through him who loved us.

Ultimately, the biblical passage best known as the definition of love-charity is in a letter from the apostle Saint Paul. The first word related to love is patience, which reveals the importance of this virtue in understanding love from the Christian perspective.

1 Corinthians 13:4 Love is patient, love is kind. It does not envy, it does not boast, it is not proud. 5 It does not dishonor others, it is not self-seeking, it is not easily angered, it keeps no record of wrongs. 6 Love does not delight in evil but rejoices with the truth. 7 It always protects, always trusts, always hopes, always perseveres.

To overcome the adversities and sufferings of this life.

"If there is meaning in life at all, then there must be a meaning in suffering." Viktor Frankl

The word patience comes from the Latin word "patientia" which basically means suffering or enduring. If we think about it, there are few things as universal to humans as suffering. It is difficult to imagine spiritual growth and to think that it will not entail some suffering. In relation to the moral life, you can suffer as a consequence of being virtuous, or as a consequence of being vicious, if we think about it, the first suffering is undeserved, and, therefore, facing it is heroic, while the second was caused by our own behavior, to face it is to comply with justice. We find a dialogue in the Bible that refers us to this difference.

Luke 23:39 One of the criminals who hung there hurled insults at him: 'Aren't you the Messiah? Save yourself and us!' 40 But the other criminal rebuked him. 'Don't you fear God,' he said, 'since you are under the same sentence? 41 We are punished justly, for we are getting what our deeds deserve. But this man has done nothing wrong.' 42 Then he said, 'Jesus, remember me when you come into your kingdom.' 43 Jesus answered him, 'Truly I tell you, today you will be with me in paradise.'

Patience is mainly related to the undeserved suffering, to the affliction that does not originates from our sins and vices. Patience is the ability to suffer without ceasing to love. We know that character is not forged instantly; resilience is developed only through the continual struggle, through our small sacrifices in the day-to-day hardships. The Bible teaches us in some passages that we will have trials and sufferings, but that ultimately, we must trust in the grace that comes from Christ, the living God, who already overcame the world.

1 Peter 2:19 For it is commendable if someone bears up under the pain of unjust suffering because they are conscious of God. 20 But how is it to your credit if you receive a beating for doing wrong and endure it? But if you suffer for doing good and you endure it, this is commendable before God. 21 To this you were called, because Christ suffered for you, leaving you an example, that you should follow in his steps. 22 'He committed no sin, and no deceit was found in his mouth.' 23 When they hurled their insults at him, he did not retaliate; when he suffered, he made no threats. Instead, he entrusted himself to him who judges justly. 24 'He himself bore our

sins' in his body on the cross, so that we might die to sins and live for righteousness; 'by his wounds you have been healed.' 25 For 'you were like sheep going astray,' but now you have returned to the Shepherd and Overseer of your souls.

1 Peter 3:13 And who can harm you if you are zealous for good? 14 In any case, if you had to suffer for the sake of justice, blessed are you: do not be afraid of his intimidations, nor be anxious, 15 but glorify Christ the Lord in your hearts, always ready to give an answer to all who ask you reason of your hope; 16 but with meekness and respect, and with a clean conscience, so that those who slander your good conduct in Christ may be confused in what they criticize you. 17 Because it is better to suffer for doing good, if that is God's will, than for doing evil.

John 16:33 'I have told you these things, so that in me you may have peace. In this world you will have trouble. But take heart! I have overcome the world.'

Suffering carries the opportunity to bring out the best in ourselves, and patience is the final demonstration of mature love. It is a great victory demonstrating how to suffer injustices with integrity; because precisely on those occasions, the strength and beauty of our spiritual life come to light.

Romans 8:18 I consider that our present sufferings are not worth comparing with the glory that will be revealed in us.

Romans 5:3 And not only so; but we glory also in tribulations, knowing that tribulation worketh patience.

James 1:2 My brothers and sisters, whenever you face trials of any kind, consider it nothing but joy, 3 because you know that the testing of your faith produces endurance; 4 and let endurance have its full effect, so that you may be mature and complete, lacking in nothing.

Hebrews 10:35 Therefore do not throw away your confidence, which has a great reward. 36 For you have need of endurance, so that you may do the will of God and receive what is promised.

James 1:12 Blessed is the man who endures trial, for when he has stood the test he will receive the crown of life which God has promised to those who love him.

2 Corinthians 12:10 That is why, for Christ's sake, I delight in weaknesses, in insults, in hardships, in persecutions, in difficulties. For when I am weak, then I am strong.

Siracida 1:23 A patient man will endure until the right moment, and then joy will burst forth for him.

Revelation 14:12 Here is the patience of the saints, who keep the commandments of God, and the faith of Jesus.

To have mercy and to forgive continuously.

"You must show mercy to your neighbor always and everywhere. You cannot stop doing it, or excuse yourself, or justify yourself."
Saint Faustina Kowalska.

This virtue is also related to mercy, which enables us to give God his place as moral judge of the world. It means accepting our human frailty and avoiding responding with evil to evil. In the Bible, we find David's story, who, to some degree, portrayed the mercy that would abound in the Messiah.

1 Samuel 24:11 See, my father, look at this piece of your robe in my hand! I cut off the corner of your robe but did not kill you. See that there is nothing in my hand to indicate that I am guilty of wrongdoing or rebellion. I have not wronged you, but you are hunting me down to take my life. 12 May the LORD judge between you and me. And may the LORD avenge the wrongs you have done to me, but my hand will not touch you. 13 As the old saying goes, "From evildoers come evil deeds," so my hand will not touch you. 14 'Against whom has the king of Israel come out? Who are you pursuing? A dead dog? A flea? 15 May the LORD be our judge and decide between us. May he consider my cause and uphold it; may he vindicate me by delivering me from your hand.' 16 When David finished saying this, Saul asked, 'Is that your voice, David my son?' And he wept aloud. 17 'You

are more righteous than I,' he said. 'You have treated me well, but I have treated you badly.

"Even in the souls that seem the most lost, there remains,
until the end, the capacity to love God again."
Saint José María Escrivá de Balaguer

Patience is also very closely related to forgiveness, which plays a fundamental role in the spiritual life; it is the proof that love as a virtue is greater than the vice of selfishness; it is the sole sustenance of any long-term friendship; it is the only way to heal so to move towards a new life. Jesus in the following parable teaches us about forgiveness and patience.

Matthew 18:21 -The parable of the unmerciful servant- Then Peter came to Jesus and asked, 'Lord, how many times shall I forgive my brother or sister who sins against me? Up to seven times?' 22 Jesus answered, 'I tell you, not seven times, but seventy-seven times. 23 'Therefore, the kingdom of heaven is like a king who wanted to settle accounts with his servants. 24 As he began the settlement, a man who owed him ten thousand bags of gold was brought to him. 25 Since he was not able to pay, the master ordered that he and his wife and his children and all that he had be sold to repay the debt. 26 'At this the servant fell on his knees before him. "Be patient with me," he begged, "and I will pay back everything." 27 The servant's master took pity on him, cancelled the debt and let him go. 28 'But when that servant went out, he found one of his fellow servants who owed him a hundred silver coins. He grabbed him and began to choke him. "Pay back what you owe me!" he demanded. 29 'His fellow servant fell to his knees and begged him, "Be patient with me, and I will pay it back." 30 'But he refused. Instead, he went off and had the man thrown into prison until he could pay the debt. 31 When the other servants saw what had happened, they were outraged and went and told their master everything that had happened. 32 'Then the master called the servant in. "You wicked servant," he said, "I cancelled all that debt of yours because you begged me to. 33

Shouldn't you have had mercy on your fellow servant just as I had on you?" 34 In anger his master handed him over to the jailers to be tortured, until he should pay back all he owed. 35 'This is how my heavenly Father will treat each of you unless you forgive your brother or sister from your heart.'

The free and personal sacrifice for love.

"Love in action is a harsh and dreadful thing compared with love in dreams." Dostoyevsky

If we look for a biblical passage on patience, we will naturally come to the account of the passion of Christ, which is the pinnacle of divine revelation. The gospel's teachings find their most extraordinary splendor on the cross, and truly there are simply no words to describe the depth and beauty of that story. Faced with this event, we can only get on our knees and be amazed by the immense love that God has for each one of us.

John 10:11 'I am the good shepherd. The good shepherd lays down his life for the sheep. 12 The hired hand is not the shepherd and does not own the sheep. So when he sees the wolf coming, he abandons the sheep and runs away. Then the wolf attacks the flock and scatters it. 13 The man runs away because he is a hired hand and cares nothing for the sheep. 14 'I am the good shepherd; I know my sheep and my sheep know me – 15 just as the Father knows me and I know the Father – and I lay down my life for the sheep. 16 I have other sheep that are not of this sheepfold. I must bring them also. They too will listen to my voice, and there shall be one flock and one shepherd. 17 The reason my Father loves me is that I lay down my life – only to take it up again. 18 No one takes it from me, but I lay it down of my own accord. I have authority to lay it down and authority to take it up again. This command I received from my Father.'

Matthew 26:26 -The plot against Jesus- When Jesus had finished saying all these things, he said to his disciples, 2 'As you know, the Passover is two days away – and the Son of Man will be handed over to be crucified.' 3 Then the chief priests and the elders of the people assembled in the palace of the high priest, whose name was Caiaphas, 4 and they schemed to arrest Jesus secretly and kill him. 5 'But not during the festival,' they said, 'or there may be a riot among the people.' -Jesus anointed at Bethany- 6 While Jesus was in Bethany in the home of Simon the Leper, 7 a woman came to him with an alabaster jar of very expensive perfume, which she poured on his head as he was reclining at the table. 8 When the disciples saw this, they were indignant. 'Why this waste?' they asked. 9 'This perfume could have been sold at a high price and the money given to the poor.' 10 Aware of this, Jesus said to them, 'Why are you bothering this woman? She has done a beautiful thing to me. 11 The poor you will always have with you, but you will not always have me. 12 When she poured this perfume on my body, she did it to prepare me for burial. 13 Truly I tell you, wherever this gospel is preached throughout the world, what she has done will also be told, in memory of her.' -Judas agrees to betray Jesus- 14 Then one of the Twelve – the one called Judas Iscariot – went to the chief priests 15 and asked, 'What are you willing to give me if I deliver him over to you?' So they counted out for him thirty pieces of silver. 16 From then on Judas watched for an opportunity to hand him over. -The Last Supper- 17 On the first day of the Festival of Unleavened Bread, the disciples came to Jesus and asked, 'Where do you want us to make preparations for you to eat the Passover?' 18 He replied, 'Go into the city to a certain man and tell him, "The Teacher says: my appointed time is near. I am going to celebrate the Passover with my disciples at your house." ' 19 So the disciples did as Jesus had directed them and prepared the Passover. 20 When evening came, Jesus was reclining at the table with the Twelve. 21 And while they were eating, he said, 'Truly I tell you, one of you will betray me.' 22 They were very sad and began to say to him one after the other, 'Surely you don't mean me, Lord?' 23 Jesus replied, 'The one who has dipped his hand into the bowl with me will betray me. 24 The Son of Man will go just as it is written about him. But woe to that man who betrays the Son of Man! It would be better for him if he had not been born.' 25 Then Judas, the one who would betray him, said, 'Surely you don't mean me, Rabbi?' Jesus answered, 'You have said so.' 26 While they were eating, Jesus took bread, and when he had given thanks, he broke it and gave it to his disciples, saying, 'Take and eat; this is my body.' 27 Then he took a cup, and when he had given thanks, he gave it to them, saying, 'Drink from it, all of you. 28 This is my blood of the covenant, which is poured out for many for the forgiveness of sins. 29 I tell you, I will not drink from this fruit of the vine from now on until that day when I drink it new with you in my Father's kingdom.' 30 When they had sung a hymn, they went out to the Mount of Olives. -Jesus predicts Peter's denial- 31 Then Jesus told them, 'This very night you will all fall away on account of me, for it is written: ' "I will strike the shepherd, and the sheep of the flock will be scattered." 32 But after I have risen, I will go ahead of you into Galilee.' 33 Peter replied, 'Even if all fall away on account of you, I never will.' 34 'Truly I tell you,' Jesus answered, 'this very night, before the cock crows, you will disown me three times.' 35 But Peter declared, 'Even if I have to die with you, I will never disown you.' And all the other disciples said the same. -Gethsemane- 36 Then Jesus went with his disciples to a place called Gethsemane, and he said to them, 'Sit here while I go over there and pray.' 37 He took Peter and the two sons of Zebedee along with him, and he began to be sorrowful and troubled. 38 Then he said to them, 'My soul is overwhelmed with sorrow to the point of death. Stay here and keep watch with me.' 39 Going a little farther, he fell with his face to the ground and prayed, 'My Father, if it is possible, may this cup be taken from me. Yet not as I will, but as you will.' 40 Then he returned to his disciples and found them sleeping. 'Couldn't you men keep watch with me for one hour?' he asked Peter. 41 'Watch and pray so that you will not fall into temptation. The spirit is willing, but the flesh is weak.' 42 He went away a second time and prayed, 'My Father, if it is not possible for this cup to be taken away unless I drink it, may your will be done.' 43 When he came back, he again found them sleeping, because their eyes were heavy. 44 So he left them and went away once more and prayed the third time, saying the same thing. 45 Then he returned to the disciples and said to them, 'Are you still sleeping and resting? Look, the hour has come, and the Son of Man is delivered into the hands of sinners. 46 Rise! Let us go! Here comes my betrayer!' -Jesus arrested- 47 While he was still speaking, Judas, one of the Twelve, arrived. With him was a large crowd armed with swords and clubs, sent from the chief priests and the elders of the people. 48 Now the betrayer had arranged a signal with them: 'The one I kiss is the man; arrest him.' 49 Going at once to Jesus, Judas said, 'Greetings, Rabbi!' and kissed him. 50 Jesus replied, 'Do what you came for, friend.' Then the men stepped forward, seized Jesus and arrested him. 51 With that, one of Jesus' companions reached for his sword, drew it out and struck the servant of the high priest, cutting off his ear. 52 'Put your sword back in its place,' Jesus said to him, 'for all who draw the sword will die by the sword. 53 Do you think I cannot call on my Father, and he will at once put at my disposal more than twelve legions of angels? 54 But how then would the Scriptures be fulfilled that say it must happen in this way?' 55 In that hour Jesus said to the crowd, 'Am I leading a rebellion, that you have come out with swords and clubs to capture me? Every day I sat in the temple courts teaching, and you did not arrest me. 56 But this has all taken place that the writings of the prophets might be fulfilled.' Then all the disciples deserted him and fled. -Jesus before the Sanhedrin- 57 Those who had arrested Jesus took him to Caiaphas the high priest, where the teachers of the law and the elders had assembled. 58 But Peter followed him at a distance, right up to the courtyard of the high priest. He entered and sat down with the guards to see the outcome. 59 The chief priests and the whole Sanhedrin were looking for false evidence against Jesus so that they could put him to death. 60 But they did not find any, though many false witnesses came forward. Finally two came forward 61 and declared, 'This fellow said, "I am able to destroy the temple of God and rebuild it in three days." ' 62 Then the high priest stood up and said to Jesus, 'Are you not going to answer? What is this testimony that these men are bringing against you?' 63 But Jesus remained silent. The high priest said to him, 'I charge you under oath by the living God: Tell us if you are the Messiah, the Son of God.' 64 'You have said so,' Jesus replied. 'But I say to all of you: from now on you will see the Son of Man sitting at the right hand of the Mighty One and coming on the clouds of heaven.' 65 Then the high priest tore his clothes and said, 'He has spoken blasphemy! Why do we need any more witnesses? Look, now you have heard the blasphemy. 66 What do you think?' 'He is worthy of death,' they answered. 67 Then they spat in his face and struck him with their fists.

Others slapped him 68 and said, 'Prophesy to us, Messiah. Who hit you?' Peter disowns Jesus- 69 Now Peter was sitting out in the courtyard, and a servant-girl came to him. 'You also were with Jesus of Galilee,' she said. 70 But he denied it before them all. 'I don't know what you're talking about,' he said. 71 Then he went out to the gateway, where another servant-girl saw him and said to the people there, 'This fellow was with Jesus of Nazareth.' 72 He denied it again, with an oath: 'I don't know the man!' 73 After a little while, those standing there went up to Peter and said, 'Surely you are one of them; your accent gives you away.' 74 Then he began to call down curses, and he swore to them, 'I don't know the man!' Immediately a cock crowed. 75 Then Peter remembered the word Jesus had spoken: 'Before the cock crows, you will disown me three times.' And he went outside and wept bitterly.

Matthew 27:1 -Judas hangs himself- Early in the morning, all the chief priests and the elders of the people made their plans how to have Jesus executed. 2 So they bound him, led him away and handed him over to Pilate the governor. 3 When Judas, who had betrayed him, saw that Jesus was condemned, he was seized with remorse and returned the thirty pieces of silver to the chief priests and the elders. 4 'I have sinned,' he said, 'for I have betrayed innocent blood.' 'What is that to us?' they replied. 'That's your responsibility.' 5 So Judas threw the money into the temple and left. Then he went away and hanged himself. 6 The chief priests picked up the coins and said, 'It is against the law to put this into the treasury, since it is blood money.' 7 So they decided to use the money to buy the potter's field as a burial place for foreigners. 8 That is why it has been called the Field of Blood to this day. 9 Then what was spoken by Jeremiah the prophet was fulfilled: 'They took the thirty pieces of silver, the price set on him by the people of Israel, 10 and they used them to buy the potter's field, as the Lord commanded me.' -Jesus before Pilate- 11 Meanwhile Jesus stood before the governor, and the governor asked him, 'Are you the king of the Jews?' 'You have said so,' Jesus replied. 12 When he was accused by the chief priests and the elders, he gave no answer. 13 Then Pilate asked him, 'Don't you hear the testimony they are bringing against you?' 14 But Jesus made no reply, not even to a single charge – to the great amazement of the governor. 15 Now it was the governor's custom at the festival to release a prisoner chosen by the crowd. 16 At that time they had a well-known prisoner whose name was Jesus Barabbas. 17 So when the crowd had gathered, Pilate asked them, 'Which one do you want me to release to you: Jesus Barabbas, or Jesus who is called the Messiah?' 18 For he knew it was out of self-interest that they had handed Jesus over to him. 19 While Pilate was sitting on the judge's seat, his wife sent him this message: 'Don't have anything to do with that innocent man, for I have suffered a great deal today in a dream because of him.' 20 But the chief priests and the elders persuaded the crowd to ask for Barabbas and to have Jesus executed. 21 'Which of the two do you want me to release to you?' asked the governor. 'Barabbas,' they answered. 22 'What shall I do, then, with Jesus who is called the Messiah?' Pilate asked. They all answered, 'Crucify him!' 23 'Why? What crime has he committed?' asked Pilate. But they shouted all the louder, 'Crucify him!' 24 When Pilate saw that he was getting nowhere, but that instead an uproar was starting, he took water and washed his hands in front of the crowd. 'I am innocent of this man's blood,' he said. 'It is your responsibility!' 25 All the people answered, 'His blood is on us and on our children!' 26 Then he released Barabbas to them. But he had Jesus flogged, and handed him over to be crucified. -The soldiers mock Jesus- 27 Then the governor's soldiers took Jesus into the Praetorium and gathered the whole company of soldiers round him. 28 They stripped him and put a scarlet robe on him, 29 and then twisted together a crown of thorns and set it on his head. They put a staff in his right hand. Then they knelt in front of him and mocked him. 'Hail, king of the Jews!' they said. 30 They spat on him, and took the staff and struck him on the head again and again. 31 After they had mocked him, they took off the robe and put his own clothes on him. Then they led him away to crucify him. -The crucifixion of Jesus- 32 As they were going out, they met a man from Cyrene, named Simon, and they forced him to carry the cross. 33 They came to a place called Golgotha (which means 'the place of the skull'). 34 There they offered Jesus wine to drink, mixed with gall; but after tasting it, he refused to drink it. 35 When they had crucified him, they divided up his clothes by casting lots. 36 And sitting down, they kept watch over him there. 37 Above his head they placed the written charge against him: THIS IS JESUS, THE KING OF THE JEWS. 38 Two rebels were crucified with him, one on his right and one on his left. 39 Those who passed by hurled insults at him, shaking their heads 40 and saying, 'You who are going to destroy the temple and build it in three days, save yourself! Come down from the cross, if you are the Son of God!' 41 In the same way the chief priests, the teachers of the law and the elders mocked him. 42 'He saved others,' they said, 'but he can't save himself! He's the king of Israel! Let him come down now from the cross, and we will believe in him. 43 He trusts in God. Let God rescue him now if he wants him, for he said, "I am the Son of God." ' 44 In the same way the rebels who were crucified with him also heaped insults on him. -The death of Jesus- 45 From noon until three in the afternoon darkness came over all the land. 46 About three in the afternoon Jesus cried out in a loud voice, 'Eli, Eli,c lema sabachthani?' (which means 'My God, my God, why have you forsaken me?'). 47 When some of those standing there heard this, they said, 'He's calling Elijah.' 48 Immediately one of them ran and got a sponge. He filled it with wine vinegar, put it on a staff, and offered it to Jesus to drink. 49 The rest said, 'Now leave him alone. Let's see if Elijah comes to save him.' 50 And when Jesus had cried out again in a loud voice, he gave up his spirit. 51 At that moment the curtain of the temple was torn in two from top to bottom. The earth shook, the rocks split 52and the tombs broke open. The bodies of many holy people who had died were raised to life. 53 They came out of the tombs after Jesus' resurrection and went into the holy city and appeared to many people. 54 When the centurion and those with him who were guarding Jesus saw the earthquake and all that had happened, they were terrified, and exclaimed, 'Surely he was the Son of God!' 55 Many women were there, watching from a distance. They had followed Jesus from Galilee to care for his needs. 56 Among them were Mary Magdalene, Mary the mother of James and Joseph, and the mother of Zebedee's sons. -The burial of Jesus-57 As evening approached, there came a rich man from Arimathea, named Joseph, who had himself become a disciple of Jesus. 58 Going to Pilate, he asked for Jesus' body, and Pilate ordered that it be given to him. 59 Joseph took the body, wrapped it in a clean linen cloth, 60 and placed it in his own new tomb that he had cut out of the rock.

He rolled a big stone in front of the entrance to the tomb and went away. 61 Mary Magdalene and the other Mary were sitting there opposite the tomb. -The guard at the tomb- 62 The next day, the one after Preparation Day, the chief priests and the Pharisees went to Pilate. 63 'Sir,' they said, 'we remember that while he was still alive that deceiver said, "After three days I will rise again." 64 So give the order for the tomb to be made secure until the third day. Otherwise, his disciples may come and steal the body and tell the people that he has been raised from the dead. This last deception will be worse than the first.' 65 'Take a guard,' Pilate answered. 'Go, make the tomb as secure as you know how.' 66 So they went and made the tomb secure by putting a seal on the stone and posting the guard.

Mathew 28:1 -Jesus has risen- After the Sabbath, at dawn on the first day of the week, Mary Magdalene and the other Mary went to look at the tomb. 2 There was a violent earthquake, for an angel of the Lord came down from heaven and, going to the tomb, rolled back the stone and sat on it. 3 His appearance was like lightning, and his clothes were white as snow. 4 The guards were so afraid of him that they shook and became like dead men. 5 The angel said to the women, 'Do not be afraid, for I know that you are looking for Jesus, who was crucified. 6 He is not here; he has risen, just as he said. Come and see the place where he lay. 7 Then go quickly and tell his disciples: "He has risen from the dead and is going ahead of you into Galilee. There you will see him." Now I have told you.' 8 So the women hurried away from the tomb, afraid yet filled with joy, and ran to tell his disciples. 9Suddenly Jesus met them. 'Greetings,' he said. They came to him, clasped his feet and worshipped him. 10 Then Jesus said to them, 'Do not be afraid. Go and tell my brothers to go to Galilee; there they will see me.' -The guards' report- 11 While the women were on their way, some of the guards went into the city and reported to the chief priests everything that had happened. 12 When the chief priests had met with the elders and devised a plan, they gave the soldiers a large sum of money, 13 telling them, 'You are to say, "His disciples came during the night and stole him away while we were asleep." 14 If this report gets to the governor, we will satisfy him and keep you out of trouble.' 15 So the soldiers took the money and did as they were instructed. And this story has been widely circulated among the Jews to this very day. -The great commission- 16 Then the eleven disciples went to Galilee, to the mountain where Jesus had told them to go. 17 When they saw him, they worshipped him; but some doubted. 18 Then Jesus came to them and said, 'All authority in heaven and on earth has been given to me. 19 Therefore go and make disciples of all nations, baptizing them in the name of the Father and of the Son and of the Holy Spirit, 20 and teaching them to obey everything I have commanded you. And surely I am with you always, to the very end of the age.'

"Do not complain. That shows a discontent with God's will in the present moment. That is also proof of impatience."
Saint Martin de Porres

The inability to face and confront evil through love and virtue.

"It is never right to do wrong or to requite wrong with wrong, or when we suffer evil to defend ourselves by doing evil in return."
Socrates

Impatience is the fact of avoiding facing evil; or wanting to battle evil through sin. By losing sight of his moral responsibility (the duty to be virtuous), the impatient person tries to solve problems through violence, which shows a lack of character and maturity in his spirituality. It is so easy to blame the outside world, it is so easy to play the scapegoat card, yet it is so unfruitful as an actual strategy towards a better life. Some verses from the Bible teach us about such type of scenarios and behaviors and warn us not to return evil for evil.

Proverbs 20:22 Do not say, "I will repay evil"; wait for the Lord, and he will help you.

Romans 12:14 Bless those who persecute you; bless and do not curse.

Romans 12:17 Do not repay anyone evil for evil. Be careful to do what is right in the eyes of everyone. 18 If it is possible, as far as it depends on you, live at peace with everyone. 19 Do not take revenge, my dear friends, but leave room for God's wrath, for it is written: 'It is mine to avenge; I will repay,' says the Lord. 20 On the contrary: 'If your enemy is hungry, feed him; if he is thirsty, give him something to drink. In doing this, you will heap burning coals on his head.' 21 Do not be overcome by evil, but overcome evil with good.

1 Peter 3:9 Do not repay evil with evil or insult with insult. On the contrary, repay evil with blessing, because to this you were called so that you may inherit a blessing. 10 For, 'Whoever would love life and see good days must keep their tongue from evil and their lips from deceitful speech. 11 They must turn from evil and do good; they must seek peace and pursue it. 12 For the eyes of the LORD are on the righteous and his ears are attentive to their prayer, but the face of the LORD is against those who do evil.'

To be consumed by the adversities and sufferings of this life.

We know that spiritual growth is gradual and that developing character and virtues takes time, so we could assume that we all start a little impatient, but we must grow until we reach patience. It is clear that when we are impatient, we lose peace and joy; that is, we become consumed and bitter not only in great sufferings but also in the small or trivial ones.

Hebrews 12:15 See to it that no one falls short of the grace of God and that no bitter root grows up to cause trouble and defile many.

A modern manifestation of this vice is playing the role of a victim when, in fact, we are not victims. Imagine the insult towards the people that are really suffering if we falsely pretend to be in their position. It is wrong to justify ourselves through self-invented limitations, problems, or evil scenarios. People who victimize themselves usually are only looking to excuse or rationalize, to some degree, their own immoral behavior.

To lose mercy and to stop forgiving.

If we dismiss the importance of forgiveness, we will live anchored or attached to the past's pains and sufferings, which will prevent us from loving by driving us through hate to seek revenge or retaliation. If we are not able to forgive, we will remain hurt, and we will end up even hurting people who were not the ones who harmed us. In Christianity, forgiving is a duty since we are all debtors of our sins and vices before God. In some sense, the evil we have done to other people count as an evil done to Christ himself. It is Jesus who commands us to forgive each other as part of the prayer He taught us.

Sirach 28:4 If one has no mercy toward another like himself, can he then seek pardon for his own sins?

Mathew 25:40 'The King will reply, "Truly I tell you, whatever you did for one of the least of these brothers and sisters of mine, you did for me."

Matthew 6:12 And forgive us our debts, as we also have forgiven our debtors.

Matthew 6:14 For if you forgive other people when they sin against you, your heavenly Father will also forgive you. 15 But if you do not forgive others their sins, your Father will not forgive your sins.

The choice to avoid sacrifice out of egoism.

If we are honest, how many times our impatience ends up denoting our selfishness? Focusing on our comfort instead of on our responsibility makes it exceedingly difficult for us to make sacrifices for love. Often from a human perspective, being impatient is positive to bring short-term solutions. But, in reality, as the years go by, we will realize that impatience has not only produced negative consequences; but it has also made situations even more complicated than they were before.

In Christianity, the ultimate denying ourselves is not devaluing our worth and dignity as human beings, but it is sacrificing ourselves freely by renouncing to follow our egoism in all its vices in order to follow God; to love.

INTEMPERANCE   INCREDULITY

IMPATIENCE   HOPELESSNESS

THE WAY OF VICE

EGOISM

PRIDE

FOOLISHNESS   AVARICE

VANITY   SLOTH

IMPURITY

Virtues are the Sublime Beauty of Holiness!

"A faithful Christian, illuminated by the rays of grace like a crystal, must illuminate others with his words and actions, with the light of good example." Saint Anthony of Padua.

The virtues we have seen are what Christianity understands as proper to a good person, which, within the language of faith, is known as holiness. It is wondrous that the Catholic Church establishes that the first step in determining a person's sanctity is to analyze the heroic virtues manifested in the candidate's life. From what can be said that virtues have universal merit and value within Christian philosophy. Saints really are the true heroes of the world.

Hebrews 12:14 Make every effort to live in peace with everyone and to be holy; without holiness no one will see the LORD.

2 Peter 1:3 -Confirming one's calling and election- His divine power has given us everything we need for a godly life through our knowledge of him who called us by his own glory and goodness. 4 Through these he has given us his very great and precious promises, so that through them you may participate in the divine nature, having escaped the corruption in the world caused by evil desires. 5 For this very reason, make every effort to add to your faith goodness; and to goodness, knowledge; 6 and to knowledge, self-control; and to self-control, perseverance; and to perseverance, godliness; 7 and to godliness, mutual affection; and to mutual affection, love. 8 For if you possess these qualities in increasing measure, they will keep you from being ineffective and unproductive in your knowledge of our Lord Jesus Christ. 9 But whoever does not have them is short-sighted and blind, forgetting that they have been cleansed from their past sins. 10 Therefore, my brothers and sisters, make every effort to confirm your calling and election. For if you do these things, you will never stumble, 11 and you will receive a rich welcome into the eternal kingdom of our Lord and Saviour Jesus Christ.

Virtues are also the irrefutable moral proofs of the living presence of the Holy Spirit in us. Chesterton said that Christians are the only reason not to believe in Christianity precisely because Catholics-Christians often fall short of fulfilling a life of virtue, love, and joy. Christ enlightened humanity by defining what virtue means through his life, which is an example of perfect and complete love, and that is precisely what places him as the most influential person in the history of humanity. All Christians are called to be a living testimony of what it means to love according to what Christ taught us. We are all called to be the light of the world by virtues reflected in our charitable behavior, through which we glorify God.

Matthew 5:14 'You are the light of the world. A town built on a hill cannot be hidden. 15 Neither do people light a lamp and put it under a bowl. Instead they put it on its stand, and it gives light to everyone in the house. 16 In the same way, let your light shine before others, that they may see your good deeds and glorify your Father in heaven.

We find a biblical passage that calls us to deepen and meditate on the fact of being loved and chosen by God to live a life of good; of virtue; and of peace.

Colossians 3:12 Therefore, as God's chosen people, holy and dearly loved, clothe yourselves with compassion, kindness, humility, gentleness and patience. 13 Bear with each other and forgive one another if any of you has a grievance against someone. Forgive as the Lord forgave you. 14 And over all these virtues put on love, which binds them all together in perfect unity. 15 Let the peace of Christ rule in your hearts, since as members of one body you were called to peace. And be thankful. 16 Let the message of Christ dwell among you richly as you teach and admonish one another with all wisdom through psalms, hymns, and songs from the Spirit, singing to God with gratitude in your hearts. 17 And whatever you do, whether in word or deed, do it all in the name of the Lord Jesus, giving thanks to God the Father through him.

The conclusion is that all virtues have a beginning: The Grace of God; and that all virtues have an end: The Glory of God. We can only be grateful for the opportunity to love, which is to freely participate in the divine and infinite life of God!

"True perfection consists in this: always doing the most holy will of God." Saint Catherine of Siena.

"Since we live by the Spirit, let us keep in step with the Spirit." Galatians 5:25

TEMPERANCE   FAITH

PATIENCE   HOPE

THE WAY OF VIRTUE

LOVE

HUMILITY

PRUDENCE   GENEROSITY

WISDOM   PERSEVERANCE

PURITY

"Moral leadership, being the most powerful, transcendent, and estimable of all, is at the end of the day, a matter of love and virtue." Unknown

"The highest form of human happiness is a fruit of virtue, which is summed up in love, which is generated through the good use of our free will, which is guided by God." Unknown

Prayer for the virtues.

Father, I ask you in the name of our Lord Jesus Christ to send your Holy Spirit and fill my soul and my body with your presence.

I want to follow you unto eternity, I want to joyfully fulfill your Divine Moral Law.

Allow my love to be like yours, complete in justice and mercy.

Grant me the grace to overcome my egoism in all its manifestations.

May my faith and my hope be only in you.

Grant me a humble, generous, persevering, and pure heart.

May my mind be wise and prudent.

Strengthen me to live with temperance and patience all the adversities and trials that await me in life.

Provide me the grace to glorify you through a virtuous, impeccable, and holy behavior.

God, may I never forget the great love you have for us.

Part 3

"You will never be happy if your happiness depends on getting solely what you want. Change your focus. Get a new center. Will what God wills, and your joy no man shall take from you." Fulton Sheen

Chapter 10: Spiritual Maturity

"He who prepares himself for grace; receives a greater grace."
Saint Thomas Aquinas

After recognizing the value of virtues and the harm of vices, we probably within our hearts the desire to grow or mature as persons. We know that spiritual development is complicated, yet to a great extent, life is about developing our capacity to love and experiencing a more complete and perfect form of charity. Thomas Aquinas wisely thought that life is a school of virtue, where we must achieve, with the grace of God, the best version of ourselves.

Interior Change

"I don't tell people, 'You're okay the way that you are.'
That's not the right story. The right story is, '
You're way less than you could be."
Jordan Peterson

If we are honest, we have all felt that we could be better than what we currently are. When our life does not satisfy us, we can blame circumstances, the outside world or we can focus on ourselves. The wise choice is introspection, that is, realizing that we must heal and change things within ourselves in order to live better. From a biblical perspective, the change that is not from within cannot be a real change, nor will it remain to bear good fruits. Jesus teaches us that change only in appearance or outward is useless and superficial in the eyes of God.

Matthew 23:26 Blind Pharisee! First clean the inside of the cup and dish, and then the outside also will be clean. 27 'Woe to you, teachers of the law and Pharisees, you hypocrites! You are like white-washed tombs, which look beautiful on the outside but on the inside are full of the bones of the dead and everything unclean. 28 In the same way, on the outside you appear to people as righteous but on the inside you are full of hypocrisy and wickedness.

Maturing as people involves continually improving our thoughts, attitudes, and decisions in function to God. All the virtues and vices mentioned above depend on these three inner realities. Some virtues or vices are more oriented to the will, others to intelligence, and others to affectivity; yet at the end of the day, all these qualities are part of our way of being.

Figure 7 Spiritual Maturity.

It is up to us to make the changes in our conscious. It is up to us to take responsibility for what no one should change for us, and for that, a spiritual criterion is essential.

"Judge people not by what they are, but by what they strive to become." Dostoyevsky

"People are usually curious to know the lives of others and reluctant to correct their own life." Saint Augustine

Self-Knowledge with Spiritual Criteria

An excellent first step towards a fuller life is to have good spiritual criterion and apply it to ourselves. That is why it was first necessary to clarify the universality of spiritual/moral concepts, by which we define what is meritorious, admirable, or worthy in human behavior.

Knowing ourselves through virtues and vices is to accurately understand the state of our souls. In the list below, you can honestly mark with which virtue or vice you feel identified. For obvious reasons, you cannot have developed the corresponding virtue where you have a vice since vices and virtues are mutually excluding qualities. Due to the fact of how difficult it is to move from one reality to the other, you likely have dominant vices and virtues; that is, your spiritual battle will probably be against the same sins throughout your life.

"To overcome the limits, you must first know yourself, then accept yourself as you are, and finally surpass yourself."
Saint Augustine

LOVE	EGOISM
✓ Faith	✗ Incredulity
✓ Hope	✗ Hopelessness
✓ Humility	✗ Pride
✓ Generosity	✗ Avarice
✓ Perseverance	✗ Sloth
✓ Purity	✗ Impurity
✓ Wisdom	✗ Vanity
✓ Prudence	✗ Foolishness
✓ Temperance	✗ Intemperance
✓ Patience	✗ Impatience

"You are not more because they praise you, nor are you less because they despise you, what you are in the eyes of God, that you are." Thomas a Kempis

"The worst deception is self-deception." Plato

"Above all, don't lie to yourself. The man who lies to himself and listens to his own lie comes to a point that he cannot distinguish the truth within him, or around him, and so loses all respect for himself and for others. And having no respect he ceases to love."
Dostoevsky

Knowing with certainty what virtues and what vices we have is the first step to internally change. It's like having a map that tells us where we are and tells us where we want to go; without that real knowledge of ourselves, we could live deceived in lies about who we really are. It is in the discovery of our evils that we see the explicit need we have for God, which moves us to conversion.

Conversion

"Because the truth of God is love, conversion to God is conversion to love." Pope Benedict XVI

In our own lives, we are all witnesses that we can choose good acts based on love or bad ones based on selfishness. It is a universal truth that all humans have fallen into vices or sins, and for that same reason, we all need an authentic conversion and a Savior.

1 Timothy 1:15 Here is a trustworthy saying that deserves full acceptance: Christ Jesus came into the world to save sinners – of whom I am the worst.

1 John 2:2 He is the atoning sacrifice for our sins, and not only for ours but also for the sins of the whole world.

Romans 3:23 For all have sinned and fall short of the glory of God, 24 and all are justified freely by his grace through the redemption that came by Christ Jesus. 25 God presented Christ as a sacrifice of atonement, through the shedding of his blood – to be received by faith. He did this to demonstrate his righteousness, because in his forbearance he had left the sins committed beforehand unpunished 26 – he did it to demonstrate his righteousness at the present time, so as to be just and the one who justifies those who have faith in Jesus.

1 John 4:14 And we have seen and testify that the Father has sent his Son to be the Savior of the world. 15 If anyone acknowledges that Jesus is the Son of God, God lives in them and they in God.

Acts 13:38 Therefore, my friends, I want you to know that through Jesus the forgiveness of sins is proclaimed to you. 39 Through him everyone who believes is set free from every sin, a justification you were not able to obtain under the law of Moses.

John 1:17 For the law was given through Moses; grace and truth came through Jesus Christ. 18 No one has ever seen God, but the one and only Son, who is himself God and is in the closest relationship with the Father, has made him known.

Ephesians 2:4 But because of his great love for us, God, who is rich in mercy, 5 made us alive with Christ even when we were dead in transgressions – it is by grace you have been saved. 6 And God raised us up with Christ and seated us with him in the heavenly realms in Christ Jesus, 7 in order that in the coming ages he might show the incomparable riches of his grace, expressed in his kindness to us in Christ Jesus.

Acts 4:12 Salvation is found in no one else, for there is no other name under heaven given to mankind by which we must be saved.

Colossians 1:15 The Son is the image of the invisible God, the firstborn over all creation. 16 For in him all things were created: things in heaven and on earth, visible and invisible, whether thrones or powers or rulers or authorities; all things have been created through him and for him. 17 He is before all things, and in him all things hold together. 18 And he is the head of the body, the church; he is the beginning and the firstborn from among the dead, so that in everything he might have the supremacy. 19 For God was pleased to have all his fullness dwell in him, 20 and through him to reconcile to himself all things, whether things on earth or things in heaven, by making peace through his blood, shed on the cross.

It is not surprising that the first message of Jesus in the Gospels is a call to repentance and conversion in order to receive the Kingdom of God Kingdom in our hearts.

Mark 1:14 After John was put in prison, Jesus went into Galilee, proclaiming the good news of God. 15 'The time has come,' he said. 'The kingdom of God has come near. Repent and believe the good news!'

Conversion is giving our whole soul to God and letting Him change our selfish heart, for a heart of flesh; a heart that can love; a virtuous heart. Conversion begins by accepting our personal vice and asking God for his forgiveness. And it ends when our behavior becomes excellent or holy.

Ezekiel 18:30 'Therefore, you Israelites, I will judge each of you according to your own ways, declares the Sovereign LORD. Repent! Turn away from all your offences; then sin will not be your downfall. 31 Rid yourselves of all the offences you have committed, and get a new heart and a new spirit. Why will you die, people of Israel? 32 For I take no pleasure in the death of anyone, declares the Sovereign LORD. Repent and live!

Ezekiel 36:26 I will give you a new heart and put a new spirit in you; I will remove from you your heart of stone and give you a heart of flesh. 27 And I will put my Spirit in you and move you to follow my decrees and be careful to keep my laws.

Conversion or choosing to love God is going from walking in the darkness (egoism) to walking in the light (love). This idea is known as a spiritual resurrection because it signifies going from living by the flesh to living by the Spirit. The mission that Jesus gives to Saint Paul is precisely the purpose of the preaching of the Gospels.

Acts 26:16 "Now get up and stand on your feet. I have appeared to you to appoint you as a servant and as a witness of what you have seen and will see of me. 17 I will rescue you from your own people and from the Gentiles. I am sending you to them 18 to open their eyes and turn them from darkness to light, and from the power of Satan to God, so that they may receive forgiveness of sins and a place among those who are sanctified by faith in me."

The word conversion means the transformation of something into what it was not. To be a convert is to be transformed into something new. It is to die to the evil person we were to be born into the goodness of God. It is losing whatever insufficient identity we had to assume a divine identity as the sons and daughters of God.

Acts 2:38 Peter said to them, "Convert, and each one of you be baptized in the name of Jesus Christ for the forgiveness of your sins, and you will receive the gift of the Holy Spirit.

2 Corinthians 5:17 Therefore, if anyone is in Christ, he is a new creation: the old has passed away, the new has already come.

Ephesians 1:3 Praise be to the God and Father of our Lord Jesus Christ, who has blessed us in the heavenly realms with every spiritual blessing in Christ. 4 For he chose us in him before the creation of the world to be holy and blameless in his sight. In love 5 he predestined us for adoption to sonship through Jesus Christ, in accordance with his pleasure and will – 6 to the praise of his glorious grace, which he has freely given us in the One he loves. 7 In him we have redemption through his blood, the forgiveness of sins, in accordance with the riches of God's grace 8 that he lavished on us. With all wisdom and understanding, 9 he made known to us the mystery of his will according to his good pleasure, which he purposed in Christ, 10 to be put into effect when the times reach their fulfilment – to bring unity to all things in heaven and on earth under Christ.

At the behavioral level, **conversion** produces a spiritual-moral alignment with God, which is made up of two natural and commonsensical stages.

1. **Repenting and stopping to sin.**
2. **Loving God and our neighbor through virtues.**

"God will not force our will; He takes what we give; but He does not give himself completely until we give ourselves completely."
Saint Teresa of Jesus

1. Repenting and stopping to sin.

If you have discovered that you have several vices, the good news is that God came into the world precisely because of people like us.

Luke 5:31 Jesus answered them, 'It is not the healthy who need a doctor, but those who are ill. 32 I have not come to call the righteous, but sinners to repentance.'

Ezekiel 18:21 'But if a wicked person turns away from all the sins they have committed and keeps all my decrees and does what is just and right, that person will surely live; they will not die. 22 None of the offences they have committed will be remembered against them. Because of the righteous things they have done, they will live.

Luke 15:7 I tell you that in the same way there will be more rejoicing in heaven over one sinner who repents than over ninety-nine righteous people who do not need to repent.

We must not drag our vices/sins to death; we must exchange vice for virtue. Staying all our life with the same vices is absurd; it is a tragedy and a disappointing drama. The first growth of the spiritual life consists in ceasing on doing evil, that is, giving up our concrete vices.

Lamentations 3:40 Let us examine our ways and test them, and let us return to the LORD.

Proverbs 28:13 Whoever conceals their sins does not prosper, but the one who confesses and renounces them finds mercy.

1 John 1:9 If we confess our sins, he is faithful and just and will forgive us our sins and purify us from all unrighteousness.

Psalm 32:5 Then I acknowledged my sin to you and did not cover up my iniquity. I said, 'I will confess my transgressions to the LORD.' And you forgave the guilt of my sin.

Acts 3:19 Repent, then, and turn to God, so that your sins may be wiped out, that times of refreshing may come from the Lord,

Sirach 21:6 Those who hate reproof walk in the sinner's steps, but those who fear the Lord repent in their heart.

Sirach 35:3 To keep from wickedness is pleasing to the Lord, and to forsake unrighteousness is atonement.

Sirach 17:21 Turn to the Lord, and forsake thy sins: 22 Make thy prayer before the face of the Lord, and offend less. 23 Return to the Lord, and turn away from thy injustice, and greatly hate abomination. 24 And know the justices and judgments of God, and stand firm in the lot set before thee, and in prayer to the most high God.

Ephesians 10:15 The Holy Spirit also testifies to us about this. First he says: 16 'This is the covenant I will make with them after that time, says the LORD. I will put my laws in their hearts, and I will write them on their minds.' 17 Then he adds: 'Their sins and lawless acts I will remember no more.' 18 And where these have been forgiven, sacrifice for sin is no longer necessary.

Quitting vices will often imply a kind of suffering or sadness, but we can be sure that the suffering experienced by giving up sin will not be in vain.

2 Corinthians 7:10 Godly sorrow brings repentance that leads to salvation and leaves no regret, but worldly sorrow brings death.

We find two prayers that reflect this act of inner contrition that seeks conversion and reconciliation with God. The first is the prayer of King David, which is considered one of the most profound prayers in the Old Testament, and the second is the Catholic act of contrition that is beseeched in confession.

1) Psalm of David:

Psalm 51:1 Have mercy on me, O God, according to your unfailing love; according to your great compassion blot out my transgressions. 2 Wash away all my iniquity and cleanse me from my sin. 3 For I know my transgressions, and my sin is always before me. 4 Against you, you only, have I sinned and done what is evil in your sight; so you are right in your verdict and justified when you judge. 5 Surely I was sinful at birth, sinful from the time my mother conceived me. 6 Yet you desired faithfulness even in the womb; you taught me wisdom in that secret place. 7 Cleanse me with hyssop, and I shall be clean; wash me, and I shall be whiter than snow. 8 Let me hear joy and gladness; let the bones you have crushed rejoice. 9 Hide your face from my sins and blot out all my iniquity. 10 Create in me a pure heart, O God, and renew a steadfast spirit within me. 11 Do not cast me from your presence or take your Holy Spirit from me. 12 Restore to me the joy of your salvation and grant me a willing spirit, to sustain me. 13 Then I will teach transgressors your ways, so that sinners will turn back to you. 14 Deliver me from the guilt of bloodshed, O God, you who are God my Saviour, and my tongue will sing of your right-eousness. 15 Open my lips, Lord, and my mouth will declare your praise. 16 You do not delight in sacrifice, or I would bring it; you do not take pleasure in burnt offerings. 17 My sacrifice, O God, is a bro-ken spirit; a broken and contrite heart you, God, will not despise.

2) Act of contrition in Christianity:

My God, I am sorry for my sins with all my heart. In choosing to do wrong and failing to do good, I have sinned against you whom I should love above all things.

I firmly intend, with your help, to do penance, to sin no more, and to avoid whatever leads me to sin.

Our Savior Jesus Christ suffered and died for us. In his name, my God, have mercy.

God takes away the evil so that the good can come out; He removes our vices so that virtues can grow. Saint Thomas a Kempis said very wisely: "If every year we gave up a vice, we would soon be saints." How much our life would improve simply by renouncing our vices and sins!

2. Loving God and our neighbor through virtues.

*"Give the world the best you have, and it may never be enough.
Give your best anyway. For you see, in the end, it is between you
and God. It was never between you and them anyway."*
Saint Teresa of Calcutta

Learning a virtue is learning to love!

God is the one who transforms and purifies our souls so that we can love. It is in the experience of any virtue that we mature as people. Each virtue is a small universe; each virtue is related to an infinity of actions and opportunities to live it. We must ask God for grace and dispose ourselves to live with the love of Christ.

2 Corinthians 3:18 And we all, who with unveiled faces contemplate the Lord's glory, are being transformed into his image with ever-increasing glory, which comes from the Lord, who is the Spirit.

1 Peter 1:22 Since you have purified your souls by obedience to the truth, for an unfeigned brotherly love, love one another intensely from the heart, 23 For you have been born again, not of perishable seed, but of imperishable, through the living and enduring word of God. 24 For, 'All people are like grass, and all their glory is like the flowers of the field; the grass withers and the flowers fall, 25 but the word of the LORD endures for ever.' And this is the word that was preached to you.

Galatians 6:9a Let us not become weary in doing good, for at the proper time we will reap a harvest if we do not give up. 10 Therefore, as we have opportunity, let us do good to all people.

2 Thessalonians 3:13 And as for you, brothers and sisters, never tire of doing what is good.

Titus 3:8 This is a trustworthy saying. And I want you to stress these things, so that those who have trusted in God may be careful to devote themselves to doing what is good. These things are excellent and profitable for everyone.

Psalm 37:27 Turn from evil and do good; then you will dwell in the land for ever.

Hebrews 13:16 And do not forget to do good and to share with others, for with such sacrifices God is pleased.

God is the one who administers the virtues through his grace. It is the Holy Spirit who works these virtues in and with us. We can remain absolutely assured that God wants us to be virtuous people and to bear much fruit.

Luke 11:9 'So I say to you: ask and it will be given to you; seek and you will find; knock and the door will be opened to you. 10 For everyone who asks receives; the one who seeks finds; and to the one who knocks, the door will be opened. 11 'Which of you fathers, if your son asks for a fish, will give him a snake instead? 12 Or if he asks for an egg, will give him a scorpion? 13 If you then, though you are evil, know how to give good gifts to your children, how much more will your Father in heaven give the Holy Spirit to those who ask him!'

John 15:7 If you remain in me and my words remain in you, ask whatever you want and it will be given to you. 8 Herein is my Father glorified, that you bear much fruit and become my disciples.

1 Peter 2:12 Live such good lives among the pagans that, though they accuse you of doing wrong, they may see your good deeds and glorify God on the day he visits us.

Chapter 11: The Best Habits

"Good habits formed at youth make all the difference." Aristotle

The three habits that we will see next, in some way, had a preponderant and recurrent place in the lives of the saints. They are very well-known behavioral patterns that we can imitate; they are activities that help us be in communion with God. They are inspired by divine revelation and common sense; they complement the sacraments and are part of the ideal of an authentic Christian life. Spending our time in these activities will be decisive to attain moral maturity. As simple as it may seem, the secret of exponential spiritual growth is hidden in these habits. It is up to us to take advantage of each day and practice them!

Prayer

Prayer is the most important habit to prepare our interior to live in virtue. In prayer, we seek to be carried away by divine inspirations; we attempt to heal and order our affectivity; we aim to reflect and make decisions based on God's will. Ultimately, we aim to have a connection with the Holy Trinity. That is why without prayer, without a real communication with God, without that living relationship with Him, we can do nothing good.

John 15:1 I am the true vine, and my Father is the gardener. 2 He cuts off every branch in me that bears no fruit, while every branch that does bear fruit he prunes so that it will be even more fruitful. 3 You are already clean because of the word I have spoken to you. 4 Remain in me, as I also remain in you. No branch can bear fruit by itself; it must remain in the vine. Neither can you bear fruit unless you remain in me. 5 'I am the vine; you are the branches. If you remain in me and I in you, you will bear much fruit; apart from me you can do nothing. 6 If you do not remain in me, you are like a branch that is thrown away and withers; such branches are picked up, thrown into the fire and burned. 7 If you remain in me and my words remain in you, ask whatever you wish, and it will be done for you.

Thanks to the Holy Spirit, we can live a meaningful and full life in imitation and unity with Christ. Praying is part of the mystical life, where we dedicate a specific time to thank God for all the goods he has given us, and thus, we ask for his grace to remain in virtue and in his love. During prayer, the most important thing we do is get ready, open our interior and let Him transform our being. Praying is seeking to live the good and the will of God despite our smallness and weakness. In the Bible, we find a passage where Jesus speaks very clearly to us about prayer.

Matthew 6:6 But when you pray, go into your room, close the door and pray to your Father, who is unseen. Then your Father, who sees what is done in secret, will reward you. 7 And when you pray, do not keep on babbling like pagans, for they think they will be heard because of their many words. 8 Do not be like them, for your Father knows what you need before you ask him. 9 'This, then, is how you should pray: ' "Our Father in heaven, hallowed be your name, 10 your kingdom come, your will be done, on earth as it is in heaven. 11 Give us today our daily bread. 12 And forgive us our debts, as we also have forgiven our debtors. 13 And lead us not into temptation, but deliver us from the evil one. "

By praying, we spiritually unite ourselves to God; we get close to Him who is the source of all good. In supplication, we cry out to God to give us the grace to live in union with his will, in holiness. In prayer, our conduct matters since God is aware of how virtuous we truly are. He will not fulfill our egoistical requests, which arise from a wicked or vicious heart.

1 Peter 3:12 For the eyes of the LORD are on the righteous and his ears are attentive to their prayer, but the face of the LORD is against those who do evil.'

Psalm 145:18 The LORD is near to all who call on him, to all who call on him in truth.

James 5:16b The prayer of a righteous person is powerful and effective.

1 John 5:14 This is the confidence we have in approaching God: that if we ask anything according to his will, he hears us. 15 And if we know that he hears us – whatever we ask – we know that we have what we asked of him.

Romans 8:26 In the same way, the Spirit helps us in our weakness. We do not know what we ought to pray for, but the Spirit himself intercedes for us through wordless groans. 27 And he who searches our hearts knows the mind of the Spirit, because the Spirit intercedes for God's people in accordance with the will of God. 28 And we know that in all things God works for the good of those who love him, who have been called according to his purpose.

Of course, God knows our interior; He knows when we really ask him for something with all our heart. We must insist to God, not in a tone of claim, but precisely with humility, purity, and faith.

Psalm 69:16 Answer me, LORD, out of the goodness of your love; in your great mercy turn to me. 17 Do not hide your face from your servant; answer me quickly, for I am in trouble.

Matthew 21:22 If you believe, you will receive whatever you ask for in prayer.'

Mark 11:24 Therefore I tell you, whatever you ask for in prayer, believe that you have received it, and it will be yours.

1 Thessalonians 5:16 Rejoice always, 17 pray continually, 18 give thanks in all circumstances; for this is God's will for you in Christ Jesus.

Philippians 4:6 Do not be anxious about anything, but in every situation, by prayer and petition, with thanksgiving, present your requests to God. 7 And the peace of God, which transcends all understanding, will guard your hearts and your minds in Christ Jesus.

In prayer, we recognize the omnipresence of God; therefore, we understand that He is always with us and that we are never alone. God will never abandon us in temptations (coming from the flesh, the world, or demons) or in tribulations (suffering-unjust circumstances); we are the ones who many times forsake Him, and that is why we fall into temptations and sin.

Matthew 26:41 'Watch and pray so that you will not fall into temptation. The spirit is willing, but the flesh is weak.'

I personally believe that we begin to live the unique beauty of the Christian life when our prayer, our virtues, and our actions become a melody in the magnificent orchestra of God.

Spiritual Reading

Reading is one of the main ways to expand, contrast and complement our knowledge; for this reason, to understand any topic, it is useful to spend time to know what other people have thought and written. At a moral level, reading will generate a significant impact; because as our spiritual ideas get sharper our potential for good explodes.

Learning through reading is exponential; it helps us build a vocabulary, relate ideas, and understand arguments; it allows us to travel back in time and explore the thoughts of very admirable people. Just imagine being able to have conversations with the brightest people from different epochs about their respective specialty areas of study; that's the uniqueness of reading.

Of course, in reading, quality is preferred over quantity. It's more about which books you have read than how many books you have read. I strongly recommend starting with reading the book that I consider most important of all: The Bible.

There is no more outstanding, powerful, and influential book in the history of mankind; we do not know of another book that has been read more, nor another book that has transformed more lives concerning the meaning of life and love.

It is no coincidence that so many intellectuals, philosophers, and scholars have been influenced by the reading of Sacred Scripture (Thomas Aquinas, Saint Augustine, Saint John of the Cross, Leibniz, Pascal, Kant, Newton, Pasteur, Mendel, Lemaître, Maxwell, Schrödinger, Dostoevsky, Shakespeare, J.R.R Tolkien, and C.S. Lewis just to name a few).

2 Timothy 3:16 All Scripture is inspired by God and useful to teach, to argue, to correct and to educate in justice, 17 so that the man of God is well disposed, prepared for every good work.

It is true that, in large part, the reason we are stuck in the spiritual life is that we don't spend enough time reading and learning about the ideas and stories of our faith. This ignorance of the Bible or the Revelation of God is the first reason Christians do not lead a truly Christian life. We simply cannot live a truth that we ignore. If we don't take the time each day, week, or month to read, we won't be able to grow exponentially in wisdom and prudence, and we won't be able to intellectually mature our love.

It is advantageous to build a subconscious knowledge within the Word of God; everything we hear, read, or see is transformed into memories, which we then use to interpret and solve the various problems or challenges of life. If we knew how vital spiritual reading is, we would understand how grave its omission is.

Reading the Holy Scriptures is magnificently complemented by the writings of the saints because the thoughts and testimonies of those people can help us develop greater wisdom. Our life will be transformed once divine words enlighten us. Our life will be another once we get to know the stories of holiness, and it will be another once we understand the Truth that is Jesus. (At the end of this book you will find a list of book suggestions. I hope you enjoy it!)

Acts of Service to Others

Acts of service allow us to put into practice all that we have seen. The virtues are thoroughly manifested or vivified in concrete experiences. Deeds of assistance are an essential part of growing and developing our love. Without works of charity, our heart turns cold. Jesus shows us that serving others is the most efficient way to overcome our ego; as we overcome it, we will grow in our capacity to love, and we will become better human beings.

Hebrews 10:24 And let us consider how we may spur one another on towards love and good deeds.

John 13:3 Jesus knew that the Father had put all things under his power, and that he had come from God and was returning to God; 4 so he got up from the meal, took off his outer clothing, and wrapped a towel round his waist. 5 After that, he poured water into a basin and began to wash his disciples' feet, drying them with the towel that was wrapped round him. 6 He came to Simon Peter, who said to him, 'Lord, are you going to wash my feet?' 7 Jesus replied, 'You do not realise now what I am doing, but later you will understand.' 8 'No,' said Peter, 'you shall never wash my feet.' Jesus answered, 'Unless I wash you, you have no part with me.' 9 'Then, Lord,' Simon Peter replied, 'not just my feet but my hands and my head as well!' 10 Jesus answered, 'Those who have had a bath need only to wash their feet; their whole body is clean. And you are clean, though not every one of you.' 11 For he knew who was going to betray him, and that was why he said not every one was clean. 12 When he had finished washing their feet, he put on his clothes and returned to his place. 'Do you understand what I have done for you?' he asked them. 13 'You call me "Teacher" and "Lord", and rightly so, for that is what I am. 14 Now that I, your Lord and Teacher, have washed your feet, you also should wash one another's feet. 15 I have set you an example that you should do as I have done for you. 16 Very truly I tell you, no servant is greater than his master, nor is a messenger greater than the one who sent him. 17 Now that you know these things, you will be blessed if you do them.

We can always find good things to do for others. It is incredible how the renewal within love is available to all people in all circumstances. I think of two exceptional saints who carried this message in the church: Saint Teresa of Calcutta and Saint Teresa of Lisieux.

These two women are superb examples of how we can transform ourselves and the world through "small" actions full of love. The church especially motivates us to do the corporal and spiritual works of mercy. For God's mysteries and the heavenly sentiments are revealed to those who set mercy in motion.

Corporal Works of Mercy.

- To feed the hungry.
- To give water to the thirsty.
- To clothe the naked.
- To shelter the homeless.
- To visit the sick.
- To visit the imprisoned or ransom the captive.
- To bury the dead.

Spiritual Works of Mercy.

- To instruct the ignorant.
- To counsel the doubtful.
- To admonish the sinners.
- To bear patiently those who wrong us.
- To forgive offenses.
- To comfort the afflicted.
- To pray for the living and the dead.

In the concrete co-operation with others, the whole culture is enriched and transformed into a divine dynamic. Without the mutual free service, society merely is unsustainable. Without love and virtue, no community can thrive, prosper, or flourish. The communion of saints is precisely the highest point of what coexistence and fraternal love mean.

Chapter 12: Human Community

"The human race is one big dysfunctional family." Robert Barron

Human beings are social creatures, so we mature and develop in our interaction with others. A community is essential to growing in virtue; it is where we learn to become virtuous. Only in communities do the virtues complement each other to achieve the fullness of heavenly dynamics.

Proverbs 27:17 As iron sharpens iron, so one person sharpens another.

Ecclesiastes 4:9 Two are better than one, because they have a good return for their labor: 10 if either of them falls down, one can help the other up. But pity anyone who falls and has no one to help them up. 12 Though one may be overpowered, two can defend themselves. A cord of three strands is not quickly broken.

Psalm 133:1 How good and pleasant it is when God's people live together in unity!

All virtues and vices will affect, impact or influence others, whether for better or for worse, so the community will always play a fundamental role in the person we become. We must seek healthy environments and stay away from toxic environments, of course, all with wisdom and prudence. We must always strive to build and not destroy, to cooperate, and not to compete.

Every community, to no small extent, is based on the bonds of friendship between its participants. The word friend comes from the Latin "amicus-amare," which means that a friend is a person you love and who loves you.

Aristotle wisely said that fellowship does not subsist under vices; friendship can only rise in virtue since only the good can substantially unite people. A healthy community seeks the reciprocity of virtues-love because they strengthen it, and it invariably avoids sins-selfishness precisely because they destroy it.

An example could explain this clearly; let's imagine that, in a group of 5 people, three are sloths and two are perseverant; although it may seem that the three sloths are united by laziness, in reality, they are not because selfishness does not unite, these people could be similar in their behavior, but in concrete life, they would be divided and would produce a dysfunctional and toxic coexistence.

On the opposite side, the two persevering ones would enhance their virtues towards the good, achieving a functional and healthy coexistence. This principle has the same effect on every virtue and every vice; two humble people build, two prideful people destroy, and so on. Of course, reality is a combination of vices and virtues, but as we saw earlier, they work in cycles since virtue attracts virtue and sin attracts sin.

Proverbs 13:20 He that walketh with the wise, shall be wise: a friend of fools shall become like to them.

It is astonishing to discover the tremendous relationship that virtues have with a healthy social life; as we become more virtuous, our social capability increases. For example, a humble, generous, pure, wise, patient person has a better likelihood or probability of building healthy and lasting friendships than a proud, greedy, impure, vain, impatient person. Vice always has a negative impact on others, and therefore, if our love for our neighbor is real, we are obliged not to be vicious.

That is why we must be attached to God and fight against our egoism to offer a virtuous friendship and thus be able to contribute to our community and society. Being virtuous or vicious has direct consequences or effects on the people around us; we really participate and influence in the sanctification or condemnation of souls. From the virtue or vice of one, thousands can be benefited or harmed.

Virtues are always friendship enhancers. We all indeed want to have virtuous friends because what comes out of those people are all kinds of goods. At the same time, we avoid vicious people because evils come from them. But as Christians, we are called to treat all people well, be they virtuous or vicious. We must always keep in mind the Church's wisdom and separate sin from the sinner, remembering that we must love the sinner and hate sin.

Saint Augustine was the one who said: "No one is naturally evil but is evil because of his vice, and by removing their vice it will result that everything in the person should be loved and nothing hated." And it is true, think of a person you really dislike; now, if we eliminate his/her vices, you will have no good reason to hate him still. However, if you would still hate him/her, then the problem is you because you do not hate evil but good.

The great challenge that all community faces: fraternal correction.

Sometimes communities seem fraternally united on the surface, but they will normally find troubles that will test their assumed perception of integration. Organizations and individuals often try to solve their problems and achieve harmony only through common agreement, and thus they forget that God is what should unite them. Unity is not only about connecting human wills, but it is mainly about following the transcendent will of God.

In reality, most human conflicts and divisions are based on some disunity with God, that is, in some form of selfishness. Sin and vices are the realities that divide us, but precisely a considerable part of the spiritual health of a community is exhibited in how it faces and cooperates to correct its spiritual problems and vices.

"All division in a community is a call to a deeper unity."
Fr. Nelson Medina

It is wise to understand that we are limited to know accurately how virtuous or vicious the people around us are; therefore, we can give our ethical opinion to help, but not to denigrate, slander, defame and misjudge other human beings.

Only God knows the absolute proportion of vice and virtue of all beings, that is, their spirituality. That is why only God judges, and his judgment is perfect. In a Gospel story, Jesus shows us how much we do not know about human reality (most of the personal conscience realm). And in a passage in the letter of James, it is made clear to us that only one is the Judge of the Law.

Luke 21:1 As Jesus looked up, he saw the rich putting their gifts into the temple treasury. 2 He also saw a poor widow put in two very small copper coins. 3 'Truly I tell you,' he said, 'this poor widow has put in more than all the others. 4 All these people gave their gifts out of their wealth; but she out of her poverty put in all she had to live on.'

James 4:11 Brothers and sisters, do not slander one another. Anyone who speaks against a brother or sister or judges them speaks against the law and judges it. When you judge the law, you are not keeping it, but sitting in judgment on it. 12 There is only one Lawgiver and Judge, the one who is able to save and destroy. But you – who are you to judge your neighbor?

But having understood why only God judges, we find ourselves with the reality that we are called to try to help people get out of their vices, which is known as fraternal correction. Jesus does not deny us the possibility of helping others by denouncing others' sins; instead, he tells us that we must first correct and overcome our vices to later help others surpass theirs.

Matthew 7:3 'Why do you look at the speck of sawdust in your brother's eye and pay no attention to the plank in your own eye? 4 How can you say to your brother, "Let me take the speck out of your eye," when all the time there is a plank in your own eye? 5 You hypocrite, first take the plank out of your own eye, and then you will see clearly to remove the speck from your brother's eye.

Sirach 8:5 Do not reproach one who is turning away from sin.

Sirach 11:7 Do not find fault before you investigate; examine first, and then criticize.

Matthew 18:15 'If your brother or sister sins, go and point out their fault, just between the two of you. If they listen to you, you have won them over. 16 But if they will not listen, take one or two others along, so that "every matter may be established by the testimony of two or three witnesses." 17 If they still refuse to listen, tell it to the church; and if they refuse to listen even to the church, treat them as you would a pagan or a tax collector.

Leviticus 19:17 "Do not hate a fellow Israelite in your heart. Rebuke your neighbor frankly so that you will not share in their guilt.

Luke 17:3 So watch yourselves. 'If your brother or sister sins against you, rebuke them; and if they repent, forgive them. 4 Even if they sin against you seven times in a day and seven times come back to you saying "I repent," you must forgive them.'

1 Thessalonians 5:14 And we urge you, brothers and sisters, warn those who are idle and disruptive, encourage the disheartened, help the weak, be patient with everyone.

In the end, the trait of excellence in a healthy community is that the strong help the weak, and thus, that the virtuous help the vicious to follow the path of virtue, which is God.

Romans 15:1 We who are strong ought to bear with the failings of the weak and not to please ourselves. 2 Each of us should please our neighbors for their good, to build them up.

Family

The family usually is our first school of virtues and vices. We are all called to love our family, and although it seems obvious, it is often the most challenging community to love, it is perhaps one of the duties that we neglect the most. Mother Teresa said, "If you want to change the world, go and love your family." And how right she was.

In the Bible, we read that we commit a great injustice if we cannot love and care for our closest ones. It makes clear the great responsibility that is to love the family. We must take care of each other spiritually, alert and correct each other about vices, and support each other to grow in virtue.

Ephesians 5:25 Husbands, love your wives, just as Christ loved the church and gave himself up for her.

Colossians 3:18 Wives, submit yourselves to your husbands, as is fitting in the Lord. 19 Husbands, love your wives and do not be harsh with them. 20 Children, obey your parents in everything, for this pleases the Lord. 21 Fathers, do not embitter your children, or they will become discouraged.

Sirach 30:7 He who spoils his son will bind up his wounds, and his feelings will be troubled at every cry.

Ephesians 6:1 Children, obey your parents in the Lord, for this is right. 2 'Honor your father and mother' – which is the first commandment with a promise – 3 'so that it may go well with you and that you may enjoy long life on the earth.' 4 Fathers, do not exasperate your children; instead, bring them up in the training and instruction of the Lord.

1 Timothy 5:8 Anyone who does not provide for their relatives, and especially for their own household, has denied the faith and is worse than an unbeliever.

Mark 3:25 If a house is divided against itself, that house cannot stand.

Friends

"Love everyone with a deep love based on charity ... But make friends only with those who can share virtuous things with you. The greater the virtue you share and exchange, the more perfect your friendship will be." Saint Francis de Sales

"The friendship that has its source in God is never extinguished." Saint Catherine of Siena

We must love all people, but we are free to choose our friends, it is wise to look for virtuous friends to fully develop our moral capacity. A friendship always implies a reciprocity in the good, that is, a positive influence in the life of the other person.

Sirach 37:12 But stay constantly with a godly man whom you know to be a keeper of the commandments, whose soul is in accord with your soul, and who will sorrow with you if you fail.

Sirach 6:14 Faithful friends are a sturdy shelter: whoever finds one has found a treasure. 15 Faithful friends are beyond price; no amount can balance their worth. 16 Faithful friends are life-saving medicine; and those who fear the Lord will find them. 17 Those who fear the Lord direct their friendship aright, for as they are, so are their neighbors also.

Proverbs 18:24 One who has unreliable friends soon comes to ruin, but there is a friend who sticks closer than a brother.

Our closest friendships have an enormous impact on the person we become. A true friend is the one who knows how to bring us closer to God, virtue, and holiness. On the other hand, bad friendships are not really friendships; they are only superficial conveniences. People who don't care about your spiritual development are probably not your real friends.

1 Corinthians 15:33 Do not be misled: 'Bad company corrupts good character.'

Sirach 37:1 Every friend will say, "I too am a friend"; but some friends are friends only in name.

I invite you to think about the people who have corrected you with justice and mercy when you have fallen into vices and sins; it is probable that at times such people caused some pain and suffering to our ego; but in the light of the charity, they were helping us heal our spiritual disorders, and, telling the truth, they have been our real friends.

"Not always the one who is indulgent with us is our friend,
nor he who punishes us is our enemy. Better the friend's wounds
than the enemy's deceiving kisses. Better to love harshly
than to deceive gently." Saint Augustine

Church

The church is the mystical body of Christ; it is the unity of souls under the true God. The church is not a building, but it is the people who believe in God's love, goodness, and perfection. They are those who faithfully try to love by following the example and standard of Christ.

Mathew 16:13 When Jesus came to the region of Caesarea Philippi, he asked his disciples, 'Who do people say the Son of Man is?' 14 They replied, 'Some say John the Baptist; others say Elijah; and still others, Jeremiah or one of the prophets.' 15 'But what about you?' he asked. 'Who do you say I am?' 16 Simon Peter answered, 'You are the Messiah, the Son of the living God.' 17 Jesus replied, 'Blessed are you, Simon son of Jonah, for this was not revealed to you by flesh and blood, but by my Father in heaven. 18 And I tell you that you are Peter, and on this rock I will build my church, and the gates of Hades will not overcome it. 19 I will give you the keys of the kingdom of heaven; whatever you bind on earth will bed bound in heaven, and whatever you loose on earth will bed loosed in heaven.'

Ephesians 4:1 As a prisoner for the Lord, then, I urge you to live a life worthy of the calling you have received. 2 Be completely humble and gentle; be patient, bearing with one another in love. 3 Make every effort to keep the unity of the Spirit through the bond of peace. 4 There is one body and one Spirit, just as you were called to one hope when you were called; 5 one Lord, one faith, one baptism; 6 one God and Father of all, who is over all and through all and in all. 7 But to each one of us grace has been given as Christ apportioned it. 8 This is why it says: 'When he ascended on high, he took many captives and gave gifts to his people.' 9 (What does 'he ascended' mean except that he also descended to the lower, earthly regions? 10 He who descended is the very one who ascended higher than all the heavens, in order to fill the whole universe.) 11 So Christ himself gave the apostles, the prophets, the evangelists, the pastors and teachers, 12 to equip his people for works of service, so that the body of Christ may be built up 13 until we all reach unity in the faith and in the knowledge of the Son of God and become mature, attaining to the whole measure of the fullness of Christ. 14 Then we will no longer be infants, tossed back and forth by the waves, and blown here and there by every wind of teaching and by the cunning and craftiness of people in their deceitful scheming. 15 Instead, speaking the truth in love, we will grow to become in every respect the mature body of him who is the head, that is, Christ. 16 From him the whole body, joined and held together by every supporting ligament, grows and builds itself up in love, as each part does its work.

The church has the mission of evangelizing the world by bearing witness to the love received from God, teaching divine wisdom, and showing the way of virtue; that is to say, the life and words Jesus. In the church, we can meet the exemplary people, and we can learn from the saints who are the great testifiers of love, all to grow with a common direction that is God. Christ tells us that if we love one another as he loved us, then we will be his disciples.

John 13:34 'A new command I give you: love one another. As I have loved you, so you must love one another. 35 By this everyone will know that you are my disciples, if you love one another.'

1 John 4:21 And he has given us this command: anyone who loves God must also love their brother and sister.

Matthew 18:20 For where two or three gather in my name, there am I with them.'

The church is a teacher of divine realities; she educates us about love and guides us on the path to salvation through the holy doctrine. The sacraments are the source of God's sanctifying grace, which allows us to fully live the gifts and blessings of the Holy Spirit. We cannot understand Christian ethics without the mystical presence of God in all the Sacraments. I believe that the explanation of the Catholic Church's Catechism is excellent to understand and deepen the seven sacraments.

- Baptism.
- Confirmation.
- Penance.
- Eucharist.
- Marriage.

- Priestly order.
- Anointing of the Sick.

I end up this book by inviting you to know and participate in the church; I am sure you can learn a lot, but I'm also sure that you can contribute a lot. God is universally calling us to a life of holiness and happiness, yet, particularly to a role in his community and ultimately, to a place in his family; the enthralling thing is that it is up to you to find out which one is yours.

Ad Maiorem Dei Gloriam!

My Lord, my God, I have no words to thank you for the love you have shown me. I was lost until you found me; I was a spiritual orphan, a sinner, and still, you called me to holiness to live in your friendship. Give us the grace to glorify you with our lives, lead us on the path of excellence in your love, and grant us the divine sentiments that come from being faithful to you and your teachings. May we, like angels, saints, and the heavenly family, be part of your kingdom of goodness by living according to your perfect will.

Luke 2:13 Suddenly a great company of the heavenly host appeared with the angel, praising God and saying, 14 'Glory to God in the highest heaven, and on earth peace to those on whom his favor rests.'

Glory to God the Father, who destined us to follow the perfect example of Jesus Christ, in whom we can fully experience all the virtues and enjoy the beauty of reality. What a great honor it is to receive and transmit the grace of the Holy Spirit. It is a complete bliss to share the life of Christ.

Galatians 2:20 I have been crucified with Christ and I no longer live, but Christ lives in me. The life I now live in the body, I live by faith in the Son of God, who loved me and gave himself for me.

Glory to God for the known and unknown saints who have made a pilgrimage through this world being living testimonies of what it means to love. Glory to God for the virtues that He infused into them; because their works of charity have left a true legacy of honor, beauty, and excellence.

Revelation 4:11 'You are worthy, our Lord and God, to receive glory and honor and power, for you created all things, and by your will they were created and have their being.'

Revelation 4:8b "Holy, holy, holy is the Lord God Almighty," who was, and is, and is to come.'

Book Suggestions!

My favorite books on **related** or **complementary topics**.

- ✓ The Philosophy of Christ – Peter Kreeft
- ✓ My Faith is not Enough to Be an Atheist – Geisler and Turek
- ✓ God or Nothing – Robert Sarah
- ✓ How to Make Decisions – Peter Kreeft
- ✓ A Life Without Limits – Nick Vujicic
- ✓ Mere Christianity – C.S. Lewis
- ✓ Orthodoxy – C.K. Chesterton
- ✓ Transformation in Christ: On the Christian Attitude – Dietrich Von Hildebrand
- ✓ Catholicism, a Journey to the Heart of Faith – Bishop Barron
- ✓ A Call to Mercy – Mother Teresa
- ✓ Holy Sex – Gregory Popcak
- ✓ The Emotions God Gave You – Art & Loraine Bennett
- ✓ Overcoming Depression and Anxiety – Bob Philips
- ✓ The Road Less Traveled – Scott Peck
- ✓ Beyond Order – Jordan Peterson
- ✓ Intellectuals – Paul Johnson
- ✓ Passions and tempers – Noga Arikha
- ✓ Boundaries: When to Say Yes, How to Say No – Henry Cloud

My favorite related to **Theology**.

- ✓ Bible
- ✓ Catechism of the Catholic Church

- ✓ Jesus of Nazareth 1-2-3 – Benedict XVI
- ✓ Handbook of Christian Apologetics – Peter Kreeft
- ✓ Theodicy – Leibniz
- ✓ Summa Theologica 1 – Saint Thomas Aquinas
- ✓ Summa Contra Gentiles – Saint Thomas Aquinas
- ✓ The Imitation of Christ – Thomas of Kempis
- ✓ Confessions – Saint Augustine
- ✓ An Exorcist Explains the Demonic – Gabriel Amorth
- ✓ *Suma Daemoniaca – Fortea
- ✓ The City of God – Saint Augustine
- ✓ The Day is Far Spent – Robert Sarah
- ✓ Faith and Reason – Benedict XVI

My favorite related to **Philosophy**.

- ✓ Summa Philosophica – Peter Kreeft
- ✓ Socrates' Children: The 100 Greatest Philosophers – Peter Kreeft
- ✓ Socratic Logic – Peter Kreeft
- ✓ Thinking in Systems – Donella Meadows
- ✓ Monadology – Leibniz
- ✓ Nicomachean Ethics – Aristotle
- ✓ Metaphysics – Aristotle
- ✓ Socrates' Apology
- ✓ Plato's Republic
- ✓ Summa Theologica 2 – Saint Thomas Aquinas
- ✓ *Lecciones Preliminares de Filosofía. – García Morente
- ✓ Man's Search for Meaning – Viktor Frankl
- ✓ *Ética Razonada – José Ramón Ayllón

Acknowledgements

First, I want to thank God for my intellectual mentors Raúl Martínez Soto and Ignacio Ruiz Velasco, who died the year I wrote this book. To them, I owe my habit of reading and the wonder and passion for the truth. It was always interesting talking and learning from them. Their humility and wisdom unquestionably shined through their thoughts, words, and deeds. Rest in peace.

Secondly, I want to thank God for letting me meet Verónica Brunkow, an amazing woman full of virtue who always displays in her smile the fruits of the Holy Spirit. She woke me up to discover the beauty of the unity of the coherence of our behavior with our Christian beliefs. She taught me ten years ago the beauty of Catholic spirituality and taught me the immense value of the sacraments; especially, she taught me to have good confessions, something I have not stopped doing since. Thanks to Lucas Cerviño, who welcomed me into the Focolare Movement, the community where I am currently happy to participate.

Thirdly, I want to thank the people who were most involved in writing this book. To my editor and great friend Bernardo Galeazzi, thank you for every moment we happily dedicate to editing and rewriting every line of this book. And to Ruth Aguilera Rocha, whom I admire very much for her great example of perseverance; thank you for trusting me and financing this charitable project.

Finally, to my mother, Ginny Martinez, who always foster my friendship with God, she inspired me to always try my best without ever losing sight of mercy. And to my father, Rogelio Anzures, who has motivated me to become more patient. Thanks to my two brothers Paola and Aldo for your sincere and generous friendship, I love you.

Bibliography

1 Leibniz Gottfried Wilhelm. Teodicea (Ilustrado) (Siltolá, Recovered Classics) (Spanish Edition). Editions of La Isla de Siltolá. Kindle Edition.

2 Plato. Plato's Complete Works (Spanish Edition). ATOZ Classics. Kindle Edition.

3 Socrates. Plato's Complete Works (Spanish Edition). ATOZ Classics. Kindle Edition.

4 Aristotle. Nicomachean Ethics (Spanish Edition). Unknown. Kindle Edition.

For most of the quotes I used well known sources on the Internet.

For quoting the Sacred Scripture I used mainly the NIV Bible kindle version, and for certain verses of the deuterocanonical books I used mainly the New Revised Standard Version Catholic Edition.

Printed in Great Britain
by Amazon

23693954R00179